Thorson Photography

Andra Putnis is a writer and social researcher based in Canberra with her partner and two children. *Stories My Grandmothers Didn't Tell Me* is her debut book.

———

'An elegant, absorbing story of ordinary people thrown into extra-ordinary crisis, and how they draw on their reserves of love, strength and resilience to survive. These grandmothers are at once both recognisable and loveable, but also heroic in their determination to bring their families through one of the most traumatic upheavals of modern history.'
**Peter Greste, Professor of Journalism,
Macquarie University**

'An Australian-born granddaughter discovering the stories of her Latvian grandmothers and their lives lived in very different times and circumstances. The personal, emotional and loving blended with the history of a nation in critical times . . . a compelling read for all generations.'
Ilze Thomas, teacher, Adelaide Latvian School

'Anyone with untold stories flowing through their DNA will find home and understanding here. I felt my own grandmother speaking to me.'
Amy Remeikis, journalist, *The Guardian*

'Deeply moving, brilliantly crafted and powerfully written, this memoir is an object lesson in how ordinary lives are rendered extra-ordinary by curiosity, persistence and love.'
Biff Ward, author of *In My Mother's Hands*

Front cover photo
The cover image, which shows refugees who left Lodz in Poland headed for Berlin in 1945, first appeared in the London *Daily Mirror* on 14 December 1945. The photographer was Fred Ramage. The image is used here to represent the plight of refugees in Europe during and after World War II.

Andra Putnis

STORIES MY GRANDMOTHERS DIDN'T TELL ME

Two women's journeys from war-torn
Europe to a new life in Australia

ALLEN&UNWIN
SYDNEY • MELBOURNE • AUCKLAND • LONDON

First published in 2024

Copyright © Andra Putnis 2024

All rights reserved. No part of this book may be reproduced or transmitted in any form or by any means, electronic or mechanical, including photocopying, recording or by any information storage and retrieval system, without prior permission in writing from the publisher. The Australian *Copyright Act 1968* (the Act) allows a maximum of one chapter or 10 per cent of this book, whichever is the greater, to be photocopied by any educational institution for its educational purposes provided that the educational institution (or body that administers it) has given a remuneration notice to the Copyright Agency (Australia) under the Act.

Allen & Unwin
Cammeraygal Country
83 Alexander Street
Crows Nest NSW 2065
Australia
Phone: (61 2) 8425 0100
Email: info@allenandunwin.com
Web: www.allenandunwin.com

Allen & Unwin and the author acknowledge the Traditional Owners of the Country on which we live and work. We pay our respects to all Aboriginal and Torres Strait Islander Elders, past and present.

 A catalogue record for this
book is available from the
National Library of Australia

ISBN 978 1 76147 132 2

Excerpts from Latvian folk songs: *Latviešu Tautas Dziesmas* [Latvian Folk Songs], edited by A. Svabe, K. Straubergs and E. Hauzenberga-Sturma, 12 volumes, Kopenhagen: Imanta, 1952–1956. Translated into English by Peter Putnis.

Pages 265–66: Extracts from Ruta U., *Dear God, I Wanted to Live* (published by Grāmatu Draugs, 1978)

Latvian motifs on chapter openers: Zanna Pesnina, Shutterstock

Set in 12/16 pt Bembo MT Pro by Midland Typesetters, Australia

10 9 8 7 6 5 4 3 2 1

Older generations who have been through terrible times don't speak very often about them. But sometimes their voices come before the end, in a roaring rush, loud and clear. Other times they are heard only through memories, hints and whispers, clues they've left behind.

I wrote this book for my grandmothers,
my family and families everywhere.

Contents

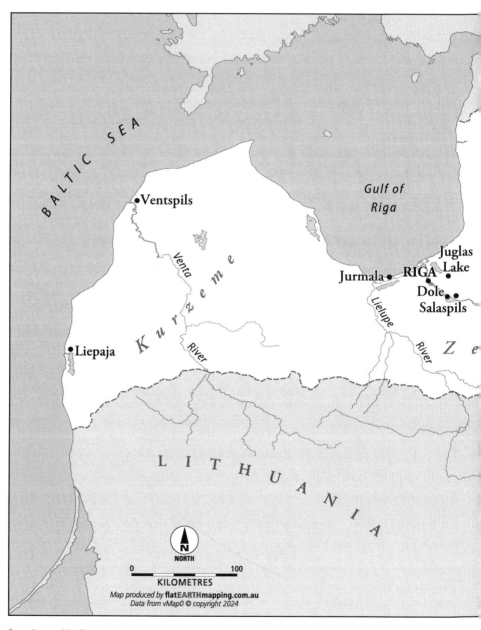

Latvia, c. 1940

Grandma Milda and Nanna Aline
Family Tree★

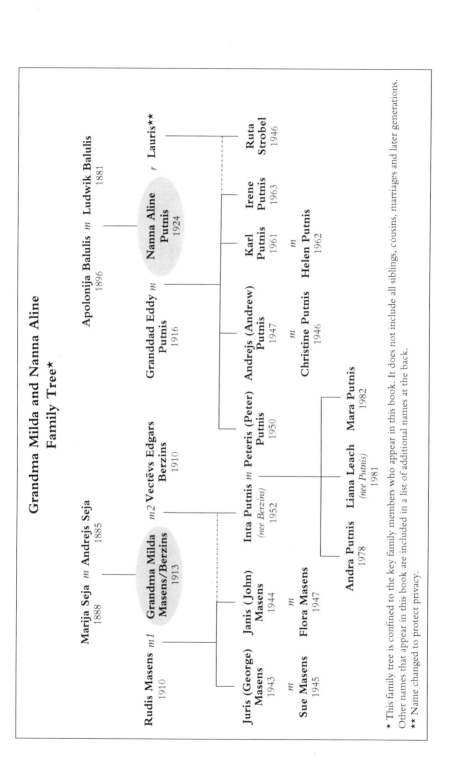

Apolonija Balulis *m* Ludwik Balulis
1896   1881

Marija Seja *m* Andrejs Seja
1888   1885

m2 **Vectēvs Edgars Berzins**
1910

r Lauris★★

Nanna Aline Putnis
1924

Granddad Eddy *m*
Putnis
1916

Ruta Strobel
1946

Irene Putnis
1963

Karl Putnis
1961
m
Helen Putnis
1962

Andrejs (Andrew) Putnis
1947
m
Christine Putnis
1946

Inta Putnis *m* **Peteris (Peter) Putnis**
(*nee Berzins*)   1950
1952

Grandma Milda Masens/Berzins
1913

Rudis Masens *m1*
1910

Janis (John) Masens
1944

Juris (George) Masens
1943
m
Sue Masens
1945

Flora Masens
1947

Mara Putnis
1982

Liana Leach
(*nee Putnis*)
1981

Andra Putnis
1978

★ This family tree is confined to the key family members who appear in this book. It does not include all siblings, cousins, marriages and later generations. Other names that appear in this book are included in a list of additional names at the back.

★★ Name changed to protect privacy.

Part One: First Light

1913–41

The girl is loved by all,
Who does as her mother asks.

Latvian folk song

1

The country in their houses

When I was little, my family would drive ten hours from Toowoomba to Newcastle to visit Nanna Aline and Grandma Milda each year at Christmas time. We'd arrive just as the sun was setting and first head to Grandma Milda's big red-brick house at Redhead on the coast, where Mum grew up. My two younger sisters and I would be tired and messy from hours of sleeping, playing and eating in the car. We'd tumble out into the ocean air and look down at the surf beach below. Then we'd all turn towards Grandma's house, suddenly shy, and Mum would have to push us forward to ring the doorbell.

The three of us would stand in a row on Grandma's giant concrete steps and wait for her doors to open. Then she'd be standing there with her slim, graceful figure towering over us, dark-grey hair curled neatly around her head like a finely wrought iron helmet.

'*Mani mazi mazuliṇi*, my little babies,' she'd cry and step back to take a look at us.

'Hi Grandma,' we'd chorus.

Satisfied by our greeting, she'd pull each of us to her thin body, then promptly propel us all inside.

'Are you hungry? I have something for you.'

We weren't, but we'd sit down warily at her dining room table and she'd ladle cold cucumber, dill and sour cream soup into little crystal bowls. We loved Grandma and were too polite to refuse it outright but I remember once whispering to Mum, 'Can't she warm it up? It tastes like grass.'

Grandma Milda overheard me.

'It tastes like summer. You eat it up.'

Grandma Milda doted on us but she could be fierce and had old European standards. When we stayed with her, Mum would help us into matching dresses in the mornings and comb our knotty hair, telling us to be good girls. Then we'd be let loose in her dark house.

Grandma's walls were covered with tapestries she'd stitched herself, large heavy squares with rows of wool forming ancient weaves and geometric patterns in forest green, red berry and pale sun colours. She had cabinets stacked full of fancy glasses and platters that rattled when the wind swept up from the beach. In one window there were small wooden dolls with vividly painted folk-dancing skirts, tiny labels listing the Latvian provinces they each represented: Latgale, Zemgale, Vidzeme and Kurzeme.

Sometimes we'd sneak into Grandma's bedroom on secret missions to see what strange things we could find. Her bedroom cupboard was filled with old fur coats, strange woven folk costumes and small mountains of glowing amber. There were blue and black gold-banded men's fraternity caps hidden up the back—we imagined they must have belonged to Latvian soldiers long ago. Some days I put on Grandma's silver Latvian rings, and they seemed to bite at me coldly until I shook them off. We'd run back to my parents, who would be eating snacks with Grandma and other elderly Latvians who'd dropped by to visit. We were half-scared, made breathless by our discoveries, but we always knew we hadn't seen it all, hadn't understood what was really hidden there, and would have to look again.

'They are Latvian things, don't touch!' Mum would say when we'd later ask her about them. I could tell she was slightly on edge at Grandma's place. She seemed to have less patience as she tried to cope with all the Latvians who'd drop around to reminisce and take stock of us, and with navigating the Christmas pageantry being orchestrated by her mother. I could sense even back then that Mum had perhaps spent too much time in her childhood witnessing old Latvians mourning the past and had decided that no good ever came from dwelling on these things.

Grandma Milda once told me I spoke Latvian before I spoke English. She wanted me and my sisters to be good Latvian girls and often remarked that we should learn the language properly. It's from her I have images of Latvians living among the birch and pine, green leaves cutting the sky into bright pinpricks. She painted pictures in my mind of Latvians dancing in patterns, arms linked, spinning around. Girls with plaits and ribbons flying. Boys with blue lakes in their eyes. The folk songs she listened to were the *dainas* and *tautasdziesmas*. Clear piped voices singing ancient songs; choirs weaving gossamer cloth around the stars.

I remember once making up my own poem inspired by these Latvian songs:

> *Saule, saule*, come out for the birds are cold
> Sun oh sun, your light breath for the trees
> The winter has been hard
> Our luck spent
> Time for green shoots and laughter
> To make the world new.

———

I don't have any memories of my dad's mum, Nanna Aline, coming to Christmas lunch at Redhead. I know she did a few times, but back then it seemed as if Nanna and Grandma lived in separate domains. Each Christmas, after a few days of presents, carols and great feasts at Grandma's place, we would drive away from the coast, heading inland around the brackish Lake Macquarie, to spend a day at Nanna's house. As we drove there, I'd look out the car window at the familiar sight of large coastal houses giving way to car yards, factories and then older run-down suburbs.

Nanna's house was a weatherboard peeling white paint on Elizabeth Street in Argenton, just down the road from the Sulphide Corporation's zinc smelter at Cockle Creek. My granddad Eddy and a couple of other Latvian men built the house in 1953 when Argenton was on the outskirts of Newcastle but, when I was young, her house seemed dwarfed by the city that had grown up around it.

We never used her front door, it seemed too formal. We would pull up on the street at the back of her place and see her waiting for us on the back doorstep in a patterned housedress and slippers. Nanna Aline was much younger than Grandma Milda, and looked plump, expressive and girlish in contrast. My sisters and I would run to receive a hug against her pillow chest, breathing in the sweet combination of talcum powder and cigarette smoke resting on her skin. She'd hold onto us with tears in her eyes as if never intending to let go.

Dad would take charge: 'Labrīt—good morning—Mum. It's okay, we're all here now.'

Nanna Aline's house always felt as unknowable as Grandma Milda's place, despite its small size, but for different reasons. While she had a decent complement of Latvian tapestries, wooden candelabras and old books, it was the crosses on the wall, statues of Mary and pictures of Jesus that made her house feel cloaked in something we didn't understand. Despite being all around us, Nanna's Catholic religion was rarely mentioned.

On our visits, Nanna Aline's main objective was always pleasing everyone and she constantly fretted about things going wrong. I remember her once wringing her hands at how her apple pie had turned out.

'It's too dry! The pastry is awful!' she wailed.

I tried to reassure her that her apple pie was delicious, while knowing nothing would make her believe me.

But she always recovered from her setbacks and made sure on every visit to connect with each of us with warmth and interest. One time she leant across to me with a chocolate caramel tucked inside her cheek to suggest we confide in one another.

'Andra, you tell me your secrets and I will tell you mine,' she whispered.

I prattled on about ballet, school and choir, trying to make her proud of me. Nanna nodded, seemingly in amazement, as if I was saying the most important things in the world. But when it was her turn, I felt uneasy.

'Things were not good when I was a girl during the war . . . I am not sure whether to tell you,' she warned.

Nanna left me dangling, but with a sense of relief at having dodged things that, once said, couldn't be taken back.

Later in the afternoon, the undercurrent at Nanna's place that seemed to cause the adults to drink too much surfaced. Nanna's voice would change with the flow of drinks, becoming high and full of regret.

'I was a silly woman,' she'd moan.

'Oh Mum, that is not true. It was the war,' Dad would say with frustration in his voice.

He often went up the road to the Argie pub when it all became too much for him.

As evening approached, my sisters and I would drift outside to the relative safety of the garden. We'd run around enjoying its neat, springy grass. I'd periodically sneak inside to grab lemon sherbet lollies and then race back outside to share the stash. There, up the back behind the garage, we'd suck on those lollies until the sherbet broke through the hard shells, a small tingle at first and then a flood of fizz spraying through our mouths, our tongues working overtime to get the last sour buzz from the hard lolly grooves. We'd be happy outside, but a part of me would worry the adults inside were going too far, getting too sad talking about the past.

On these visits, our grandfathers would also be around. They were in the background, reading Latvian newspapers and sitting in their favourite chairs. Sometimes Nanna's husband, my granddad Eddy, would make us take turns sitting on his knee while he played a game of lunging forward to try to catch our ears in his mouth. He had yellowing Tic Tac teeth and we hated that game, but would sit there for a few rounds, knowing instinctively he was a volatile man who might upend the day if he perceived too many things not going his way.

When we returned to Grandma Milda's place, her husband, my *vectēvs* Edgars (*vectēvs* is Latvian for grandfather), would hug us all, cry and go back to sleep in his black leather rocking chair sitting in the corner of the lounge room. He wasn't very active because he'd had a stroke when he was 65. His tears would catch in his stubble and shine on his face for the next few hours as he dozed.

But it was my grandmothers who took centre stage as we grew up. They were in charge of their houses, Latvian islands sitting on opposite sides of Newcastle. Two different matriarchs, fussing over, loving and feeding us their special *pīrāgi*, delicious bread-like crescents filled with fatty speck and onion. They were both remarkable storytellers in their different ways, fluent in Latvian and English in their later years, well-educated women who often chose to share their opinions about life and all those around them. Characters with hidden pasts, still very much present in our lives.

2

Catalyst

When I think back, it was the life I started to make away from my family that led to my decision to seek out my Latvian grand-mothers' stories. After studying law and history at university and working for a few years for the public service in Canberra, I moved to Darwin in late 2004, wanting to learn more about Aboriginal and Torres Strait Islander peoples and cultures. I worked initially for the Northern Territory government, but soon moved into advocacy, spending most of my time trying to get more funding for Aboriginal and Torres Strait Islander ranger groups working on environmental and cultural protection projects. I lived in a share house with my now husband and other flatmates; we were all trying to figure out where we fitted and what we wanted from life. I learnt about Country, land and sea rights, and started to think more deeply about my place in the world.

Being more than 4000 kilometres away from my family gave me space to forge my own way and then turn around and look back at where I'd come from. Darwin is a place that strips people bare. All that sweat and unrelenting humidity makes pretence difficult and helps people see parts of themselves that may have been previously hidden. In the heat, I slowed down and started to wonder about my family's past.

I began reading books about Latvia and the Second World War. This led to nights lying awake on top of sweaty sheets watching the ceiling fan stir the heat, wondering whether it would be crazy to dedicate serious effort to finding out how my grandmothers survived the war and what my connection to Latvia really was.

Back then, I felt almost completely Australian, with little claim to Latvia. I'd grown up on a seven-acre block on the outskirts of Toowoomba, looking up at tall gum trees swaying in the wind and attending a small local school where I'd stood on the parade ground each morning to sing the national anthem before filing into class. Most weekends consisted of adventures in the bush with my sisters, Liana and Mara; picking our way through the long grass to visit our chooks and horses, ducking under barbed-wire fences and running down the gully to the trickle of a creek at the back of our place. Sometimes we'd visit the Jondaryan Woolshed for hayrides or go to the local pub, where we'd successfully wheedle from our parents the purchase of multiple packets of Samboy chips and pink lemonades.

Latvia was a faraway and mysterious place to me, despite my connection to the country through my grandparents. When I was very young, I thought it was a made-up fairy country. I used to play a game with my younger sisters that involved putting on Mum's old ballet costumes and twirling around to try to get there, spinning and giggling until we were giddy.

One time, I ran to tell Dad it wasn't working. He was outside whipper-snipping the long grass by the front shed. I hovered near him, my bare feet standing on a rock to avoid the bindis, until he turned off the machine.

'What sort of magic do you need to get to Latvia?' I asked.

He wiped the sweat off his face.

'What do you mean?'

My voice wavered as I became less certain.

'You need magic, right?'

Dad started to laugh. 'You silly moo! Surely you know Latvia is a real country. You can see it on the map.'

I shrugged and looked down at the yellow clumps of grass.

'Come on, I need a drink of water anyway.'

I wanted to run back to my sisters but followed Dad and

10

watched as he dragged out our orange *Jacaranda Atlas*. He set me on his hot, itchy knee.

'See, here it is. Up at the top of the world.'

The little country was smaller than the tip of his finger. It seemed miniature and weird.

When I went to the atlas a couple of days later to look for it, I couldn't find it within the hundreds of green and brown lands and foreign-sounding places. For many years I thought I was missing something. I wondered if it only appeared on the map sometimes and disappeared at others.

I couldn't have been much older when I came to understand that Latvia was not only a fairytale country, but also a place of nightmares. One night Mum came into my bedroom to check on me before I went to sleep. I'd already turned off my light, so all I could see was her black outline. She sat on my bed and whispered, her breath smelling of beer. 'You don't understand how lucky you are.'

I lay quietly under my faded navy doona, wishing she would go away.

'I grew up hearing about the Russians. How they forced splinters of wood under people's fingernails during the war.' The image flashed—a woman's hands, bloody nails with dark purple moons. 'You have to understand,' she said, 'sometimes people do awful things to each other.' She bowed her head.

I waited but she didn't move. Eventually, I slid my small hand out from under the covers to hold her hand. At my touch, she threw her head up. I knew she was looking at me, but it was too dark for our eyes to meet. 'You're lucky. Our family is lucky. We escaped Latvia. You hear me?' She leant over to give me a sloppy kiss and swayed out of the room. I rubbed away the wet imprint of her mouth and curled into a ball. I knew Mum wasn't trying to scare me. She was trying to warn me. But the depth of her pain terrified me.

All in all, it felt safest to keep Latvia well away. When asked at school about where my name came from, I kept my answers short. 'Latvia . . . a small country near Finland and Russia.'

As I got older, I added a bit more. 'Umm, it's part of the USSR at the moment, but we don't really talk about that in my family.'

'Can you speak Latvian?' I'd sometimes be asked.

'Only a few words like *čības*, that's slippers, and *slota*, that's broom. Apparently, I used to speak more when I was little. Now I can sort of understand my parents and grandparents when they are speaking to each other,' I'd mumble.

People would look at me strangely and I'd change the subject.

————

It took months of reading books in Darwin to build up momentum and courage to the point where it seemed like finding out more about my grandmothers' lives was the inevitable way forward. I didn't tell my parents. I felt too exposed and imagined their many possible reactions—all of them bad: *Why would you dredge it all up? We left it behind us when you were born. We've given you everything, the freedom to be anything; and kept you away from stories of starving people and crazy soldiers. Why would you drag everyone through it? You aren't really Latvian, anyway!*

I sometimes woke after dreams about running from disintegrating mediaeval stone buildings in some far-off European city, my parents lurching and sleepy behind me, unable to keep up.

My fears were pushed back by the hundreds of books I'd read over my life, extolling the virtues of mythic quests and the power of stories—some real and others fantasies. I remember the first time I read *The Lord of the Rings*; I was eleven or so, tucked away in my room, eager to get inside the tale. I went forward through ancient forests, boggy plains and under and over mountains, taking it all extremely seriously with my heart in my throat.

At the end, when Frodo left Sam for the Grey Havens, I cried so hard my eyes closed up into small slits.

I was not so crazy as to think that in learning more about my grandmothers' lives I would become some sort of Frodo. Yet the diet of books I had fed myself over years reinforced the importance of stories, propelling me to wonder whether fully discovering my grandmothers' stories might be a noble quest, a chance to face the past and reckon with it.

As the eldest of three girls, I had always sat at the table the longest, listening to the adults and finding out snippets about Latvia and my grandmothers' lives. With a fair amount of naivety, I suddenly felt it was my task to press pause in the forward rush of my life and look back before it was too late.

I already had parts of Grandma Milda's story, shards and frag- ments revealed throughout my childhood before she passed away when I was nineteen. The urgent task now was to go and visit Nanna Aline. I thought there was a good chance she would tell me her story if I finally, and properly, asked for it. I resolved to set out on the journey and worry about my parents later.

———

At my first interview with Nanna Aline in February 2006, we sat down across from each other at her small kitchen table in Argenton, the room warm with the smell of bacon and sweet onion left over from breakfast. Nanna's row of pale yellow and orange 1950s flour, sugar and salt canisters sat above her stove. In fact, her whole house seemed preserved like a comforting diorama, so many things just as they had been when I was a child.

After we'd fussed around each other, eating and talking to re-establish our connection, we got down to business. Nanna changed tack and started sizing me up in shrewd fashion to get to the bottom of what I thought I was doing.

'So, you want to know about Latvia and the war?'

She stared at me over the top of her glasses. I could hear a lawnmower a few houses down and took a deep breath, telling myself it was just a normal Tuesday outside.

'Just some stories from your life, Nanna. The ones you want to tell . . . I want to find out more about our whole family. Grandma Milda's story too . . .'

'You are lucky she is not here to see you poking around! Our story is just like all the others—Polish, Hungarian, Ukrainian. Read a book!'

I felt flat-footed and underprepared.

'I don't just want the facts in the history books. I want to know your story.'

Nanna nodded as if she'd caught me out. 'I used to want to talk about my life. Nobody wanted to hear it. Now, I am not so sure. I know what people like your grandma Milda said behind my back!'

I squirmed on the vinyl kitchen chair.

'All right, then. I don't remember everything. But I have my own point of view. Some old Latvian women go on about how wonderful things were before the war. How they used to help their mothers collect mushrooms in the woods and weave by the fire. How the boys were strong, helping their fathers chop the wood. You heard these stories? Well, it was not always like that. Not all the boys were good and I was not as kind to my *māte* as I should have been. If you want that story, you are talking to the wrong grandma.'

Nanna paused and I put down my pen.

'You see, Milda always thought she knew best. She was much older than me. She thought she was the proper Latvian. A Lutheran. That was the main religion in Latvia. My family were Catholics. That was a big thing. We were in the minority. Catholics were looked down on. My mother mostly spoke Lithuanian and Polish, she wasn't even a proper Latvian. People thought we were unsophisticated, you know? Your grandma Milda thought that about me.'

'No, Nanna . . .'

'Yes, she did! I remember the first time I saw her was at a Latvian concert at the Broadmeadow Rotary Hall here in Newcastle. I could see straight away she thought she was in charge. She had on a dark-green dress with pearl buttons and was organising the food. My legs were wobbly under my plain skirt. I had brought some *pīrāgi* but they were burnt. Of course, Milda had made a proper chocolate torte. It stood almost a foot high.

'It's not as if she came from a rich family back in Latvia. Her father started out as a timber worker. I once heard he had to stand on the logs and use his feet to sort and send them down the Daugava River to the mill. He had permanent bruises from getting his feet crushed. Her mother worked as a housekeeper for German families. Your grandma Milda was born out in Dole. She only moved to Riga when she was a young woman, but she acted as if she'd lived there all her life. Definitely turned her nose up at the sight of me.'

Nanna spoke slowly, her voice rising and falling at the end of her short sentences, often pausing to punctuate them with self-admonishments and conclusions. Still, my head spun trying to keep up with her. I hadn't imagined we would start with all this stuff about my grandma Milda.

'We don't have to talk today, Nanna . . . if it's too much,' I offered, attempting to buy myself time to get back some control.

Nanna waved her hand as if shooing me away. 'You think I haven't gone over my life many times? Okay, now we will start from the beginning.'

I vowed to just stay quiet and listen.

3

 Nanna Aline

To be a good girl

I was born in Kraslava in 1924. A farming town, on the Daugava River. My family lived right up against the south-east border of Latvia, next to Poland and Byelorussia (now Belarus) but we never went to those places. In winter, parts of the river froze. In spring, there were thousands of flowers. Everyone looked after the land, worked hard and tried to be good people.

Latvians have a saying, 'You must have your own little corner, your own little place'. In Latvian it sounds very good, '*Savs kaktiņš, savs stūrītis zemes*'. Some people called us peasants. Well, we were! In Kraslava, people worked the land. But you have to understand, back then in Latvia people were also very educated. I went to good schools. I learnt German, Russian, even a bit of Latin.

Everyone made things at home. Once I asked my mother if we could live in a flat and buy things from the shop like my friend Marta's family did. She got very angry and shouted, 'Bread you make by hand tastes better than bread from the shop!' That was how it was. Most people found their worth from making things with their own two hands.

But I was not such a useful child. One time my mother asked me to help my grandmother sort out the potatoes from the garden. The good ones were to go in a barrel for us to eat, the bad ones were for the pigs. It was autumn and my fingers were frozen. I must have been around eight years old. Maybe I had a few tears? I didn't want to do it and was being slow on purpose—trying to use my white handkerchief to pick the potatoes up. I didn't want cold dirt on my hands. Well, of course, the handkerchief became black. My grandmother saw it and yelled to my mother, 'What have you taught this girl? She doesn't even sort potatoes properly!'

But I was loved. Never again in my life did I have love like the love from my parents and my aunty Adela. I was the only child, see? Something to cherish. I was always with my aunty. We slept together in a small room with the beds placed right next to each other. There was only a small gap—maybe fifteen inches between our heads. I thought my dreams might pass into Aunty's head at night. We were that close.

We were a religious family. As a child I loved saying prayers. My mother was so happy to have a daughter who wanted to pray. When I was little, we lived in the church dormitory because my father was the church organist and choir master of the famous St Ludvigs church. We lived near the nuns and the priests. There was a passage we could walk down from our rooms to the main church. We didn't need to use the front entrance. I thought I was special to go down that passage. When we were all going along to church, the priests' robes would be all around me. Black like the wings of birds.

If the war had not come, I might have been a nun. Maybe like little Saint Thérèse. She is known as the Little Flower of Jesus. She didn't do any special deeds but gave herself wholly to God and was not tempted. But I didn't have any sisters to show me the way.

St Ludvigs was a grand white church for a small place like Kraslava, famous throughout Latgale. It sat on top of a hill looking over the town and had an upper level where the choir stood. I remember once sneaking into that church by myself when I was still very little. I crept from our dormitory and went all the way outside to the front of the church; it did not feel right to use the priests' passage. I hid behind the pine trees and looked at the front doors for a long time. I waited until no one was around and then ran past the statue of Mary up to the entrance. But I almost couldn't open those doors, they were heavy.

When I finally got inside, it was very quiet and dark. Jesus was hanging up on the cross near the altar. I went to our normal pew and knelt down. I started to do the Stations of the Cross. I said the words looking at the pictures on the walls around the church: Jesus as he is nailed to the cross; Simon of Cyrene as he walks with him; and later, Veronica, dressed in purple, as she wipes the blood from Christ's eyes. I think maybe in my heart I felt good, swollen, because I was being pious, you know?

Eventually, my mother and aunty found me. They'd been looking for a long time but I was not in trouble. My mother had tears in her eyes, she was so happy. 'Oh! So little and you came here to do the Stations of the Cross. You must have Jesus in your heart,' she cried.

That mattered to my mother. I had to be a girl of good character. Once when I stole some of Aunty Adela's cherry jam, I was sick until I went to confession. Maybe my mother and aunty smiled at that behind their hands, but it was a big thing to me. I was ashamed. I knew, you see, how my mother liked people who lived their life the right way by God.

I had a cousin, Jekabs, who was training to be a priest. He stayed with us for a while on a bed in the kitchen, and how my mother talked about him. 'Look Aline, you see how Jekabs is saying his prayers! He is reading the Bible with such love in his voice. Hear how he speaks.' Jekabs would look up from his Bible across at me and the corner of his mouth would lift just a little. Sometimes I wanted to pinch him.

But it was true. Jekabs was a very religious and serious boy. He was good at his studies. Once I was crying because I had to draw a beanstalk with little pods for homework, and Jekabs did it for me.

But when I handed it in, the teacher gave me just a small smile. She knew I hadn't drawn it.

I found it hard to be a good girl. One time I complained about my winter coat for days—it was too short for my arms, but my father said I had to keep wearing it. I was embarrassed at school and wanted very much to have a new coat. You know what my mother did? She made one for me from her old coat. That's how good she was, but I wasn't grateful. I wanted the coat to be new.

What a silly girl I was. I think that now! There are many Latvian folk songs about how important it is to be hardworking, useful to your family. See, I'll sing one to you.

> God, let me die the way,
> My father and my mother died:
> Father died on the threshing floor,
> Mother kneading dough.

Well, my life turned out nothing like that. Goodness me, I was stupid! I was a girl who didn't know what was going on, that's for sure.

Another thing. Don't you believe your grandma Milda was always picking berries. No! She wanted a fancy life. She wanted to have other people picking berries for her!

4

 Nanna Aline

The announcement

I was there, you know! At the very beginning, when the war started for Latvia in 1940. I was there at the Daugavpils Song Festival on 16 June when the first announcement was made. Me, just a girl from Kraslava. There, for that moment.

Everyone around me was happy the song festival was being held in Daugavpils because they were usually in Riga. We were proud it was in our part of the country. Choirs are everything in Latvia. Voices are treated like instruments. Everyone wants to be a good singer.

You must go and see a song festival one time in your life. They still happen. Can you imagine the sound a choir of 14,000 people makes? Music soft like rain and then like thunder. Only Latvians have choirs that big. We sing the *dainas* and *tautasdziesmas*—folk songs, simple songs about land and nature. Sad songs, happy songs and deep old songs about fate and life. They often have a message, like how to keep a good home. Some have warnings, like men should not drink or they will fall in the pigpen. Some songs are full of pride. You see, Latvia was a young country, only formed after the First World War. Lots of people, including your grandma Milda, thought Latvia was God's most favoured country on Earth.

It was the first time my mother had let me go to a song festival. I went with my father and the rest of the Kraslava folk group. My best friend, Marta, was with me. We travelled on the back of a farm truck. The fields were green with little white daisy flowers everywhere. It was only about 30 miles away but it took half a day because we had to go here and there to pick people up, and the roads were bumpy. Lots of times the girls and I flew up and then landed down hard on the wooden seats.

What a thing it was when we finally entered the city and saw the crowds. There were so many people, our truck had to crawl down the road. All the men had big oak leaf *vaiṇagi*, like crowns, around their heads. The women had flower wreaths. Everyone had on folk costumes; it was like a field of red, green and white around us. I remember Marta telling me to fix my scarf. It had slid down my neck and we didn't want to look messy in front of the Riga girls.

But one thing, I wished my father had stayed home. I thought he would stop me from having a good time with my friends. He was a very serious man with a long snowy beard. He always wore his black church robes. As we went through the town, he kept looking over and shaking his head when I laughed with Marta loudly or waved at someone. He did not eat during the whole trip. You see, he always ate alone at home, everything just right, bread cut neatly and so on. He was a very particular man, not good at travel.

It took hours for us all to walk into the park and be arranged on the Stropi Stage. My father went with the men to one side. All of us girls joined the crowd towards the back. I felt dizzy with so many people around me. Thank goodness Marta was standing next to me. There were banners for all the districts and the red-and-white flag of Latvia. We all had bunches of wildflowers to hold. Mine were yellow buttercups and stalks of white yarrow. I was worried because the stems went soft in my hands before we'd even started singing.

Then everything went quiet. A roar of clapping started and I looked down to see if the President had arrived. Everyone knew he was coming to open the song festival but the conductor waved his hands for everyone to be still. I reached out and took Marta's hand. Then there was the announcement.

Andra, go and get the history book on the bottom shelf in the lounge room. Yes, you find the page, you tell me what the conductor said:

> Ladies and Gentlemen. I regret to inform you that our President, Dr Karlis Ulmanis, has been unable to travel to Daugavpils to open our Latgales *Dziesmu Svētki* concert. In a moment, we will broadcast an announcement from the President. He is to address the country from Riga.

People started to turn to each other. I didn't know what was going on, just that something big was happening. The speakers on the side of the stage started to crackle. Then we heard his voice on the radio—Ulmanis, the 'Father of Latvia', as everyone knew him.

> *Labdien* to you all across the country, and especially those of you at the song festival in Latgale. International events this week have moved with a rapidity far exceeding all precedents any of us have ever witnessed. The present situation demands that I stay in Riga, and I hope you all understand . . . Latgale borders directly with our large eastern neighbour, with whom we share extremely important items of mutual interest. These items deal directly with our security and with the security of the Soviet Union. We must deal with them from a position of mutual faith and trust. I ask for patience in these times, do not panic and keep true to the Latvian spirit and no harm will come.

Everyone started to talk at once. I heard one lady cry out, 'The Russians are coming!' Too many people were moving and turning to one another. I felt afraid and took hold of Marta's arm as a horn rang out over the crowd. Everyone stopped and looked down. Our conductor was waving his baton from side to side, and then it was announced over the loudspeaker that we would sing the national anthem.

What a sound! I'd never heard anything like it. '*Dievs, svētī Latviju!*—God bless Latvia!' As soon as the anthem ended, the conductor raised his baton and we went again. We all joined hands and swayed. '*Dievs . . . svētī . . . Latviju!*' Then again. '*Dievs . . . svētī . . . Latviju!*'

I looked across at Marta and saw she was crying. We hugged each other tightly, as if we were joining as one. We both felt the anthem strongly in our hearts. We all did. We sang it three times. That is important to remember. I'll never forget that sound as long as I live.

After the concert, everything became confusing. It was close to midnight but my father did not want to wait for the truck home in the morning. He wanted to get back to my mother, so we went to the train station. There we found hundreds of people trying to leave, pushing to get past one another, running all over, carrying their bags. Everyone wanted to catch the trains going west, but we were going to Kraslava, east of Daugavpils towards the Byelorussian border.

When a train came going in our direction, the guard would not let us on. My father's robes were flapping as he tried to explain we needed to get home. He looked ridiculous. The guard kept yelling that the train was going the wrong way. My father kept nodding and shouting that he knew. The guard let us on when he finally understood we lived in Kraslava.

Our carriage was empty. You wouldn't think it but my clearest memory from that day is how strange it was to be in the carriage by myself with my father on the way home. That was the thing that made me feel like my world was turning upside down.

We were never alone just the two of us. He never spoke directly to me at home but now he kept clearing his throat. I held tight to the handle of my suitcase and looked out into the dark.

I jumped when he finally spoke. 'Don't worry, Aline. It won't be that bad if the Russians come. I lived under the Czar, it wasn't too bad,' he said. I just looked at him and nodded.

When we got off the train, we had to walk a mile to our house. The sun was coming up. As we went through the town, I checked to see how everything looked, but it still seemed the same, all the houses and trees. Then I saw my mother. Her hair was blowing out of her scarf in the wind. She normally kept herself very tidy but she'd been waiting for us in our front vegetable patch all night. She fell down to her knees in the dirt and held on to me. 'It will be hell!' she cried.

You see, she knew. One of her brothers had died in 1918 when Latvians fought Russia for independence the first time. She could remember the fields full of graves. When we got up to go inside, I saw she had big wet patches of dirt on her skirt.

We all sat down at the kitchen table and looked at each other. Soon there was another announcement from Ulmanis on the radio. People have never forgotten his words:

> As of this morning, Soviet armed forces are entering our country.
> This is taking place with the government's knowledge and
> agreement, which results from existing friendly relations between
> Latvia and the Soviet Union. I therefore wish that the population
> of our country meet the arriving armed forces with friendship . . .
> Do not allow panic or bloodshed . . . I will stay in my place and
> I ask you to remain in yours.

5

Sweet Riga

When I was ten, my family made plans to move from Toowoomba to the Gold Coast. This coincided with Grandma Milda deciding she could no longer take care of my *vectēvs* Edgars by herself. My parents bought a new house with a granny flat, and many of Grandma Milda's mysterious Latvian things were moved up from Newcastle. At first, my sisters and I were wary of having our grandparents living right next to us with their strange art, old books, fermented food and proper ways of doing things. Initially, my grandma Milda was busy taking care of my granddad, who was very ill. But once my *vectēvs* Edgars passed away, she had more time for us. Grandma Milda seemed to soften and we became used to running into her granny flat to see her whenever we felt like it, often preferring her company to that of our parents.

My sisters and I started to spend hours each day after school sitting next to her as she sewed with the TV on in the background. On Monday and Tuesday nights, we'd watch *A Country Practice*.

'I like that Georgie Parker and that Cookie,' she'd often say. 'She's a lovely girl and he's a funny man.'

Our three little heads would nod and she'd break into a smile.

At the first ad break, we'd ask for lollies. Grandma would huff and puff but struggle out of her leather rocking chair to her kitchen cupboard and peer in.

'Ha! There is nothing left in here. You girls keep coming in and taking things without asking.'

My sisters and I would squirm around and look at each other.

'There are more lollies up the back, Grandma. The skittles . . .' I'd venture.

She'd turn around and stare at us.

'How is it that you know what's in my cupboard better than I do?'

We'd wait as she'd mutter to herself and then turn back to keep searching.

'Ha! Here is something. I must have forgotten about them.'

She'd take out the red packet and, grinning at us, count out ten brightly coloured skittles, tinkling each one down carefully into three little glass bowls.

'They have to last the rest of the show.'

We'd all jump up to kiss her old cheek.

'Thanks, Grandma, thanks.'

'You girls are lucky,' she'd retort.

'Yes, we know.'

'I am not sure you do!'

After the show, Grandma Milda was sometimes in the mood to talk and would paint small careful scenes from her childhood in the Dole district, countryside south of Riga.

'In summer, my mother was always busy working for the German families who came to stay in their big country houses. All the children in the district would go out picking cherries. We would eat so many, everyone's stomachs would be aching. But I never said a word about it to my mother and father. They were hardworking people and I knew I would get no sympathy at all.

'Winter was another world altogether. When the snows came, they were a thick white blanket over the fields. But every day I still walked more than 3 miles to our school and back. Can you imagine walking every day in thick snow to school? Of course, you can't. Your parents drive you girls. But there was no way I wanted to stay at home with my mother, even when the snow was thick. She would have put me straight to work!'

26

But when I took the initiative and asked further questions about what her childhood was like, it was often difficult to get more details. Her sentences became shorter.

'What was your bedroom like?'

'You know, four walls, a bed and cupboard,' she'd shrug.

'Were you close to your brother?'

'Well, of course, but I liked my own company, and we had different friends.'

'Did you go to church?'

'Religion was important, particularly on special occasions.'

Even as a young girl, I could feel her reticence to lose control and open herself up to painful topics and memories. But when I stopped asking questions, Grandma Milda seemed more comfortable to hold forth again on her own terms. She sometimes ended our evening with variations of the same story, speaking proudly about how, when she was eight years old, Latvia finally won its independence in 1920, freeing itself from the Russian Empire. Her eyes would glow as she spoke of how Riga had flourished with new industries, buildings, music, art and culture.

'Riga became the Paris of the North. Yes, it did! It was such a wonderful time, our town transformed with our big central markets and grand government buildings. Our five *lati* coin was the most beautiful silver coin in Europe. Do you girls know what I mean? We even started making our own cars and aeroplanes! People wanted to be able to enjoy their lives, not stay labouring down in the dirt. Our art and music—everything came alive.'

From listening to Grandma Milda, I imagined Riga to have been re-made during this time into a glowing city filled with majestic institutions alongside Art Nouveau stone buildings and thatched gingerbread cottages. When she moved there with her parents and siblings in the late 1920s it sounded to me like she was at home in the city, but that her parents were out of place, shifting between different labouring and domestic jobs in Riga and heading back out to the family home in the Dole district when they could. I sensed that in her early twenties, Grandma Milda had sought to go her own way.

One time, Grandma Milda told us the story of her beloved Café Luna.

'When I finished school, I worked as a bookkeeper, first at the post office and then at Lino, a stationery company. I very rarely made mistakes. When I finally had some money for myself, I wanted to buy something nice. I often walked past a well-known Riga place, Café Luna, on the way to work.

'Once I went there by myself to have just a small treat. When I opened the door, I could see rows of sugar and nutmeg scrolls, chocolates and pepper cookies. *Wunderbar*! The smell! Warm and sweet!'

We breathed and sighed as Grandma's eyes sparkled with remembered joy.

'I chose a simple almond chocolate and sat down. The waiter brought it to me in the middle of a white plate with a beautiful golden rim. I almost laughed. It was resting there all by itself. So small! I could see the rise where the almond was buried just underneath the chocolate.'

We sat there captive, the vision of the perfect chocolate in front of our eyes.

'I had to nibble to make it last. What my mother would have said if she saw me eating chocolate in the middle of the day! All her life, she cleaned and cooked. She would never have imagined her daughter sitting in Riga eating chocolate. But I thought, why not? I wanted to have that chocolate very much.'

We leant back and listened, amazed as she went further than she usually did, and spun a magical tale of her beautiful city.

6

Grandma Milda

'I want this life'

How wonderful my Name Day was in 1938. I was 24 and it was 11 May but spring was nowhere to be seen. There were grey clouds racing across the sky as I walked across the Akmens Bridge. The Daugava River was full of melted snow rushing past. There were white caps on the surface of the water.

I was almost swept down *Kaļķu Iela*—our famous Lime Street in the oldest part of the city—into the Town Hall Square. That was where I was to meet two of my closest friends, Tedis and Edite. I checked my watch. Midday. The Doma church bells started ringing, then St Peter's and St Jacob's over the red rooftops. It was like our famous weathervane roosters were crowing up high on their steeples. I wanted to laugh and sing into the wind: *Rīga dimd!* Riga rings! *Rīga dimd!* Riga rings!

I turned the corner and saw my friends waiting for me, their bodies hugged in tight up against the wall to try and escape the cold wind. Edite was wearing her big brown coat and her eyes were excited. '*Labdien*, Milda. *Labdien!*' they both cried. At that moment, the sun broke through the clouds and Tedis lifted his golden head to the sky. 'The sun has come out for your Name Day!' he shouted. I looked up at the stone walls decorated with vines and heavy bunches of grapes, turning silver in the sun.

We linked arms and wove our way through the loud trolley buses, screeching on their wires. 'Where are we going? Is it the opera? Is anyone else coming?' I asked. Tedis grinned. 'Ah, wait and see,' he waggled his finger. I think he knew I was wondering if Rudis Masens might join us. We had all met him at a dance hall a few months earlier and they knew I liked him very much.

As I walked through the city, I felt as if I was flying. Tedis wound us through the streets, down around the back of the market and along the river. We went through the *Vermanes dārzs*, our special gardens, and saw the stone lions. There were only a few green shoots in the flowerbeds. I knew Tedis was trying to confuse me and keep me guessing. He could be a cheeky one.

At last, we stopped in front of the grand white columns of the opera house. 'Oh, Milda! See who is there,' said Edite. That's when I saw Rudis at the top of the stairs in a navy suit. My legs were shaking but I managed to climb up towards him. He looked handsome, and it was hard for me to meet his eyes. '*Lūdzu*, Milda.' He handed me a bunch of yellow daisies and bent forward to kiss my cheek. '*Lūdzu, paldies*,' I managed but couldn't find any other words to say.

The silence between us grew when I walked into the dark foyer. My shoes clicked too loudly on the wooden floor and I knew I should say something to cover the sound but couldn't. I was grateful when we reached the deep-green carpet. When we entered the theatre itself, I could see its famous red velvet stage curtains falling from the ceiling to the floor. The four of us sat down in the third row. Rudis rested his arm next to mine, his wool suit pricking my skin through my thin blouse. After a few minutes, the gold lamps along the side of the theatre were lowered. My mind was singing, 'I want this life. I want it to be mine!'

Rudis and I took time getting to know one another. Ha! I wondered whether he liked being an eligible bachelor too much. He came from a wealthier family than mine but we learnt how to talk easily, back and forth with one another. We got along very well and shared our favourite poems and books. When he took me to eat at *Otto Schwarz*, I felt as if I was a woman out of a story. Back then it was the best restaurant in Riga. They had all the fine dishes of Europe—fillet Rossini with foie gras and crêpe suzette! But there were also good Latvian *kotletes*, the mince very moist with a tasty tomato cabbage sauce. Also food from the forest—white partridge with lingonberries, wild boar and deer. Our food was there with all the food of the world!

In summer, we went out to his family's country house in Ape to pick berries and on train trips to the beach at Jurmala with Edite and Tedis. Rudis also took us out rowing boats on Juglas Lake. The water was very calm, like a mirror, and we often saw the reflections of huge stork nests up high in the trees. In winter, we went skiing and ice-skating. Rudis was quite brave and energetic. A real Riga man! I was brave too. I became a Riga girl! Maybe it was because Latvia was a young country, but we were all brave back then.

I remember the *Jāņu Diena*, our St John's Day, in June 1939. It was our big national celebration for the summer solstice. We all went out to Cesis, where there was a field set up with places to dance and sing. In the middle was a special old oak tree that had stood there for centuries. All the food and drink stalls and tents were decorated with tree branches and flowers. There were big bonfires to jump over for good luck and lots of beer. It is our tradition to stay awake the whole night.

In the early morning, I went with Edite and some other women to the forest where we washed our faces in the dew. It is our custom to bring beauty and good fortune. You girls should know about these things.

It worked! Rudis and I got married on the twentieth of October 1939. The Lutheran pastor who performed the ceremony was a very respected man. Lots of people wanted him to do their ceremonies and we were lucky to get him. My wedding dress was beautiful, white waves of chiffon to the floor. People admired how we looked as a couple. My mother was surprised, I can tell you that! She could not ever have imagined such a wedding for herself, even that such an event could happen. Latvia had changed, and I was a part of it.

I believed *Laima*, the Latvian goddess of luck, was looking over me. But we only had eight months before the Russians came and occupied our country. Their filthy tanks rolled into Riga on 17 June 1940. The Russians took all the wonderful things we had built between the wars and ground them into the earth.

7

Linen bags and red candies

I was only sixteen but even I could see that everything changed as soon as the Russians arrived in Kraslava only days after the song festival. There were pretend elections and a new Communist government. Important buildings were covered in big red sheets stamped with the hammer and sickle. It sounds scary, but to me, it just seemed ridiculous in the beginning. I had no idea what was really going on, even though my mother knew. I'm ashamed but I will tell you the truth, a story so you know what it was really like for me.

A few months after the Soviet Army had occupied our country, I came home from school one day to find my mother sitting and sewing in the dark. My mother had drawn the curtains and was sitting with big squares of rough grey linen in her lap. I had no idea how she could see the needle in the dim light.

'What are you doing?' I asked. She told me she was sewing huge bags to put all our belongings in. 'In case the Russians come for us,' she said.

I felt angry and upset. I was not a small child so I should have understood what was happening but I looked at my own mother as if she was crazy. I went to the room I shared with Aunty Adela and buried my head in a book. I thought my mother had gone mad because of the stories of the Russian secret police, the Cheka, taking people. They were just stories to me then, not real. I didn't come out until my father was home. I couldn't stand to see my mother sitting there like that.

It wasn't long afterwards that a Russian inspector turned up at our school. He was a fat man with small eyes. As he entered our school room, some of the boys whispered, 'He looks like a *cūka*.' A pig! Poor Sister Anna, our teacher, heard them and went completely white.

The inspector made her stand at the back while he tested us. 'How do you say "bread" in Russian? What about "table" and "chair"?' It was lucky we knew the right answers.

After our test, he didn't leave. He stood around and then sat down on a chair at the front. 'I will tell you something,' he said. 'It's Stalin, not God, who is number one. I will prove it.' We all just stared at him.

'Everyone close your eyes,' he said. 'Everyone say, "God, please give us lollies".'

We sat there. None of us said anything. You see, we thought it was a trick. We knew the Communists hated God.

He kept going. 'Come on. You won't get into trouble. Say it.'

Well, we all closed our eyes and went along with him. 'God, please give us lollies.' We had no idea what was happening.

My shoulders jumped when he cried out, 'Open your eyes and see!' We looked around. Our classroom was just the same. The inspector shook his finger at us. 'See? It didn't work. There is no such thing as God.'

Everyone thought it was over but then he said, 'Let's try again! Close your eyes and say, "Comrade Stalin, please give us lollies".'

We all went along with this and then I heard lots of small cracking sounds. I opened my eyes and saw the inspector jumping like a madman. There were little red candies all over the floor.

He pointed directly at me and I froze. 'Now you know, Comrade Stalin is the one to ask when you need something!' he said.

Things became worse. When we saw two Russian soldiers coming up the path to our house, my mother told me to stay quiet. She went straight over to the front door, opened it and welcomed them in. I just stood there. I didn't understand what she was doing. She sat them down. 'Would you like a drink of *balzams*?' she asked. I couldn't believe it. The soldiers also looked surprised but happy as they drank their drinks.

Then they told my mother that an officer and his wife were being given our house. I remember my mother just nodded. Perhaps I looked rude because she spoke crossly to me. 'What are you standing there for, Aline? Start making the bread. Can't you hear we have people coming?'

As soon as the soldiers left, my mother's shoulders started shaking. 'Where will we go?' she cried. I had no idea what to do and I tried to put my arms around her but she wouldn't stop. We'd only just moved from our rooms in the church dormitory to our own place. Can you imagine how my mother felt? I've told you how hard Latvians work to have their own piece of land.

A couple of hours later Aunty Adela came home and calmed my mother down. The two of them sat and talked. Aunty had heard that other people were giving their homes to the Russians but asking whether they might also stay and pay rent. That is what my parents did. Can you imagine? They had saved for so many years to have their own house and then they had to turn around and pay rent.

It happened quickly. A day later a Russian officer and his wife turned up with their suitcases. We moved upstairs and they lived downstairs. My mother and aunty carried my parents' bed down and made it up with blankets for them. That helped start things off the right way with the officer. He appreciated it. His wife was very young, only a few years older than me, and away from her family. She seemed almost embarrassed to be taking our home.

I remember once the officer gave me some chocolate and I was afraid I'd say the wrong thing, so I did a curtsy. How stupid! I think that now. Sometimes the officer brought my mother brandy and ham. He had all sorts of things because of his position. My mother said over and over to me, 'Be polite but don't talk to him.'

Well, of course, the arrangement got harder as time passed. We had to be careful never to show our emotions around the house. Then came 14 June 1941 and everything changed. People started talking in whispers, 'Have you seen so and so?' 'Where is Mrs Lapa?' 'I heard some people are being sent to Siberia.'

My friend Marta told me most of the big houses near the forest were empty. People said it was the Cheka. My mother had known what was coming when she'd sewn those linen bags. It became suffocating at home; no one could talk to one another with that Russian officer in our house.

One thing I remember is the story of my mother's friend, Mrs Rozitis. One day our neighbour leant over the fence and whispered to us about what had happened to her. Mrs Rozitis was near her window sewing when she saw a black truck stop outside her house. She'd been terrified for weeks she was going to be taken to Siberia, and she'd been waiting for it to happen. She took her sewing scissors and stabbed herself in the chest before they'd even knocked on the door.

It turned out the truck outside her house wasn't the Cheka. It was just a normal truck.

8

Baigais Gads

The year 1940–41 is known by Latvians as *Baigais Gads*—Year of Terror. On 14 June 1941 simultaneously across the country, Red Army soldiers and several wings of the Russian secret police launched an operation. Small groups of men drove into the streets at night-time and started knocking on doors to detain whole families. They rounded up over 15,000 people in 24 hours and denounced them as 'enemies of the people'. Many were civil servants, landlords, priests and university teachers. Half of them were women and children.

People were herded into cattle cars without food or water. Some of the trains sat at stations across Latvia for days in the sun, with people dying of dehydration. It was summer, only days away from *Jāņu Diena*. People should have been baking bread and preparing caraway cheese.

When the trains got going, they headed to gulags in Siberia, harsh-sounding places—Vyatlag, Norilag and Rechlag. People peered out between the dark wooden slats to try to work out where they were going. Each morning, those who hadn't survived the night were carried out in bundles and dumped in shallow pits beside the train tracks.

That was the beginning of Latvian deportations to Siberia and constant oppression over the decades to come.

———

I went to visit Aleksis, an old Latvian friend of Grandma Milda's, to see what he might be willing to share about those terrible times.

'My family lived in Rezekne, in the east, on the train line to Leningrad and Moscow. I was only seven years old when the Russians came. My mother heard there were trains filled with hundreds of deported people going through our station. She met up with our neighbours to talk about what we could do for them. One of the women at the meeting spoke up. "I am old," she said. "Maybe the Russians will let me through to give the mothers some milk for their babies?"

'I was surprised when she turned and asked me, "Will you help me carry the milk pail?"

'I wanted to be brave in front of everybody. My mother wasn't sure at first but everyone talked further, and in the end, it was agreed a woman and a boy would be seen as the least threat by the soldiers. Somehow it was decided; it all happened very quickly.

'When we got close to the train, I saw the soldiers with their guns and was petrified. I stopped walking, but the old lady took the canister from my hand and kept going. All of a sudden, one of them strode over to her. I watched as he grabbed the canister and threw it to the ground. "What have the babies done?" the old lady spat at him. "They are not criminals!"

'He swung his rifle around and smashed her in the face.

'I just stood there as she crawled back to me. I watched that white milk soaking into the dirt. The old lady's nose was broken. We had to walk all the way back to our street with her face covered in blood.

'The babies on the trains needed that milk to survive.'

9

❋ Grandma Milda ❋

The cupboard

I taught you that it is better to remember the wonderful times. What did you expect to learn? Some of us escaped and some of us didn't!

During the Russian occupation, Rudis and I were sharing a flat in Pardaugava over on the western side of Riga with another man, Egerts, as our lodger. Egerts had a mouth on him and didn't like Russians.

One day when Rudis was at work, Egerts saw a black truck on the street. 'Hide!' he cried. But I didn't know where to go. My mind kept thinking of places but they were not good enough: *Under the bed? Behind the door? Under the sink?*

Egerts shook me. He grabbed me by the hand and dragged me into the big oak cupboard in our hall.

It was half-empty and dark in there, only the hinges showed a crack of light. I stared at that bright line to stop my body knocking against the cupboard. I heard Egerts' chair scrape along the floor and knew he was sitting down at the kitchen table to pretend he was eating a normal breakfast. He did that for me. I know he did.

Then they were pounding at the front door. I kept my eyes on that bright line. 'Who is there? I am coming!' Egerts called. All at once, the men rushed past the cupboard and the room was full of the sound of their filthy boots. 'Come here! Get here!' they yelled. I couldn't block out the sounds. They kicked him, over and over. After a long time, they dragged him out of the room.

I could hear his body banging on each and every stair down to the street.

I stayed hidden in that cupboard for hours. The rushing in my ears was too loud for me to hear anything else. My mind kept clicking over: *Is one waiting? Waiting me out?* There was such an ache in my legs. I tried to keep my eyes on the bright line, but somehow, without deciding to, I stretched out one of my legs. I started to fall and tried to catch the sleeve of a coat to pull myself back. Its hanger swung out and I crashed against the cupboard. The noise was such a bang!

I waited but no one came. When I inched the door open I could see the kitchen. Egerts' plate still had his hard-boiled egg on it but his chair had been knocked over. The blue rug was stained black, and I knew it was his blood. After a long time, I crawled out, then managed to get up and run to our bedroom. I put my pillow on the floor, curled up and waited for Rudis to come home.

Hours later I heard his whistling outside. When it stopped I knew he'd seen our front door was open. 'Milda?' I couldn't speak. I felt the floorboards moving under me as he ran over. 'What's happened? What's happened?' he cried.

For a long time I did not want to speak. I found I could not begin to tell him.

Thank God the Germans came when they did. You know the Russian soldiers set our precious St Peter's church on fire before they left. In the middle of Riga, it made a huge bonfire. I could see the sky from my flat, a huge stain of awful black smoke. It looked like the world was ending.

Latvians brought buckets of water, but the Russians shot them. They didn't want anyone to get close enough to put the fire out. All we could do was watch as the church burned down to the ground.

10

Sanctus Donatus

The Russian officer and his wife left Kraslava with no notice. They just took their bags and went because there were rumours the Germans were coming. Mother and Aunty Adela scrubbed the house from top to bottom, then we moved our furniture back the way it had been.

My father came home and poured drinks to have a toast. My mother let me have some cherry brandy. It was like a small party for a couple of hours and then we had to think about what might come next.

Kraslava soon became a dangerous place to live. Russian soldiers started arriving from all over Latvia as they needed to get back across the eastern border. My father sent my mother, aunty and me to my grandmother's place out near Indrica in the country, but he wouldn't leave his church. My mother begged him, but he wouldn't come with us. On our way to my grandmother's house, I remember seeing my school. It had rows of windows along one side, and every one of them was smashed.

It was awful to be at my grandmother's place, not knowing what was happening. The sun was shining but we had to stay inside. Every time we heard a dog bark, we thought it might be soldiers coming. My mother wouldn't speak to anyone. She just sat and counted her rosary beads. She was sure my father would be shot. I brought her food but she wouldn't eat it. She was like that for two days.

Eventually, a neighbour came and told us the Russians had left. My mother jumped up. She wanted to walk the 10 miles back to Kraslava straight away. Everyone told her it was too dangerous but my mother wouldn't listen. Aunty Adela couldn't walk such a long way because her leg was not good. In the end, it was just the two of us who left for home.

It took most of the day to walk back along the forest road. We could see smoke on the horizon but there was no one about. When we reached the edge of Kraslava, we could see burnt houses. I was afraid for my father.

We ran into a friend and he started to cry when he saw my mother. 'Apolonija, I have heard the priests have been shot and the vicar was arrested to be tortured!' My mother's knees collapsed and she fell to the ground moaning. I stood there in the middle of the road.

Then I saw him! My father, running towards us. '*Māmiņa*, he is here! He is here!' I yelled.

He ran up and pulled us close to him. He was crying and trying to talk to my mother. He told her that when the soldiers came, he'd hidden in the forest. A big part of him was ashamed about that, but my mother and I were grateful he was alive.

Our church was ruined. Part of the roof was missing, and the wooden beams were like the ribs of a giant black skeleton. The floor was covered in ash. You have to understand, it wasn't just a church to us. It was where we had lived for many years. It was where my father played his organ every day and conducted the choir. It was where my mother prayed. Her soul was in that place.

'How could they burn the bones of Sanctus Donatus?' she kept asking. Decades earlier, the Catholics in Kraslava had paid for his bones to be brought there, consecrated and placed under that church.

For the next few months my mother was part of a group that helped sort through the ruins searching for the ashes of Sanctus

Donatus. What a thing to look through ashes for ashes, but that is what they did. They bent down, going through the ashes until they found the place where they thought he was buried. My mother was the one who collected him up and laid him to rest again.

Part Two: No Light

1941–45

Daugava, black-eyed
Flows dark as night falls.
How could it not flow black,
Filled with precious souls.

Latvian folk song

11

The Germans

The attack by Nazi Germany on Soviet-occupied Latvia on 22 June 1941 caught the Red Army unprepared. Within days, divisions of Russian soldiers fled over the border, looting and burning as they went.

Given their recent experiences of deportations and other Communist atrocities, a large part of the Latvian population welcomed the Germans and hoped the country might find its way back to independence. For a brief moment, it must have seemed as if the light had returned. But it soon became clear that Germany considered Latvia a part of German-occupied territory and that Nazi ideology and policies would be enforced.

I wanted to understand my grandmothers' experiences of those years of the German occupation but knew I'd not chosen an easy path and could end up hurting everyone. I can recall a conversation I had with a friend in Darwin when I told her I was going to research the lives of my grandmothers.

'Lucky you're looking into them and not your grandfathers,' she blurted.

'Huh?'

'Weren't lots of Latvian men part of the German Army?'

'I think one of my grandfathers joined the Latvian Legion, but they weren't involved with killing Jews, if that's what you mean. The Legion went to the frontline. Latvians of all faiths lived side by side before the war came along.'

'Right then, okay . . .'

'What are you saying? Most Latvians weren't Nazis!' I declared.

'Maybe not. But that means some were. Most people will do anything to survive.'

———————

For many years in the Australian–Latvian community, the Holocaust was a taboo subject, only spoken about in whispers of grief, denunciation and shame. There has been more open discussion in the last 40 years, initially led by historians living in Latvia. Major Latvian historical institutions such as the Museum of the Occupation of Latvia now hold themselves to high standards of accuracy and truth in presenting information about this time.

Throughout the Nazi occupation of Latvia, approximately 70,000 Latvian Jews were killed. This annihilation was organised by the *Einsatzgruppe A*, a special operational unit of the Nazi Security Service. While most Latvians tried to stay out of the way of the Nazi machine, work has been done exposing the stories of Latvians who were heavily involved with the Nazis—men like Viktors Arajs, whom the Germans put in charge of a commando unit that killed approximately 25,000 Jews, many of them buried in pits in Rumbula Forest on the outskirts of Riga.

Still, it was a shock when I started to research the German occupation more deeply and saw the black-and-white photos of Jewish families lined up on the streets of Riga with the Star of David pinned to their clothes. I don't remember my grandma Milda ever mentioning the Riga ghetto but she must have known about it. Those photos brought the Holocaust much closer to home than studying the Second World War and Nazi Germany at school had.

One evening Nanna Aline and I were sitting together on her couch in the lamplight as she tried to explain the survival instinct that settled over Latvian families during that time of chaos.

'It is no excuse, but it was the terror of the Russians and the gulags that stuck in the mind of the country. That is why people welcomed the Germans.'

'Unless you were Jewish,' I added.

'Yes.'

'Many Latvian families came to have bad experiences at the hands of both the Russian and German occupations. Here, I will show you.'

Nanna got out one of her Latvian leather-bound photo albums. She started to go through the pages until she found the grainy grey photo she was looking for.

'That is Boleslavs, my uncle. He was taken to Siberia by the Russians.'

Nanna leant in for a better look at him before turning the page. I murmured sympathies and scribbled in my notebook.

'That one is Stani, another uncle, see right there, near my mother. He was a youth teacher in Bauska. He was accused of being a Bolshevik and was arrested in Salaspils by the Germans.'

I nodded to show I understood.

'Lots of Latvian families could share similar stories. One person taken by the Russians; another person taken by the Germans. But at first, the majority of Latvians were happy to see the Germans. Anyone that tells you differently is not telling the truth.'

12

 Nanna Aline

Candlesticks and children

In the beginning, many Latvian people kissed the ground the Germans walked on. There were celebrations in the streets. People put on their folk costumes, picked bunches of flowers and went to the tall Freedom Monument in Riga. Even in Kraslava, we had a small parade down the main street.

I got caught up in the feeling I could live again and I wanted to get back to having a good time with my best friend, Marta. I know how it sounds now, but I'd just turned seventeen. That's how young people are: they want to have a good time. I begged to be allowed to go out, but time and time again, my mother told me to stay home. She still often sat at our window to keep a watch on what was happening in the street.

Finally, she agreed. I told her I was going to the market down the road, but instead Marta and I went for a walk in the Count Plater's Forest on the eastern side of Kraslava. It was a lovely place with paths through the trees. I knew my mother would not approve of us going there but I thought I was old enough to do as I liked.

At first, Marta and I enjoyed ourselves. It was warm. She was wearing a new dress with yellow flowers and looked very pretty. I felt good to be close to her, like I was somehow prettier myself, you know? We had our arms linked and we were singing childish songs, like this sort of thing . . .

The little girl farted when watching the cow.
The little girl farted when taking a bow.
The little girl farted when working the mill.
The little girl farted when climbing the hill.

We were laughing and walking, but when we got deeper into the woods, Marta and I started to wonder if we'd made a mistake. We could hear lots of rustling; at first we thought it was hares and squirrels, but then we were not sure. We'd just decided we should turn around and go home when we heard someone running through the trees and then sounds like sharp firecrackers in the air.

'Shooting!' hissed Marta. We took off running back down the path but my legs were heavy. I was too slow. It was as if I couldn't move properly. I stopped to catch my breath.

Then I saw him in the trees, a man's eyes among the green leaves. I knew he saw me. I felt as if I had frozen to ice, and it was hard to turn and walk away. Somehow, I was convinced that if I started running, he would come after me. I don't know why. I just walked as fast as I could and only caught up with Marta once I reached the edge of the forest.

For some reason, I was truthful with my mother when I got home. She was very angry with me. 'You must listen, the war is not over!' she cried. She thought the man must have been a Russian soldier hiding from the Germans.

A couple of months later, there was a loud knocking at our door. Two German soldiers came in with their rifles yelling, *'Jude! Jude!'* My mother grabbed my shoulders. 'Aline, what do they want? Tell me, tell me!'

You see, she could not speak German. I told her they were looking for Jewish people. 'No! Tell them no!' she cried.

The soldiers went through the house. They tossed the blankets from our beds, looked in cupboards, went down to our back cellar, where we kept our jars of pickled cucumbers. Then, it was over. Afterwards, it was hard to believe it had even happened.

But a few weeks later there was a second shock. A German officer turned up at our place and said he was moving in. My father was the one who had to speak with him because my mother didn't understand a word.

It was not like it was when the Russian soldier and his wife had taken over our house. The German officer told us he would have the back room. It was more like he was a guest, but we knew we had no choice.

When he came back, I looked up from my book to see my school friend Abrams with his head down, carrying the officer's bags. I was about to say hello to him when Abrams shook his head. I knew that meant I shouldn't say anything. I watched Abrams as he set down the bags and then backed away to stand outside our front door. It was as if he was not allowed to stay inside. I looked down at my book and kept my eyes there.

Abrams was good at maths and used to tutor me. We were in the same class. He was nothing different from me, but he was Jewish and so had been taken from his family. I saw him only a few times after that, carrying heavy boxes and sacks around town.

It was around this time that my mother came home one day weeping. She'd seen a long line of Jews sitting on the side of the road near the market with their suitcases. She was very upset. Kraslava was a small place and my mother knew a lot of those people. They were our shopkeepers and neighbours. 'Where will they take them?' she cried.

'I have heard they are going to Palestine,' my father said, to reassure her. It seems crazy now but many people thought this. Now I think we wanted to believe that, but we must have known the truth, even from the beginning.

A few days later, one of our priests came to our house to talk to my mother. I was surprised when he asked me to join them. We sat down in the kitchen together and he told us that a Jewish mother had given her children, a young boy and girl, to the nuns who lived near our house, explaining they were to be baptised to keep them safe. He asked whether I would be their godmother.

I was shocked that he would ask me! It's hard to admit now, but I felt special that I was chosen to do such an important thing.

My mother wanted to know the baptism would be done properly. That was the main thing for her—that the children were going to take the Father, Son and Holy Spirit into their hearts. I know how it sounds but people didn't think the same way back then as they do now. These days, many people think God is so forgiving he doesn't mind what you do as long as you try your best. Not back then!

My mother was humble and fearful of God. She believed it would be a sin to be part of a baptism that wasn't real—that we would both go to Hell. The priest told her all would be done correctly. That was very important.

Later that night, we walked to the house where the nuns lived. It was cold but I remember we went quickly without our coats. We were shown into a back room that was lit by candles. Everything was set out. An altar had been arranged with a wooden cross and some candlesticks carved with our Latvian *raksti* symbols taken from the church. The priest delivered the prayers and sprinkled the water on the children's heads, just as would have been done in the church. I had to come forward, to put my hands on the children's shoulders and say their new names.

The little girl's shoulders jumped when I touched her. I wanted to tell her not to be afraid, but I didn't say a word. When it was finished, the nuns took them to the kitchen to have some milk and bread.

When we got back home, Marta was at our door. 'You went for a walk? Why aren't you wearing your coats?' she asked.

'We just rushed over quickly to give the nuns bread,' my mother said. My whole life I had never heard my mother lie, until then.

The next day my mother could not forget the lie she'd told and so she did bake some bread to give to the nuns. She told me not to tell Marta what we had done. I kept that promise, I know I did, but I don't know what happened to those children. Such important things I can't remember now. I can't even remember their names.

13

Imagine two houses burning

The few times Grandma Milda talked about the German occupation, she'd never describe it in any chronological way. Instead she would fire out warnings and metaphors aimed at educating us. Once, when I asked her directly whether back then the Germans were in fact worse than the Russians, she angrily spat out her answer, 'Imagine two houses burning, one completely in flames and the other with only one room burning. Which one would you live in? The Russians had a list of people they were taking away. Under the Germans there was a different list: Jews, Gypsies and Communists. We were not on it!'

When I was growing up, she occasionally made remarks about 'filthy Russians' and 'clever Germans'. I'd squirm, uneasy that she was saying something wrong. At school, we'd learnt more about the German atrocities of the Holocaust than anything the Soviets had done.

'Everyone is terrible in war. All sides are the same,' I mumbled once, wringing my hands.

'All sides the same? Not to the people being shot at, they aren't,' she retorted.

I sat there, stung, as she grabbed the ornamental sepia globe that sat on her bookshelf next to her leather recliner.

'You want to know? See here, Latvia! See here, USSR!'

She jerked her finger at the tiny pink dot of Latvia up against the boundless Soviet Union, her eyes fierce. I watched as she then spun the globe on its small gold axis, her jaw jutting out, indignant.

'And here, Germany! And here, Australia! The further away from the Russians, the better!'

I felt like a small bug. Her gaze through her glasses felt hot and magnifying as she directed her rage towards me.

'Sorry, Grandma,' I whispered.

'Don't talk about things you know nothing about.'

I stayed by her side for a few more moments so it would seem as if I wasn't running away.

I now wonder whether the year I spent learning German at high school was partly an effort to show I had some understanding of Grandma Milda's connection to Germany and therefore Latvia, at least so it seemed to me back then. Her eyes twinkled brightly when I announced I'd received third place in the German-speaking contest at school and recited the winning poem for her.

'Your pronunciation is good! Just like a little German!'

She patted my arm and I felt a queasy pride. I had wanted her to think I was a bit more European than she'd surmised, but being a good little German was going too far.

'Not all Germans are good, Grandma,' I quietly muttered. 'And not all Russians are bad.'

She paused and looked at me speculatively. I held my breath, wishing I could take the words back, but all she said was, 'I suppose that is true. It didn't seem like it back then.'

Then she waved her hand as if to dismiss me.

———

I knew Nanna Aline had also had to navigate the 'two burning houses' of the Russian and then Nazi occupations. Sitting in her kitchen one day, I asked her about the complex relationship many Latvians, including her, had with the occupying German forces.

'You want to know how I could have been involved with baptising those Jewish children but still look up to Germany?' she asked.

I shrugged weakly.

'All I can say is that a lot of people held those two opposite ideas in their heads during that time. Latvia had a long history with Germany going back centuries; our upper classes all used to be German people. We had to keep living our lives.'

I slowly nodded and kept listening.

14

Reichsarbeitsdienst

In late 1941, my parents agreed to send me to boarding college near Daugavpils. I wanted to go very much because Marta was going. My mother convinced my father I needed more of an education. The nuns ran the college and she thought I would learn useful things from them.

But even at boarding college, I did not stand on my own two feet. All our meals were cooked. All our laundry was done. I just followed Marta and the other girls. I didn't know my own mind. I didn't think about what I should learn to set up my own house one day. Nothing like that!

We studied German language and culture, but also Latvian history. The Germans did not ban all Latvian things. It was more like they wanted us to think Latvians and Germans had always been close and that we belonged together.

I didn't think it was unusual when three German officers came to visit our school. I didn't connect them with those Jewish children. The officers looked handsome in their dark-green uniforms, their chests pinned with gold medals. People who talk on TV shows always think they would see through the propaganda if it happened to them, that they would never be so stupid. But propaganda is powerful. Never forget that.

We held a concert for the officers as it was close to Christmas. I was responsible for decorating the hall with pine branches and cones, and I brought in bundles from the trees that grew near the fence. The hall looked very good and smelt fresh. I was proud of the way it looked.

The students all sang—some German songs, some Latvian ones. I looked over and saw one of the officers had tears in his eyes at the sound of our voices. He stood and announced it was their turn to share something. The three of them wrapped their arms around each other's shoulders and sang 'O Tannenbaum'.

One of the officers told us Wagner wrote it when he lived in Riga. It sounds stupid now, but I remember there was a good feeling in the hall from all the singing. Lots of girls were whispering about how kind the officers were.

After the concert an officer stood up and told us about *Reichsarbeitsdienst*. It was a program where young Latvians could go to Germany to work as part of the war effort against the Communists. He spoke about what a good thing it would be to do and how we would learn more about German culture.

After the concert, Marta jumped out of her chair and said she was going to sign up. I thought: *Well, why not?* What an adventure it would be for us to go together. I could see a new place and improve my German. I didn't think about how far away I would be from my parents as I put my name down next to Marta's. I did this in a blink. Just like that. But later in bed that night I thought of my name on those papers. I had smudged the ink of the final 's' in my last name—Balulis. I kept seeing it over and over, that messy ink. I started wishing I could get those papers back.

When I returned home for Christmas, I didn't tell my mother what I'd done and tried to push it out of my mind. We made plans for me to study nursing in Riga. I thought I could become a better person if I were a nurse. I imagined myself caring for others and having younger girls admiring me.

A few months later, I was accepted. 'Aline, you have found your life's work,' my mother said. I will never forget it, she looked at me with such love. I went to Riga for training and stayed in a boarding house with some of the other students and senior nurses.

During the second week, one of the nursing sisters came into the room where we were having our lesson. She called out, 'Balulis, I have a message for Balulis.'

I walked to the front while the other girls watched. The nurse told me she had a message from my mother. I felt a bit important I was getting a message rather than worried.

Outside the room, the nursing sister told me my mother had called from the Kraslava post office. 'There is something wrong,' the nurse said. 'Your police station received a letter asking you to report for *Reichsarbeitsdienst.*'

My cheeks went hot. The sister looked at me and knew straight away. 'It's true! How could you do such a thing?' she cried.

She marched me to the office. 'Your mother is waiting for you to call her back. You tell her there is no mistake!'

The telephone was big and black, sitting right in the middle of the desk. My hands shook, so the sister dialled the numbers for me. I heard the operator connecting the call, then my mother's voice. It was faint but I could hear she sounded confused. 'The policeman has just shown me your signature . . . I don't understand,' she said.

I took a deep breath. 'It will be okay, *Māmiņa*. Marta and I will go together. It will be good for us both.'

I will never forget what she said next. 'Oh Aline! You don't know how it will be!' She told me they were only taking people born in 1924. Marta was two years older. She cried and told me they could arrest my father if I didn't go. 'Your father could not survive jail!' Such a terrible feeling came over me but I knew I could not share it with my mother.

When she calmed down, she told me there was very little time and I had to report to the *Reichsarbeitsdienst* office on *Stabu Iela* in Riga in five days.

Soon everyone in my school knew what had happened. Some of the nursing sisters felt sorry for me, but there was nothing they could do. Each day I talked to my mother on that black telephone, she said the same thing over and over. 'But you have always had someone to take care of you, Aline. What will you do?'

At first, my mother planned to bring my clothes and food to Riga, but she couldn't get a ticket for the train because all the seats were going to the army and government people. At the last moment, she had to send them with a lady she knew who was already travelling. My mother had wanted to say goodbye to me in person, so she was devastated she could not come.

Five days later I was off to Germany. My carriage was full of Riga girls, all dressed in their fine coats. They were all confident, talking and laughing. I felt sorry for myself and ate the bread and liverwurst my mother had sent. She'd also packed my rosary beads and a small prayer book along with my clothes. That was all I had.

I looked out the window at the fields and farmhouses for hours. I didn't really know where I was going. All I had was the address: RAD Lager 6/31, Kloddram, Über Boizenberg. I heard one of the girls saying it was near the Elbe River. Maybe I shed a few tears? I don't know. I didn't talk to the other girls and sat by myself the whole way.

This is how it can be. Sometimes one small moment changes the course of your life, just one decision.

15

 Nanna Aline

Kloddram

When we got to Kloddram, south-east of Hamburg, it was not too bad. The fields were green with crops. You might have thought the bombs had ruined everything, but it wasn't like that. It was lovely, with lots of trees along the Elbe River. The war seemed to be somewhere else, far away.

We were put into dormitories. I was lonely the first few nights, but then I met a girl from Riga named Elizabete. She became my only friend. It's like a rare pearl to find a true friend when you are on your own. She had curly dark hair and laughed all the time. She was nothing like me. I was a little blonde mouse.

It was hard, but I grew used to it. Each morning, we got dressed in our blue dresses and red scarves. They gave us coats. We had an armband and the letters 'OST' on our sleeves. That meant we were workers from the East. We would get on our bicycles and ride to the farms and factories where we worked. I was not such a good rider and the tracks were very muddy, but I learnt. After a while, I even liked the feeling of riding fast.

The people I worked for were kind—an older couple who had no children. They wanted us to work, but they never yelled or hurt us. All the farm workers ate meals with them. We had potatoes, leeks, milk and good sausages. Many OST workers were not that lucky.

There was a French prisoner of war also working on the farm. He was not allowed to be with us at the main table, but had to sit on his own at a small wooden table by the door. The Nazis thought prisoners of war were unfit to share meals with German families. Those were the rules, but I don't think the German couple really thought that way. He ate the same food as us and it was my job to pass it to him. No one was awful to him, but we simply knew we had to stay away from him. Yet we still sometimes shared a smile together. He was tall with a big jaw; I don't think he was a bad person.

One day we were working together in the same field. The Frenchman was near the road and I was further back in the middle. A shiny black car stopped at the side of the road and two German officers got out and headed towards him. I crouched down, but I wasn't behind any trees. I thought the officers would see me for sure.

The officers started to yell and the Frenchman took off, running towards the fence. I pushed myself further down so I was lying on the dirt. The ground was cold. I waited for a gunshot, but it never came. When I opened my eyes, I saw the officers had caught the Frenchman and pulled him to the ground. They dragged him back to the car and drove off. Now I think those officers must have been able to see me the whole time, but just didn't care.

I lay there until I was sure they weren't coming back and then ran to the house. When I got there, the farmer's wife met me at the door, reached her arms out and brought me to her. She'd seen everything.

She took me to the kitchen and helped me wash the dirt off my face and arms. We both cried for that Frenchman and then she told me we must never speak about it again.

I did tell Elizabete when I got back to the dormitory that night. No one else, only Elizabete, because I could trust her. She lit a candle for the Frenchman. We prayed together and it helped. I don't know what happened to him. It was very rare to know what happened to people back then.

Soon afterwards, I was granted leave to travel back to Latvia to visit my parents. You see, *Reichsarbeitsdienst* was a proper work scheme with conditions. When I arrived home, everyone was talking about how the Germans were losing the war. My parents thought I should stay in Kraslava.

I had been assigned to work in a munitions factory by then. It was serious work and the rules were strict. Every bullet had to be counted and packed properly. People could be shot for doing the wrong thing.

We knew I might be arrested if I didn't go back to Germany, but we were desperate. My father tried to arrange for me to marry a man he knew because he thought that if I was somebody's wife, I might be allowed to stay.

The man had terrible black teeth and there was no way I wanted to stay at his place even for a week. The idea of marrying that man was awful.

'It's a crazy idea. He's a drunk,' yelled my mother. 'The Germans will know it's a trick.'

Eventually it was agreed I had to go back. There was no other choice.

16

Articles and letters

The same day Nanna told me about her life in Kloddram, I decided to share with her something I'd found out about the fate of Jewish children in Kraslava. I had been going back and forth between Newcastle and Canberra visiting the National Library to research the German occupation, and had come across mention of a few Latvians in Kraslava baptising some children to try to keep them safe. It felt wrong to hold back this information when Nanna was sharing so much.

After dinner, we went to sit on her patio, resting big glasses of white wine on the small table beside us. I took a deep breath.

'Nanna, when I went to the library in Canberra a few weeks ago, I found something. About Jewish children being christened in Kraslava.'

Nanna turned to me, her eyes wide. 'They had information about such a thing?'

I went inside to retrieve the excerpt I'd had translated from the *Daugavas Vēstnesis* (Daugava Gazette) and stored in a beige manila folder in the front flap of my suitcase. I decided not to voice the terrible Nazi propaganda statements at the beginning and began reading from when the article mentioned Kraslava, my voice quiet and unsteady.

In recent times, many Jews, with the aid of some clergymen, have tried to convert to Christianity and so save themselves from the Star of David. In this respect, particularly scandalous conditions stand out in Kraslava. According to information from the Kraslava police, an entire Jewish family was 're-christened' in a local church—the merchant Barkans with his wife and two children.

At the time when the deportation of Kraslava's Jews to encampments occurred, other such enterprises were uncovered . . . One Agata Tomane, Miesnieku Street 5, accepted for upbringing two Jewish children. But Tomane . . . gave them to her friend Paulina Silava, Vienibas Street 45. Tomane gave her a hundred roubles to look after the children for a few days. But a week went by and Tomane never showed so Silava informed the authorities. On questioning she revealed that Tomane had taken on the children's upbringing for a large amount of money . . . Resident of Kraslava, Anna Garancareka, of St Ludviga [church] estate no 2, after the Jewish deportations, took in for upbringing a certain Jewish girl . . . She gave the child in for christening . . . Marija Umbrasko in the same way took on . . . a child and had it christened in the local church. Olga Jurevica of Pils Street 9 took a boy and girl from the Jewish Pasternak to raise . . . Acting in the same way was Marija Vasala, Pagraba Street 12, who took on upbringing of two unknown Jewish children.

These Jewish children were taken from their obliging stepmothers and sent to Jewish camps. The guilty women will have to answer to the courts and a harsh penalty awaits them . . .

Daugavas Vēstnesis [Daugava Gazette], 31 October 1941

I handed the piece of paper to Nanna.

'Goodness me, you really found this?' she asked, her voice wavering. Nanna shook her head in pain and confusion.

'Could any of those children be the same ones you were trying to help?' I gently asked.

'I don't know. They could be . . . I don't remember the name Jurevica but we lived near Pils Street. I don't know those other names . . . I never talked about those children with my mother. It was like it never happened.'

Nanna pulled her handkerchief from her sleeve and started to squeeze at it. 'Those poor children.'

'It's okay, Nanna.'

She leant over to take a sip of wine, her hands trembling. 'It was a long time ago . . . I am not sure they are the same children . . .'

'Yes, maybe they are different children,' I echoed.

I looked out over the garden, pink and silvery now the sun had set. The silence built between us. I wondered whether it would have been better to keep the article from her and started to think perhaps we should stop for the night altogether, but then Nanna cleared her throat.

'Now I want to tell you something,' she said.

I looked across, saw hesitation in her eyes and then the decision to keep going. An uneasy feeling swelled in my stomach. 'It's okay, Nanna. We've been drinking too much. Maybe we should go to bed?'

'No. I want to tell you,' her voice grew firmer. 'Every Sunday I was in Kloddram we got dressed in our good clothes. All the girls wore green skirts and white blouses with the swastika on our sleeves. We had to sit in our dormitory and write letters home to our families. We all sat at our desks and were given one sheet of paper. We were told to write about how we were in a lovely part of Germany and that we had good food to eat. It was true and so I did write about those things.

'When they could, my parents sent letters back to me. They were written with such care. Each time I got a letter from them, I would hold on to it longer than anyone else before I opened it. I felt guilty, you see, for leaving my parents.

'I kept those letters. But a few years ago, I decided to burn them.'

Her words hit me: *There were letters! But she burnt them!*

Nanna nodded as if understanding the magnitude of what she was saying. She jutted her chin out, as if goading me to say she shouldn't have done it.

'They were my letters to burn. I was sitting out here on this patio, tired of the pain. It was just over there, near the clothesline. I lit a fire in a big tin drum, threw one letter on and watched it burn. A thrill came up in me. I threw on another one. Perhaps I felt a bit guilty, but I told myself to keep going. The fire was very hot. I had such a strong feeling in my chest that if I burnt them all, I would be free.'

My mind churned. *There were letters. She burnt them. They are gone!*

'Suddenly, I stopped. I have no idea why. I was determined to burn them all, but I realised in that moment that I would never feel love like the love from my parents in those letters. The rest will stay with me now. They will be cremated alongside me.'

Nanna rubbed at her eyes and then slowly pushed herself up from her chair and shuffled into the house. My mind started to race: *Is she upset? Is she going to get them?* I sat there, not knowing what to do.

Nanna soon reappeared, holding the thick bundle carefully with both hands out in front of her, as if she was carrying a precious jewellery box. My mouth went dry. The letters were tied together with a thin pink gauze ribbon.

Nanna eased herself back into her chair. Her hands worked at the knot, her short nails picking without traction. I wanted to help, to take the bundle and do it for her, but I knew it wasn't my place to touch the letters.

The knot finally came free and Nanna opened the yellowing squares of paper, some of them faded and torn. The pages were filled with two different styles of writing, some paragraphs dense with black ink, others filled with loopy letters.

'My mother wrote in Polish and my father in Latvian,' she said. Nanna read in silence for a while, putting pages aside until she found what she was seeking.

'Here, this is something. I will translate it for you. This passage was written by my mother on 20 December 1943. I had been in Kloddram for a few months.'

Aline, thank you for your letter. We are happy to hear what
you are eating there and how you are working. Also, thank you
for your apology. My heart was aching very much that my dear
daughter did not listen to the advice I gave her. I saw how your
future life would be away from us in Germany and I worry that
it will be very hard.

  I am crying and praying for you every day, Aline. Aunty misses
you so much, particularly when she is going to sleep at night and
looks across at your empty bed. We are all safe here and waiting
for your return.

The air felt thick between us.
'Is there more, Nanna?' I stammered.
She scanned the page.
'Well, then my father writes something.'

Make sure you do not cry, Aline. For Christmas, the choir will
sing the same old pieces of music. 'Adeste Fideles' and the others.
We have not learnt any new pieces. Do not cry during Christmas
and remember you are always in our thoughts. We know you
have a difficult life there. We are always saying prayers to Holy
Mary and we ask you to say the prayers we used to say together
every day.

Nanna carefully folded the letter away. It gently slid into its well-worn creases. I willed myself to be still as she selected another one.

'This one is from twenty-seventh of March 1944. The Russian front was heading back towards Latvia. My mother writes first.'

69

I am remembering how it was when you were with us last Easter. You sang with such a beautiful voice. Now God must be punishing his people as the Bolsheviks are coming back again.

'My father was always brighter than my mother in the letters. See, here . . .'

Dear Aline, do not worry about your mother. We will both have each other at Easter time. I believe that life will turn out better than your mother says. I am still optimistic for the future. But there are big storms nearing and you must stay in Germany. The world is in tears. With God's help we will meet you again next year. You shouldn't lose your courage and when you come back to us, I am sure you will speak perfect German.

But ultimately even the optimism of Nanna's father began to falter.

'This is the letter he sent me when the Red Army was approaching Kraslava, a few months before they arrived in Riga,' Nanna said. Her hands shook as she started to read.

Dearest Aline,

I am not intending to write you a proper letter. Only to let you know that the position here is very serious. Every single hour we are awaiting changes. Lots of our possessions are in the country already and your mother is in the country as well. Our postal service is not working properly but despite that I will return to Kraslava after I leave for the country to check to see if we receive a letter from you. A letter from you would bring us such happiness.

You have to be brave because everything will be in God's hands and in a future life we will meet one another. Look after yourself and we will look after ourselves too. Now we are happy you are in Germany and not here. The situation is very grim. Today is 7 July 1944. I am writing this letter still from Kraslava but I think it will be the last one. But if you send a letter, write to our old address and, somehow, we will get it.

I kiss you very sincerely. Do not cry and do not forget God and prayer. And we pray for you.

Your Father,
Ludwik Balulis

'That's enough for now,' Nanna's voice wobbled.

She folded the papers and then slowly re-tied the bundle. I stared out at the garden, the trees now silhouetted against the grey light, then looked back at Nanna. Her head was bowed.

I swallowed and forced out a question. 'Nanna, how often do you read these letters?'

Her fingers tightened around the bundle. 'Too often. Some-times when I am on my own, I think about my life and I read them. Some of them I have read more than a thousand times. They are my burden but also my bond. All I have from my parents.'

Nanna looked up, her pale watery eyes pouring into me.

It was then it hit me—nothing I'd heard was in the past! Nanna carried around all that had happened with her every day. She walked with these millstones of grief around her neck, still managing to clap and laugh. I looked at her through new eyes, as if I could now see all the layers upon layers of past events within her.

17

Fog

It was difficult to piece together what Grandma Milda's life had been like in the first year of the German occupation. She had rarely spoken about such times to me when I was a girl. The period was a grey fog with only spotlights of information here and there, her muttered comments and the occasional outpouring of words to set ignorant grandchildren straight.

When I visited our old Latvian friend Aleksis, he revealed that Grandma Milda had told him a few stories of that period when they were both living in Newcastle many years later. His impression was that after the Germans arrived, Grandma Milda and Rudis had continued on with their lives in the Pardaugava flat. Milda initially tried to find her way back to the life she once led. However, she'd lost much of the sense of joy and freedom of her pre-war years in Riga.

'Depression. People didn't use the term back then but I think that is what it was. Your grandma once confessed how hard it was to keep putting one foot in front of the other after the Russian occupation. Then life became horrible under the Nazis.'

I baulked at the idea of Grandma being depressed. She'd always seemed to be a strong and forthright woman.

'Milda and Rudis needed money and she went to work for a time in a paper and stationery store. That helped for a while. She was proud that her boss, Mr Jansons, felt he couldn't do without her. Your grandma Milda was good at mathematics and very organised.'

I could imagine her in the back room, immersed in columns and rows of figures.

'But then they also started trying for a family. It didn't happen straight away,' Aleksis told me.

In March 1943, three years after they married, my uncle Juris was born. Perhaps Milda hadn't wanted to bring a child into the world during the Russian occupation if she could help it.

'That was a hard period,' Aleksis recalled. 'Rudis worked as a radio and telephone technician for a national company and studied at the polytechnic at nights. The way I understand it is that your grandma Milda withdrew, but she also needed help running the house after your uncle Juris was born. Her mother, Marija, moved in but Milda had a mixed relationship with her. They often didn't get along. Marija was very bossy and Milda wanted to do things her way.

'She had somehow drifted apart from her brother. People were caught up with their own obligations, trying to survive. Her brother had been through an awful time. His wife had been pregnant through the Russian occupation and his first son was born just after the Germans arrived. He was an engineer and was soon co-opted to help the Germans.

'Those were difficult months. I think Milda stayed in her room with Juris a lot of the time to try and escape it all.'

I closed my eyes and imagined Grandma with her baby son. She must have wanted more than anything to keep him tucked away safe from the world outside. I had read enough to understand that the streets of Riga had been incredibly dangerous. The hammer and sickle had been replaced with Nazi posters and new sheets and banners appeared on the government buildings, a darker red this time, with the swastika emblazoned everywhere.

18

Stay safe inside

I used to stare at Juris while he slept. His little eyelashes were very fine. Not that my mother approved. She was not the sort of person who had time to watch children sleep. But I was a new mother, and he had given me a good reason to stay at home in the flat.

Would you want to go out and see the burnt buildings and broken streets? There were new posters everywhere shouting 'Žīds nepieder pie jums. Sviežiet viņu laukā!' 'The Jew does not belong with you. Throw him out!' The newspapers were full of pictures of dead bodies, including all those that had been found inside the Cheka headquarters. Every day the Germans wanted to remind us of what the Russians had done.

There were work gangs on each corner, all prisoners of war dressed in filthy rags. Army round-ups for more men. Queues for food. People informing on one another. 'I heard he was part of the Russian group that took people.' 'She has a family hidden in her attic.' 'So and so is working for the Nazis.' How could I take Juris outside?

Once I saw a big man yelling at the young Jewish boy who helped serve customers at the shop on the corner. He was accusing him of getting the change wrong after selling him a loaf of bread. 'Thief!' he was yelling, 'Thief!' The man kept looking over at the open door to the street outside. We all knew he was hoping to get the attention of the Nazi police. He wanted that boy taken away. I don't think the boy had even made a mistake with the change.

It was better to stay inside. The safest place to be was sitting and sewing next to Juris while he slept. He was a good baby, tucked up in his woollen blankets. I used to sew clothes for him—little blue overalls, shirts with nice buttons and warm brown trousers. Sometimes I would hold them, half-finished, against his body, trying to imagine how they might look if we went out for a walk near the river. But there was no way I was going to do that. The clothes were just for us. All I wanted was to be left alone.

Rudis and my mother wanted me to go back to living a normal life. What normal life? I can remember Rudis wanting to start going to the opera again. 'The Germans have started it again. I can get tickets. It's *Der Freischütz*,' he said. There was no way I wanted to go. I kept my eyes on Juris's cot. 'No, Rudis. He is too little,' I said.

There were many occasions when I would hear my mother moving around the kitchen, banging pots and pans. I knew she was trying to make a point. 'You have to go out with Rudis, or do something useful here,' she often yelled. She took over the whole flat and I was grateful for her help but it was not a good situation. 'The carrots need to be chopped, Milda. Come and help with the *kotletes*!' Juris just slept through all her noise, his little eyes closed.

Sometimes I tried to pull myself up. I knew Rudis wanted to keep moving ahead. He kept studying and wanted to be promoted in his company. A couple of times I went to his work gatherings. I dressed up in my best cream blouse and blue skirt and said all the right things. There were many Germans as well as Latvians at these events. He wanted people to have a high opinion of him, of us both. I wanted that too and could speak German very well. Many Latvians could. But I was just too tired.

Can you imagine the fear we felt when the radio started reporting the Germans were losing the war? You can't! Only those who have been through something unbearable know how it feels when you hear it is coming back. The dread was like a sack of rocks in my stomach.

There was nowhere safe for us to go. My mother suggested we move back to Dole. What did she think? That we would be safer back in the orchard? Those times were gone. I just wanted to stay with Juris where we were. I couldn't think about doing anything else.

19

Uncle George

He doesn't go by the name of Juris much anymore. Juris the little blond baby became 'George' the knobbly-kneed kid, his name anglicised once Grandma Milda arrived in Australia. I've always called him Uncle George.

One day I decided to drive to his house in Belmont to ask him some questions about Grandma Milda's life. Before I could knock, he opened the door with a smile and a loud welcome. 'If it isn't one of the little miiiices! Or is that nieces? Don't just stand there. Come in!'

We went into the kitchen and he made us tea. Then we moved to the back veranda. I took off my sandals and rested my feet in the fur of his big 'Bear Dog' who lounged under the table.

'Such awful stuff,' Uncle George jumped in. 'I rarely asked my mum what happened during the war but her mother, Old Battleaxe Marija, your great-grandmother, shared some things with me. She was a very matter-of-fact person. Quite fearsome, actually. You've seen a photo of her?'

I made a face as I recalled her broad square chin and frown lines around her mouth.

'You know what I mean then.'

I heard the sliding door open and looked up. It was my aunty Sue in floaty peach linen, her nails painted to match. She came over and kissed my cheek.

'Good to see you, but I'm off to lunch to give you two space to talk.'

Aunty Sue was warm and no-nonsense as always. I wanted to ask her to stay.

'But there is one thing I need to get off my chest first,' she said. 'Your grandma could be a real witch sometimes, perhaps because of all she went through. She could be very judgemental of others.'

I blinked but nodded. I knew that what Aunty Sue was saying had truth to it.

'She went through hell during the war, but that certainly didn't stop her putting others through misery. I remember when I was really young, in my own world, pregnant and excited to be having my first son, she wanted to burst my bubble and told me horrific parts of her story to try to "wake me up". It scared the living daylights out of me. George was angry at her for that, weren't you, love?'

He sighed and shrugged.

I watched, startled, as Aunty Sue changed tack, tears forming in her eyes.

'She could be a witch but she was a tough lady, I'll give her that,' she choked. 'George will tell you what we know, but God only knows how much of it is true.' She turned away, rummaging for her car keys in her bag as she went.

Uncle George cocked his head and opened his palms as if the gist of everything was now on the table, then leant back in his chair and began.

'The way I understand it is that in early 1944, my father, Rudis, started coming home from work each night telling your grandma they needed to leave Riga. The Russians were slowly pushing the German front back west towards them. All Mum wanted was to stay in the flat with me. She couldn't stand to think about it. She kept begging Rudis, "Not tonight, let's not talk tonight. Tomorrow, I promise." He'd shake his head because he knew they were running out of time.

'By then Rudis had been formally conscripted into the German Army and he was then stationed in Liepaja, a day's train ride from Riga. They needed technicians to help with their communication systems. Mum begged him not to go, but they both knew he had no choice. After Rudis went, I think everyone started to tell her it was too dangerous to stay but Milda didn't want to leave Riga. Her father moved into the flat in Pardaugava. He listened to the radio all the time and left the Old Battleaxe to do all the yelling.

'In May of 1944, Mum told the Battleaxe she was pregnant again. It explained a lot about why Mum didn't want to leave. Now they waited together to hear from Rudis. Every day there was more news confirming the Germans were losing the war, but they heard nothing from him. The Red Army was marching back towards Latvia. People started to leave Riga in droves. Mum's brother, Rudolfs, left with his family for Germany and I think ended up in Denmark.

'Finally, the telephone rang. It was Rudis, but the line was bad. Mum could hardly hear him. He told her she had to leave but that he would try to get to her. Then she thought she heard something about meeting in Liepaja, but the line went dead. She didn't even get to tell him she was pregnant.'

I looked up at Uncle George, stricken.

'God, that is awful!'

'Yeah, it was a real mess . . . When there were reports the Russians were only weeks away from Riga, the Battleaxe put her foot down. She told Mum they couldn't wait for Rudis any longer. The German authorities were already evacuating German and Latvian civilians to Germany and its territories. Mum finally agreed to go. She sewed money into the lining of her two warmest coats—three big five lat coins.

'But then it started—the arguments about where they should head. The Battleaxe wanted to go to Ventspils, because there were boats leaving from there and it was the closest point. Mum wanted to go to Liepaja to try to find Rudis, and then for all of them to get a boat together. Her father stayed quiet and packed their stuff. In the end, I think they agreed to go to Liepaja.'

'How pregnant was Grandma by then?'

'About seven months. It was a nightmare that kept getting worse. God, it must have been truly horrific. I was only a baby of one and a half, but apparently I was a dream kid. Never cried.'

20

 Grandma Milda

Fleeing Riga

Only once. I will tell this story once and never again. It was September 1944, grey and wet on the street. I stood there and watched my mother place Juris into the pram. She squashed him in with all of his clothes and blankets, but he didn't cry. He had on his warmest little fur booties. I had on two coats, one over the other. Winter was not far away, but I felt too hot. I thought that surely Juris must also be too warm but I didn't say anything.

My father started to push the pram towards the train station. I held onto the side to stop myself from slipping on the wet cobblestones. My stomach was big. I knew everyone could see I was pregnant. I felt their pity. I wanted it and yet I hated it at the same time.

It took us over an hour to get across the Akmens Bridge. There were thousands of people going in the same direction. Some people were pushing wheelbarrows filled with suitcases. I saw one man with a cart that seemed packed with his whole house. 'What good will it do him?' my mother sniffed. 'What is he going to do with it all?'

It was chaos when we arrived at the station. 'You must leave the suitcases here to make room!' the German soldiers were yelling. There were huge piles of people's belongings on the platform. Blankets, crates and even a goat. Scavengers were already going through everything. People were crying and knocking against each other in the crowd. I was shoved forward, and felt as if I was going to faint.

Suddenly, a young soldier was at my side. 'Let her through!' He couldn't have been more than fifteen, but he pushed people back so as to let me and my parents board the train. Juris stayed in his pram as a couple of people lifted it over the crowd. I rushed forward, but Juris sailed smoothly over people's heads onto the train, managing to sleep through it all.

On the journey to Liepaja, people started singing some of the old folk songs, but I didn't join in. There were cheers when we went over the rivers—first the Lielupe, and then the Venta. I kept staring out of the window. The fields looked green in the rain. There were small white *pīpenes*, daisies, in the long grass by the tracks. Some of the birch leaves were starting to turn pale yellow.

As soon as we got off the train at Liepaja, we headed to one of the German headquarters down by the port to ask about Rudis. My mother marched straight up to one of the officers and demanded to be told where he was. 'Look!' she said, pointing. 'His baby is about to be born!' The man turned deep red. 'What do you want me to do?' he shouted.

Everything went a strange brown and grey.

The next thing I remember I was on the floor, surrounded by people. A German woman was bringing me some water, her brass buttons popping out from her chest. She looked important. I said to her: 'Please, can you help me find my husband?'

As I sat up and drank some of the water, the woman scolded me: 'It's no use. You must think of the baby first. There are boats leaving for Danzig and Gotenhafen tonight. You cannot be foolish!' But as we waited, I kept looking for Rudis in the crowd. I hoped that I would feel his hand on my shoulder; that I would turn around and see him standing there.

Late that night we boarded a steam boat, intending to cross the Baltic Sea, leaving Juris's pram behind on the docks. The boat was packed with Germans and Latvians trying to escape. We had to sit crowded together on the deck up against a big wooden crate. I heard a man talking about how the Allied planes were bombing the boats, to prevent German supply ships retreating. Such a tightness started to squeeze my chest that I tried to cover my ears and cried, 'Stop!' My mother shouted over to them, 'Will you be quiet! We don't want to hear about it!'

As soon as we left the port, the Germans turned off the lights so the Allied planes would have difficulty seeing us. Everything turned black. When we got further out to sea, the waves started to rock. I felt my stomach heaving, but I willed myself to stay still. Then it began to rain. My coats became cold and heavy as they soaked up the water. But Juris slept on in my mother's arms under a thick shawl.

Then I heard them! Bombers roaring over the ocean, their droning filling the sky. They were coming closer. I ducked down and thought: *This is it! Any moment!* I held my breath, wishing Juris was in my arms. Then . . . nothing. The droning slowly eased off. It became softer until all I could hear were the waves against the boat. Somehow, we had been spared.

The hours kept rolling on. Everything stayed black. Everyone was seasick. We finally arrived in Gotenhafen just before dawn. The sky was grey-pearl. My legs were frozen stiff and I could hardly get off the boat. Yet when I finally stood on the docks in a sea of people, I looked across at my mother and a burst of hope filled me. 'We need to look for Rudis,' I said. But my mother just stared at me and said nothing.

The German soldiers started to move everyone off the docks, shouting they needed to clear the space for more arrivals. We spent days in some army barracks on the outskirts of the port. Then one morning soldiers came and herded our group towards waiting trains that were to take us south-west to safety. I had no idea where we were going. Some people said we were going to Stettin and others said we were being taken towards Dresden.

My mother pushed herself into action. She started to yell, 'See, she is with a baby! Let us through!'

She kept shouting and pushing me forward until we were next to another long train. I dragged myself up into a carriage. There was no room to sit down. My back was aching with a pain that rolled all the way up my spine to my jaw.

A group of Latvians finally made room for me on the floor. I didn't care that it wasn't a seat. The floor was such a relief. My mother rubbed my lower back, and let me close my eyes and rest.

When I woke up, I could hear people praising Juris and finding him small pieces of apple and bread to suck on. I looked over and saw an old man making funny faces at him. I sat up then and a young Latvian woman next to me introduced herself. Her name was Alise. Her light blonde hair reminded me of an angel.

'He's such a beautiful little boy,' Alise said. 'You can close your eyes again. I have your suitcase.'

21

✸ Grandma Milda ✸

Little Lācis

Hours later I woke on the floor of the train to people yelling: 'The line has been damaged! We have to get off!' Everyone was moving about, collecting their belongings. 'What's happening?' I cried. I stood up and tried to pull my suitcase out of Alise's hands. 'I have it!' Alise said and looked hurt. In that moment, I knew I could trust her.

The old man placed Juris back in my arms and we all got off the train. I watched as my mother forced her way through the station crowd. She was charging around, talking to this group of people and then the next.

Alise found a place for us all to sit down, off to one side. I pointed to my mother. 'What is she doing?' My father looked across at her, both helpless and amazed. 'She's trying to work out what we should all do.'

We stayed in Gotenhafen in a camp for a few days, but my mother finally assembled a group of about a dozen Latvians who all thought we should get further west. 'Milda, get your money,' she ordered me. Alise helped me unpick the seam of my coat and locate the coins I had hidden there. A German farmer was offering to sell us a large enclosed truck and petrol. This was lucky as the army had confiscated most trucks. Everyone gave whatever money they could. A deal was done. One of the Latvian men agreed to drive and a plan was made to head towards Berlin. I piled into the back of the truck with everyone else. Juris was the youngest by far.

It was dim in there. All I could see were flashes of light between the planks of wood on the side of the truck as we drove on. Each time we hit a bump, it felt like my baby was going to drop out of me. The pressure on my back was unbearable.

I heard one man say that we were following a German convoy at a distance because they could be attacked. He said, 'It is still better. They will hit any trouble before us.'

Juris started crying. My mother passed him over to me. I took him onto my lap and he felt heavy. I prayed we would stop soon to have a rest.

Then it happened. We came over a hill and the driver yelled, 'Russians ahead!' Everyone started shouting and crying out to each other: 'They have a machine gun! They're shooting the Germans!'

We lurched to a stop. Then suddenly bullets were hitting the side of our truck. My whole body was shaking with the awful sound. Soldiers were screaming in Russian. The big bolts at the back of the truck were opened and the doors flung wide. At first, all I could see were the dark outlines of men against the light. Then I saw their leering faces and uniforms stained with mud.

The soldiers were yelling and waving their arms. I couldn't move, but my father reached out his hand. He helped me to pick up Juris, then stand up slowly and step down from the truck. Outside, the noise of the machine guns split my ears. It was as if the shots were bursting through my head. A group of about fifteen soldiers stood in front of us.

One of the soldiers told us to line up. They started to pull our bags out of the truck and go through them. On the ground I saw the old man who had been so kind to Juris on the train. The soldiers were kicking at him and ordering him to get up.

Then everything stopped. I watched one of the soldiers picked up Juris's small teddy bear, *Lācis*. My heart jumped into my

My maternal grandmother, Milda Seja, at the beach before her marriage to Rudis Masens, Jurmala, Latvia, c. 1938.

Rudis Masens at Jurmala, Latvia, c. 1938.

Milda and friend, fashionably dressed and strolling down the streets of Riga, Latvia, c. 1939.

Milda on a boating trip with Rudis Masens on Juglas Lake, Latvia, c. 1938.

A view of the beginning of Kalku Street from Brivibas Boulevard, Riga, Latvia, 1930s. National Library of Latvia.

Milda and Rudis Masens on their wedding day, Riga, Latvia, October 1939.

Milda skiing with Rudis and friends, Latvia, c. 1939.

A Soviet BT tank with a truck and troops in the centre of Riga in the early days of the Soviet occupation, 1940. PD-RUSSIA/Wikimedia Commons.

Mass deportation of Latvian residents to Siberia in cattle cars—many were civil servants, landlords, church members, university teachers and their families, 1941. Wikimedia Commons.

Damaged buildings of the Riga Old Town and St Peter's Church, 1939–1945. Carl Kadelke, National Library of Latvia/Wikimedia Commons.

Welcoming German soldiers, Riga, June 1941. Bundesarchiv. Photograph by o.Ang/
Wikimedia Commons.

Juris aged one dressed in clothes made
by Milda, Riga, early 1944.

Andrejs and Marija Seja (Milda's
parents) at Memmingen displaced
persons camp, Germany, 1949.

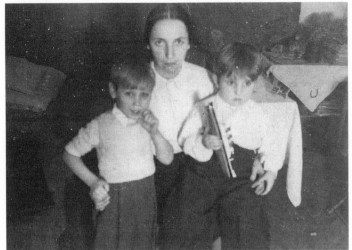

Juris, Milda and Janis in Italy before boarding the USS *General Harry Taylor* to Australia, 1949.

Milda (back row, third from right) with Latvians and other migrants, Greta Migrant Camp, NSW, 1950.

Milda folding sheets with fellow migrants as part of her work in the camp storeroom, Greta Migrant Camp, 1950.

Milda and her sons with friends, outside their 'Chocolate City' dormitory, so named for the brown weatherboard huts, Greta Migrant Camp, 1950.

Milda posing in front of a tent at Greta Migrant Camp, 1951.

Milda and husband Edgars near Greta, 1951. Edgars was apparently smitten with Milda from the moment he met her.

Milda, Juris, Janis and Inta (my mother) at the house Edgars built for them in Redhead, Newcastle, c. 1956.

Inta in the garden at their Redhead house, c. 1956.

Aline (front row, left), Milda (back row, second from left) with Latvian community members at an event, Newcastle, 1962. Photograph by Mr Ozolins, Universal Photography.

Regular Latvian society party at the Broadmeadow Hall. Milda and Edgars are in the middle on the left-hand side, Newcastle, c. 1958.

Milda wearing traditional dress at a Latvian event, c. 1970.

Milda and Carl Masens (her eldest grandchild), Newcastle, c. 1988.

My paternal grandmother, Aline Balulis, at around age fifteen, Kraslava, Latvia, c. 1939.

Kraslavas Romas Katolu Baznica, Roman Catholic Church, St Ludwig. Aline's father was the organist and her family lived in the church dormitory during the 1920s–30s, when she was a young child, Kraslava, Latvia. National Library of Latvia.

A street scene near Aline's family home in the small town of Kraslava, 1930s. National Library of Latvia.

Aline (back row, second from left) with extended family and friends (occasion unknown), Kraslava, c. 1936.

National Song Festival in Daugavpils, attended by Aline at age fifteen, when it became clear to her and the crowd that the Soviet Union was soon to invade Latvia, June 1940. National Library of Latvia.

German Armoured Personnel Carrier at crossing, Latvia, June 1941. Bundesarchiv. Photograph by Hugo Tannenberg/Wikimedia Commons.

Aline in *Reichsarbeitsdienst* (German Worker Scheme) uniform, Kloddram, Germany, 1943.

Aline as part of the choir heading to perform at a nearby displaced persons (DP) camp, Alt Garge DP camp, Germany, 1946.

Aline and Andrejs aged two in Butzbach DP camp, Germany, 1949.

Aline and Andrejs en route to Australia, 1949.

Aline and husband Eddy, in their International Resettlement Organisation photos, Butzbach, Germany, 1949. National Archives of Australia.

Eddy and Aline enjoying a moment of peace together at Redhead Beach in Newcastle, c. 1952.

Andrejs and Peteris (my father), enjoying playing in their (temporary) red pedal car, 1952.

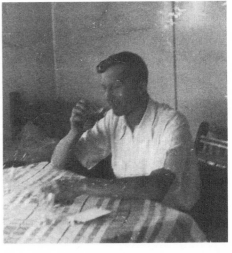

Eddy having a drink in the kitchen of his home in Redhead, Newcastle, c. 1952.

Aline, Eddy, Andrejs, Peteris and baby Karl, on the occasion of his christening, Argenton, near Newcastle, 1961.

Aline's parents, Apolonija and Ludwik Balulis, back home in Kraslava, Latvia, in 1950, sent to Aline by her mother a few years after correspondence became possible.

Apolonija at Ludwik's grave, in Kraslava, 1958, sent to Aline in Argenton by mail from Latvia.

Aline in bed in her home in
Argenton, 1960s.

Aline posing for a photo in the bush
on the outskirts of Newcastle, 1960s.

A small party in Aline and Eddy's kitchen, Argenton, 1960s.

Aline dressed to go out to a Latvian society event, Argenton, late 1960s.

Aline. This photo appeared on the order of service for Nanna's funeral in Newcastle, November 2021.

throat. The soldier slowly turned and grinned. He held the bear up and pretended to make him walk, pushing his little brown legs forward. He laughed.

Everyone stared at him. The soldier started spitting and screaming in Russian, 'Who owns this bear?'

I froze. Suddenly, the soldier tossed the bear up in the air. I watched it go up, flung like a rag against the grey sky. The soldier aimed and fired. *Lācis* fell to the ground and lay in the dirt. I could see a hole where one of his golden eyes used to be.

I held Juris tight against my side. The soldier looked over. I saw understanding dawn on his face. He knew the bear was ours.

'Stop! Stop!'

I turned to see a Russian officer yelling and waving his soldiers over. The one who had shot the bear pointed directly at me and smiled, but then walked off towards the officer to get his orders. The rest of us were left standing there, lined up next to the truck, waiting. I felt as though I was going to collapse. Then I heard my father call across loudly in Latvian to the officer. I was shocked at the sound of his voice. 'We are not German, we are Latvian!' he yelled.

I could not believe it because I was used to my father staying silent while my mother took charge of things. We all watched as the officer came over to my father and stood in front of him. He cocked his head, thinking for a while, and then the officer opened his mouth and started speaking in Latvian about how he had studied in Riga before the war. My father replied that he had recently lived in Riga. They exchanged more words, going back and forth. After a few minutes, the officer clapped my father on the back and shook his hand. I was stunned. It took a while for relief to slowly seep into my body.

We all piled back into the truck and drove away. Juris fell asleep as soon as the truck started moving, but it took hours for me to stop shaking. Little *Lācis* was left behind in the mud. All my life, I have not wanted to think back to this time. But when I have, one question has come to me: 'What could have gone so wrong in the world that a man would shoot a little boy's teddy bear?'

22

✺ Grandma Milda ✺

Survival

I stayed quiet in the truck as we drove further south to avoid the fighting, but other people started to speak up, wondering if our driver knew what he was doing. I had no idea where we were. 'We are lost,' my mother cried. We stopped to ask a German farmer directions. He sent us even further south and a few hours later the Latvian man sitting opposite me insisted, 'That farmer lied to us, we are going the wrong way!' Finally, our truck came to a stop. A local man told us we had arrived in Böhmisch Leipa. Sudetenland! We were much too far south and out of petrol. Everyone filed out. We all looked half-dead.

I was standing near the truck, eating a small piece of bread when I felt a wet rush between my legs. Such a feeling of dread came over me. My mother hurried to me with a couple of the other women. They walked me to a shed and we went inside. I was told to lie down on the dirt floor, to stop my contractions from starting.

Alise went out into the streets, asking people if they knew where I could go to have my baby delivered. She was told about a nursing home that was being used as a small hospital on the other side of town. The women decided I needed to be taken there, but our truck was out of petrol so we had no choice but to walk.

My skirt was wet and freezing between my legs. The contractions started along the way.

At first sight, the nursing home looked fine. Its roof was whole, without any signs of bombing. But as we approached its doors, a strong smell of rotting flesh hit us. It was a charnel house!

My mother forced me to go in. There were rows of soldiers lying in beds on the ground floor, blood soaking into their bandages. Some of them silently stared up at the ceiling. Others were moaning in pain.

I clung to my mother's arm. A nurse came over and told us to go straight to the third floor. It was hard to climb the stairs. When I got there, a long line of women were waiting. All these women? The sight was unbelievable. I had never imagined so many women would be giving birth during wartime. I thought, somehow, I would be the only one.

The matron in charge stormed down the corridor, yelling, 'Nobody goes in until I can see a baby's head between your legs!'

I stood in that line for more than six hours, staring at lights on the ceiling above me, flickering on and off. I tried to breathe evenly and stay quiet. My mother rubbed my back. There was nothing else to do.

When I finally started groaning, the matron pointed towards me and shouted: 'It's her turn.'

I went into the delivery room. The floor was slippery with blood. I got up onto the bed and pushed until I was unable to keep going.

'A boy!' the nurse finally cried. I had given up hope and, at first, my mind could not comprehend the news: *He is alive? He is here?*

Straight away, the nurses wrapped part of a small mattress around his little body. They sewed up the sides to create a kind of cocoon. They warned me to take him out only to feed and change him, because he would freeze to death if I didn't keep him in that cocoon.

I was put in a room full of newborns and mothers. It was very cold. There was only one potbelly stove to heat the room.

I named my second boy Janis. They gave me his German birth certificate. I remember staring at the swastika on it and wondering whether he would ever get to see Latvia.

My mother left to give the news to the others. A few days later, she returned to the hospital and told me we would have to keep moving. 'There is no petrol left here, we have to walk,' she said.

I looked at her as if she was out of her mind. I didn't want to leave, but the matron told me I had to. 'There are too many germs,' she said. 'Your son will be safer outside.'

It started snowing as we left Böhmisch Leipa, and I doubted I could do it. I kept Janis wrapped up tightly and everyone took turns carrying him. I have never felt so cold in all my life. I kept hearing the matron's voice, over and over: 'Keep him wrapped in that mattress.'

We walked more than 300 kilometres on foot through Sudetenland and into Saxony, always heading south-west. We passed near Chemnitz and then headed further south to avoid more fighting. There were too many mountains and rivers to cross. At one point, our group stayed at a farm to rest for a few weeks. Just as we were about to leave, someone saw a small group of soldiers in the distance. My mother and I buried ourselves at the bottom of a haystack with the children. Juris started to cry. I put my hand tightly over his mouth. Inside, my brain was screaming at me: *Take your hand away!* I knew I might suffocate him.

When he stopped crying, I was too scared to look down and check that he was still alive. But I put my hand on him and could feel his little chest going up and down. The soldiers passed the farm without stopping.

We were always looking out for both Russian and German troops. Nobody knew who they could trust anymore. Once when an old German priest rushed us into his church to escape a group of soldiers, we had to hide under the wooden floorboards. With my back on the frozen dirt, I felt as if I was already in a grave. Even after we left that church, the cold continued to seep into every part of me.

There came a point when I no longer wanted to live. I simply couldn't bear it anymore. My mother kept pushing me, but I was getting weaker.

I walked onto a bridge and decided this was it. I made my way through a crowd, walked to the very edge and looked down. The river was half frozen over and the trees were covered in snow. Some of the branches looked beautiful, with ice hanging down in long crystals. I told myself that my heart would stop as soon as I entered the water.

But then my mother and father were beside me. They grabbed me and dragged me back to our group. My mother was yelling at me, but I could hardly hear her. Tears were running down my father's face. I slipped on the ice, but my mother gripped my arm hard and kept me standing up straight.

My mother didn't let go of my arm for weeks. Alise kept shoving Janis towards me at night so I could feed him.

Our group walked along more slowly now, often having to stop and rest. The roads were crowded with other people. All of us were trudging together in the sludge and ice. Many people were like walking corpses, not really there anymore inside their bodies.

Eventually, we arrived in Bamberg. When we entered the town, I saw people sitting around in the streets and lining up in great long queues for food. No one was walking onwards. No one was running. They almost looked alien.

My father shook me and cried, 'It's over!' I felt empty. *It's over?* I repeated the phrase to myself and tried to believe it.

Red Cross workers were trying to organise people. I found myself heading towards them with Janis in my arms. I was taken to a medical tent, where I was given a place to lie down underneath a clean grey army blanket. There was a stove, and I began to feel warmer.

A nurse took Janis to examine him. She came back to me with sorrow in her eyes. I looked over to where he lay on the examination bed and saw that his bottom was covered in red sores.

I choked and tried to explain. 'The matron in Böhmisch Leipa told me to keep him in his mattress. I changed him when I could.'

The nurse nodded. 'You did well. He would have died if not for that mattress. The sores will heal.'

Part Three: Grey Light

1945–50

Brightly, brightly, the fire burns.
In the small dark corner
There Laima is writing a life story
For this little child.

Latvian folk song.
Laima is the Latvian goddess who
sets people's destiny at birth.

23

No place

Historians have estimated approximately 150,000 people left Latvia in the final year of the war. They became refugees, trekking westward away from the Soviet forces that were driving back the Germans. The roads, filled with people from all over Eastern Europe, were destroyed, becoming pools of half-frozen mud. Bodies lined the edges—those who had frozen to death trying to flee.

The trek through the German-occupied territories had been terrible chaos. Refugees had tried to weave their way through different war fronts and often run into groups of Russian and German soldiers. Before researching this phase of the war, I'd imagined the fronts of armies as long neat lines sweeping across the landscape, but it had been nothing like that at all. As well as the major battles, there had been pockets of fighting between military units across a vast expanse of land, and increasing desperation and lawlessness had sent some soldiers completely berserk. It was extraordinary for Grandma Milda's group to have gotten through to safety.

I remember my Uncle George saying: 'It was the Battleaxe who pushed them through Germany. Of course, my grandfather was also there when it counted, yelling out to the Russian officer that they were Latvian, but he could also give credit where it was due. With admiration, my grandfather used to refer to the group of women who had got them all through, his wife included, as the "female contingent".'

The vast number of people from all over Europe who ended

up stranded in Germany after the war was staggering. There were millions of refugees, deportees and prisoners of war, milling around shell-shocked and sick. Accounts of the time describe long lines of cattle cars filled with people entering refugee camps and queues of shawled women with haggard faces fumbling to show whatever identity papers they had to officials when words failed them. It was all some people could do to pull up their sleeves and bare the numbered tattoos they'd received in concentration camps running from their wrists towards their elbows.

At the Yalta Conference of the three Second World War allies—the United States, Britain and the Soviet Union—held in February 1945, the Soviet government requested the repatriation of people from the Baltic states, as they now considered them citizens of the USSR. Of course, most Latvians, Estonians and Lithuanians refused to go because they knew prison, deportation or execution would likely greet them if they returned home. Instead they moved into displaced persons (DP) camps in Germany run by the United Nations Relief and Rehabilitation Agency (UNRRA) and then later the International Refugee Organisation, becoming displaced persons, *dīpīši* in Latvian slang.

24

No happily ever after?

After breakfast one morning at Nanna Aline's place, I gingerly broached the idea of continuing her story beyond the end of the war. For the last couple of days I'd sensed she thought we might be approaching the end of our conversations but I knew if I was really going to understand her life, we needed to press on.

'Nanna, can we talk about what happened after the war?' I asked her one morning. 'Is that okay?'

I was surprised by her sharp bark of laughter. 'I have to warn you. If you thought that because the war was over, things would be all right for me, well, my life didn't work out that way.'

'It's all right, Nanna. I know you were trapped alone in Germany.'

I'd managed to pick up at least that much from the hushed conversations between family members at Christmas and Easter events over the years. Nanna being in Germany and separated from her parents was somehow the catalyst for the next chapter in her life, although I did not have any of the details.

'What do you know?' she shot back in an accusatory tone.

'I mean, I don't know,' I quickly demurred. 'But I want to know . . .'

She took a deep breath and I sat pincered between thoughts of finding out more and declaring that we should let it rest to give us a way out. As the clouds blocked the sun outside, light ebbed from the kitchen and I felt very unsure. But then Nanna gave me a small fateful smile.

'All right then. I'll tell you two important things. Point one. It doesn't matter how your life is, you just have to go through it.

You have to live every single day. Doesn't matter how you feel. Maybe you spend all day crying? The next day could be better, you might not cry anymore. Then something bad comes and you cry again. That is how it was for me.

'Point two. When you are alone and have left the world you grew up in, your house with parents' love, you are desperate for someone to come along. When you have no experience of managing your life, then you want someone to help you.

'My mother was right. I ended up on my own at the end of the war. You think I was part of the big celebrations in the streets? No! I was sitting on the bed in my dormitory in Kloddram. I was happy the war was ending but I didn't have any idea what to do. I was just like a small piece of wood out on the ocean. How do you say it? Flotsam? Jetsam?'

The image of small pieces of wood rushing up and hurtling down immense waves in the middle of the lonely ocean filled my mind. An immeasurable sadness came over me.

But still I leant forward and nodded.

'Can you tell me, Nanna? What did you do?'

25

Getting to Alt Garge

I knew I could not stay where I was but had no thoughts at all about where to go or how to live. I watched my friend Elizabete rushing around, putting all her clothes and blankets in her brown suitcase. You see, she had fallen in love with a German man and was going to head south with him and his friends. 'Come with us,' she said. But I didn't think there was a real place for me with them. I was worried about what my mother would think of me running off with a group of German men. I should laugh about that now given everything that happened!

It was too quiet after Elizabete went. I sat and cried to myself for a long time. Eventually, my eyes rested on the small wooden cross on the dormitory wall. Maybe God gave me some energy because I took off my red scarf and combed my hair. I shoved my swastika armband under my pillow. It felt good to be rid of that thing! I pulled my suitcase out, packed my things and walked towards the door before I could change my mind.

There was no one in the hall. I went downstairs to the garage to get my bicycle. It was dark, and at first I couldn't see it and thought someone had taken it. But there it was, right in the corner. I tried to balance my small box suitcase on the front handlebars and get on, but it kept falling off. I very nearly went back to the dorm. I ended up pushing my bike with one hand and carrying my suitcase with the other.

101

It was hard to get my legs moving. Very slowly, I walked onto the main road. There were hundreds of people on the streets—it was not like I was the only one. I kept my head down.

The road was muddy, so I couldn't have ridden my bicycle anyway. Out of nowhere a man ran straight towards me with bare feet, black with dirt. He was so thin that the top part of his body looked like it was going to fall off his hips. He was a skeleton, right in front of me. I cried out, but he went off into the crowd.

There was nothing to do but keep walking. At first, I didn't know where I was headed but then I found my feet travelling on the same road that I used to take to get to the house of the German farmers. Maybe God was helping me? It was 8 miles to their farm but I kept going. The last hour was hard. It was dark and I couldn't see properly. A few times I almost decided to leave my bike but held on to it. It felt good to have something in front of my body.

When I arrived at the door, I was unsure of myself. I knocked and the farmer's wife opened it just a crack. Her eyes went wide when she saw me and she closed the door! I stood there not knowing what to do. I didn't think she was going to let me in but she came back with her husband.

'Is anyone else with you?' he asked.

He looked into the dark and then decided to let me in. The wife gave me fried bread with hot milk. She put pillows down on their floor and gave me a quilt. I remember it was made of different flower patches—maybe from a little girl's old dresses. That is how it seemed to me.

That night, I lay awake, wondering what I should say in the morning so they might let me stay. I decided to tell them I would help preserve food from their vegetable garden. I knew anything that could be picked should be taken inside straight away because there were thousands of people on the roads looking for food to eat. I thought maybe I could become like a daughter to them until I went back to Latvia to find my parents.

As soon as I woke up, they asked me to sit down at their table. Straight away the farmer told me I couldn't stay. 'You have to go and find your own people,' he said. 'There are camps. I've heard Latvians are joining together at Alt Garge.'

It was as if I was in a bad dream when I left their house. Nothing seemed real. I don't even know how I got up to walk. They gave me a piece of speck as a trade for my bicycle. I was glad to have it because in Latvia, speck has always been seen as something you might give a person who needs strength. They told me to head south and follow the Elbe River.

Just before I left, the farmer's wife whispered to me, 'You can come back if things get bad.' I was grateful for that.

I went along by myself for a while but was completely terrified. I thought someone was going to jump out of the bushes at any moment. Then another hand came from God. I met a Latvian family on the road, a couple with a daughter named Ade. I don't know if I would have made it without them. They let me walk with them for the few days it took to get to Alt Garge. I remember we had to cross to the south side of the river and we were lucky because the bridge had not been blown up. They had a cart and we all took turns to push it. I shared my speck with them and they gave me bread.

When we arrived, there were hundreds of people queuing to get through the big gates. There were lots of Latvians—men, mothers with their babies and children—all standing in the mud. But it was such a thing to hear the Latvian tongue all around me. When you are in a foreign place, it is a gift to hear your own tongue surround you.

It took hours but eventually the gates opened. I had my passport and birth certificate. The British soldiers let me in.

As soon as everyone was registered, we rushed towards the kitchens. I was not starving but very hungry. The UNRRA camp officials were waiting to serve people through big kitchen windows and had huge pots of soup and crates of bread. Everyone was overwhelmed by their generosity.

I will never forget what I saw next. A man pushed through the crowd, knocking two little children over into the mud. He rushed forward and started to stuff bread into his mouth. Pieces and pieces of it he jammed in, right in front of everyone.

Whispers started among the Latvians. People knew him. That man had been a famous person in Latvia. It was such a shocking thing to see him spitting and choking on that bread. Everyone understood. They knew it could be them. Still, they turned their faces away in disgust. People with university degrees, famous people and farmers—we were all equal for once.

After we had eaten, the men and women were separated. We had medical checks and the officials sprayed DDT down our blouses to kill any lice. We were all allocated dormitories. I was in one with about 30 other women, the same one as Ade and her mother. It was an old army barracks so there wasn't much to it—beds, a concrete floor and a few tiny windows—but we were grateful. The officials tried to get everyone to put their bags into storage sheds, but no one would do it. Our dorm was packed halfway to the roof with suitcases. There was hardly anywhere to stand and we had to crawl over our beds to get out.

A few days later, I got a big surprise. I went for a walk with Ade and saw one of my childhood friends from Kraslava, Mikels, sitting alone on a log in the middle of the camp. I ran over to him.

'Mikels, it's me, Aline,' I said. He just stared at me with wide eyes.

'Aline, from Kraslava,' I repeated.

He rubbed his head so hard I thought he might wear his hair away. It was then I realised there was something broken in him. I tried to sit with him on that log. He kept staring at me and apologising and jumbling his words. It was like his mind was full of holes. I couldn't stand it. After a few minutes, I squeezed his arm and walked away.

Years later, I heard he recovered and became a priest in Dortmund. I still feel ashamed I couldn't bear to sit with him for longer on that log. We used to catch the same train back from our different boarding schools in Daugavpils at the end of term. We both liked each other. We might have even got married in another life.

After a few months, we knew we would be at Alt Garge for a long time. Most people had no news of their families. I didn't know where my parents were, if they were dead or alive. What could we do? There is only so long people can sit and stare at each other and cry.

26

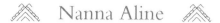

When you are on your own

We all had to make a life in those camps, but the path was different for each person. It was easier for us younger ones without families. People began to live in the moment. Some Latvians started to band together in choirs and put on plays. It was strange but the war had changed the natural order of things. In a way, I had more freedom than I'd ever had before. I was twenty-one and not as shy as I was as a girl. I wanted to find some sort of life. Sometimes I felt like we were on an adventure. I feel stupid telling you that, but it is true.

Ade and I were washing clothes in a big tin tub on the fire when I first met Lauris. He came striding across the wooden planks the camp officials had set out to stop people walking through the mud. I remember him shouting, '*Labdien*, girls!'

He looked handsome, but then he slipped and one of his feet sank all the way up to his knee. I started to laugh. He grinned and pulled his leg out. It was black with mud. He limped over, introduced himself and told us he was helping organise the Latvian choir that would be performing for the upcoming *Jāņu Diena*. 'Two more girls are just what we need,' he said. You see, it was important that we mark such an important occasion as Latvians in exile.

Lauris told me he knew I was from Kraslava and that he too was from the Latgale district. We'd both been at the Daugavpils Song Festival in 1940. He was a few years older and far more worldly than me, but because we had come from the same place, I dared to imagine we could be friends.

Ade and I started going to choir practice. There were moments we would be singing and Lauris would catch my eye. I knew he had lost his wife. Many people had stories like that. I felt sorry for him.

But Lauris was also strong. He knew how to work the black market and trade cigarettes and coffee powder for other things. He was involved in the Latvian camp committee. Maybe I felt a bit protected by him. Also sophisticated, you know? I could hardly believe someone like him might be interested in me. He told me that my eyes reminded him of the sky.

Oh God! What did I know about love, or men and women? Nothing! Before I met Lauris I had never even had a proper boyfriend. The only romance I'd had was once in Kraslava when a boy from Riga, who was visiting for a wedding, threw a red rose through my window.

Lauris was not a boy! Of course, that *Jāņu Diena* every one of us was full of strong feelings—sadness at all the people who had been lost, fear at what was happening in our country—but there was also a sense that we needed to keep going with life. There was such dancing and singing, everyone caught up in the moment. I didn't know how to look after myself.

Lauris was very charismatic. You have to understand how it was. People just wanted to live after coming so close to death.

I kept the baby inside me a secret for a few months. Most of the time I didn't believe I was pregnant myself. I didn't tell Lauris and I was too ashamed to tell any of the women in the dorm.

Of course, eventually Ade's mother worked it out. I was in the laundry washing sheets when she marched up to me and placed her hand on my stomach. 'Foolish girl!'

I froze and then found the words to say I was going to be fine.

She shook her head. 'He hasn't told you? His wife and daughter have been found. They are in another camp. He's leaving to join them!'

I could hardly breathe. I didn't want to believe her; I put my head down and kept washing the sheets.

Everything seemed to happen quickly after that. It didn't take long for Ade's mother and the other women to start talking. 'What can she do?' they whispered to each other.

Ade tried to help. She walked with me to places, so I didn't have to go alone. One time I ran into her father near one of the storage sheds, and he turned his back on me.

I was never alone with Lauris again. I saw him a few times around the camp. He always gave me a small wave, and his eyes seemed sad. But, you know, as soon as I knew his wife and daughter were alive, I never thought we would be together again. I would never have broken up his family. I was proud of myself for knowing that. Within a few weeks, he was gone.

The older women in the camp kept talking. 'Who will look after her?' I knew they were trying to help me in their own way. Some of them did it like a duty. I was a young woman and they thought it was their role to offer advice. A few did it from kindness. They passed me extra food and one old woman sometimes came to my bed at night and rubbed my back.

One of the Latvian women in the camp was a midwife named Lina. We had been friendly for a while. I felt she didn't judge me like the others, but that she really enjoyed my company. One day she told me she was leaving Alt Garge with her husband to rent out a small house in Greven that belonged to a German woman whose husband had died in the war. She planned to take in lodgers and asked whether I wanted to go with her. She promised she would help deliver the baby.

Soon talk of this plan got around. All the women seemed to think it was the best idea, so I went. Like a puppy, I followed Lina. I think now that she saw me as her pet. It made her feel good to be above me, helping me.

Lina's house was near Münster. She gave me a small room to myself at the top of the stairs. There was just enough space for a bed. There was another lodger in the house but he kept to himself. Most of the time it felt like it was just me, Lina and her husband living there. I found work at a potato farm nearby. We had enough food and it was not a bad place. Really, it could have been much worse for me.

One day Lina came to my room and told me she'd found a Latvian couple who couldn't have children and had heard about my situation. Oh, how she talked and talked at me! 'They are good people. The baby will need a proper family. You won't be able to take care of a baby by yourself.' What she said was true. But I was like a rag doll. I did not know my own mind.

There was a priest, Eduards, who was helping to look after the Latvian Catholics around Münster. Lina invited him to her house to talk to me, and he came up to my room. I was nervous at first. He was dressed very neatly and had a Bible in his hands. I thought he might condemn me, but he looked at me kindly and suggested we kneel and say the Lord's Prayer.

One day as we knelt, I told him how bad I felt. 'God's will is God's will,' he said. He was never in a hurry to leave. 'I will come back next week,' he said at the end of each visit. He always did.

Lina didn't like that Eduards and I were getting closer. Maybe she wanted me to rely only on her. I started to call him Eddy. As time went on, he said he was developing love for me and wanted to get married. 'I will leave the priesthood,' he said.

I was very worried and knew it would be a major sin for him to do that. 'Even if you don't want to marry me, I will still leave,' he said.

Perhaps I was like a tragic figure sitting there in that room? Maybe I made him feel strong? But one thing I know: there was an unspoken deal. He never talked about life with a baby. It was as if he thought our lives together might begin after I gave the baby to that couple.

'We must start fresh together,' he said. But he put it on me. He never said exactly what I was supposed to do. He always said I had to think of what was best.

I went to the hospital when the time came. Lina was my midwife. How hard it was! I was in labour for two days and finally a lovely little baby girl was born. I named her Ruta. I held her in my arms and wanted very much for her to have a good life. She was small and perfect in her white blanket.

Lina had organised for the couple who wanted to adopt her to come to the hospital as soon as I was in labour. I think maybe she even arranged a minor operation for the woman so they had a reason to be there. I was nervous when they came into my room. Lina had helped me wash so I looked presentable. Ruta was in the bassinet beside me, sleeping soundly. I had to hold my hands together to keep them steady.

First, the lady came into the room while her husband waited outside. She looked smart in a dark-green coat and had a nice smile. She kept patting my arm. 'You did well! You just rest,' she said.

After a while she asked if she could bring her husband in. I agreed. He was very polite but got to the point. 'We have money and will take good care of her. We will cherish her as if she was our own child,' he said. The two of them standing there looked like they would be good parents. Really, they did.

Lina didn't tell me she'd already written up Ruta's birth certificate with them listed as her mother and father. It was her signature on the document as the midwife that made it official. I went white when she showed me. You see, I hadn't realised that was how it would be. I hadn't understood I wouldn't even be listed as Ruta's mother.

The couple kept saying over and over, 'We will take good care of her. She will have a good life.' They promised me they would not change her name, that it would stay the same as on her birth certificate. I remember thanking them for that.

The lady brought a bag into the room and, when she opened it, I saw it was full of woollen blankets. I was glad to see those blankets. 'Thank you, you did so well,' they kept saying. 'You must rest now.' Then it was over and they left with her.

My whole life I have had to live with my actions. I once went to see Ruta not long after her birth. She looked content with her new parents. I don't know. Maybe I wanted to see how they were taking care of her? Maybe I wanted to change my mind? Maybe, if I had been stronger, could I have kept her? I think that now. Maybe I could have learnt to look after her? I have heard people talk on TV about adoption. I always watch if I see a show about it. It hurts, but I watch.

Someone always asks the most important question. How can a mother give away her child? I have asked myself that a thousand times. How did I give her away? I know all the reasons: how I was on my own, how I couldn't take care of her and that her new parents were good people. Those things were true. Still, I wonder whether there was something wrong in me. I was her mother. She was my blood. The bond between a mother and child is meant to be strong enough to survive anything. I should have been stronger.

Don't say anything, dear one. There is nothing to say. Let's just sit together.

27

The rubble of the world

Grandma Milda was 32 when she entered the Bamberg DP camp on 11 June 1945 with her parents and two little boys. To her it felt like she was standing in the rubble of the world, completely destroyed. She could not believe she had to start over again. For a long time, she wanted more than anything to reclaim what she had lost rather than discover a new way forward.

Her old friend Aleksis told me that Milda had insisted to him a number of times that she'd tried hard at first to find news of Rudis. She hoped she would be one of the lucky women reunited with their husbands.

'She told me she often dreamed he would just appear out of thin air. Maybe just there, suddenly, at the gate,' Aleksis said.

It wasn't a crazy notion. In my research I found that quite a number of people reunited with family in those camps.

As she waited for news of Rudis, Grandma Milda also found purpose in the Latvian projects that were being established. It is estimated that approximately 70 per cent of the country's writers, artists, musicians and actors had fled west by 1945 and a lot of these people ended up in the camps. Many members of the Latvian ballet had escaped to Lübbeck and half the cast of the Latvian opera was at Oldenburg. Given this, most Latvians, including Grandma Milda, felt a deep sense of responsibility for upholding the Latvian culture through music, plays and art, particularly as they could imagine the suppression of their culture taking place under the Soviet reoccupation back home.

Some of these Latvian events must have been incredibly

poignant as people held concerts and plays that aimed to keep the soul of Latvia alive. I have read stories of American and British officials working in the camps feeling overcome by the haunting sound of Latvians singing folk songs in the evenings, longing for the homeland they might never set foot in again. People gathered in the twilight to sing songs such as '*Pūt Vējiņi*'. As Latvians sang, the words took on different meanings as old words were overlaid with the experiences people had just been through: 'Blow wind, drive my boat, drive me to Kurzeme.'

Church services were held to pray for family members back in Latvia and those who had been lost. Afterwards Latvians would gather half-stunned, a heady mix of grief, guilt, desperation, nationalism and love swirling around in the air.

Later they would come back to Earth to pool and trade the items they'd managed to flee with, and to distribute the clothes and food people had collected from the camp officials.

Grandma Milda initially tried to stay out on the edge of these events and hold herself apart, but she couldn't help turning to those around her to seek solace and form new friendships. Very few people were able to manage on their own.

28

 Grandma Milda

Searching for news

Can you imagine how we felt to be in those camps? Of course, we were grateful for the food and somewhere to sleep, but those Americans knew very little about what we had been through. They had no idea what to do with us. Some of them even thought we were Russian! They couldn't understand why we would not just return home. One time I was standing next to a Latvian man trying to tell an American officer how terrible Stalin was. That officer got angry and said we should remember that Stalin had been part of the Allied forces!

At first, there were many transfers to different camps as the officials tried to group people from the various countries together. In February 1946 we moved from Bamberg to Hanau DP camp near Frankfurt. It was a bigger place, more organised and there were lots of Lithuanians there as well.

Over time, the camp officials realised we were not going anywhere. There were protests when they let Russian government people in to try to persuade us to return home. People were terrified they were Cheka! We thought we might be taken back without our permission or that the Russians might get information that would be bad for people left back in Latvia. Eventually, the camp officials understood what we were saying and stopped letting them in.

Of course, I wanted to find news of Rudis. Everyone was trying to exchange information, and I was no different. Sharing news among ourselves was very important. We had to work to try and piece together what had happened to our families.

Each day I would make my way through the dormitory sheds to the concrete bunker at the entrance of our camp that was the central office. There was always a crowd of people around the huge noticeboards where the officials would put up cards with messages they had received from other camps. That was the main way people were being reunited with members of their families.

You had to look carefully for your *dīpīsī* number. That was how all the messages for us were arranged. No one pushed. Everyone moved politely around one another as they hunted. It was often quiet, but then a cry would break the silence when the fate of someone had been discovered. It was sometimes good news, sometimes bad news. You could always tell from the sound of the cry.

One day, I had only been searching for half an hour when I heard my mother call out to me. I was annoyed at first and wondered what she wanted me to do next. She was always at me to try to get more food or supplies to better our situation. I walked over to her and she told me she'd just heard from another Latvian couple that a man named Rudis was working with radios at Wildflecken DP camp, about a day's travel north-east from us. My whole body felt as if it was about to burst up into the sky and my mind was buzzing: *It must be him! Who else could it be?*

I spent the rest of that day caught up in hope. I traded my cigarette rations so my father could catch a lift in one of the army trucks heading to Wildflecken that evening. I prayed to God and hugged the boys. My father whispered in my ear as he climbed onto the back of the truck. 'It is promising,' he said. That meant a lot as my father didn't often feel positive.

That night I couldn't sleep because I was too excited. I tossed and turned in my narrow bed, imagining how it would be when Rudis saw me with our second son, Janis, in my arms. I imagined how he would rush over and swing Juris up into the air. How he would have a huge smile on his face. How proud of his sons he would be!

The next day, a Lithuanian lady from our dormitory lent me a good dress. The word had got around and all the women were happy for me. The dress was dark blue with a smart brown leather belt at the waist. It was very kind of her to lend it to me. I put it on and sat on my bed waiting, feeling as if years had fallen away.

There I sat for hours, until my mother walked into the dorm. Her mouth was set in a grim line. 'Your father is outside,' she said. I could tell by her face that the news was not good. I opened my mouth, but no words came out. My heart started to thump very loudly.

I walked slowly to the door. The late afternoon sun had come out for a change and my eyes had to adjust to the light. I saw my father a little way off, standing under a small tree, and I managed to walk over to him.

He pulled me straight to his chest and cleared his throat. 'The man I met knew Rudis. He was in Liepaja with him, working on the radios,' he said.

I didn't want to hear anything more, but my father kept going. 'He's not sure Rudis made it out of Latvia at all.'

I buried my head in my father's woollen coat and cried.

All I wanted was for night to come, but it was light for many hours. My mother let me lie in bed while the rest of the women talked and worked around me.

The next day I decided not to go to the noticeboard to see if there were any messages about Rudis. Overnight, something had changed inside me. I knew that if I did not find something to keep me busy, I would not survive. There were broken people around me, just sitting blankly and waiting for the camp officials to bring them food. I knew I could not end up like that.

Juris stayed by my side as I slowly walked around the camp to get a better sense of what I needed to do to look after the boys. It helped to have Juris's small hand in mine, although I didn't want to look too closely into his eyes. They were too sad.

29

 Nanna Aline

'Why did he marry me?'

I was lost for weeks after Ruta was taken away. I went back to my room in Lina's house. I remember the wallpaper. Rows of lavender. I kept thinking it might have been a girl's nursery before the war. It was driving me crazy to be in that room but I couldn't be with other people. The only time I came out was to eat. I had just one visitor, Eddy. He was the only one who looked into my eyes. He talked so earnestly. 'God knew best. What's done is done.'

Eddy was eight years older than me. He understood the world. He kept swearing he would leave the priesthood even if I didn't marry him. Perhaps I agreed in the end because I'd grown up with priests around me as part of my childhood. I remember when I was little, peering through the windows when they entertained the lady schoolteachers from our parish. Sometimes after too much wine there would be touching and kissing. I never told my mother what I saw. She would have been angry to hear me talk of our priests in such a way. She thought they were men of God, but I knew the truth: they were just normal men, not always holy.

That's how I think it was for Eddy. He was very clever and had studied in the seminary. He loved being seen by other people as a scholar more than he loved God. He became stuck on me. Now when I look back, I think to myself: *Why did he want to marry me?* I was a fallen woman. Was that perhaps what he found attractive? I was also a good-looking woman back then. That must have had something to do with it.

Lina and I had a terrible fight when I told her I was thinking of marrying him. I went down to the kitchen to talk to her about it one evening. I wanted her blessing. She yelled at me, 'Do you want to make another mistake? Can't you keep to yourself?'

Lina never supported any idea she didn't come up with. I tried to make her understand. 'I can't be a burden to you anymore,' I told her.

She became angrier as we talked and finally flung her hands up. 'Be it on your shoulders! Why should I say "yes"? I don't want that weight when it goes wrong.'

So that was that. I packed my bags and went to Kassel–Bettenhausen camp, where Eddy had organised for us to live. We married at the registry office in Kassel. I have no idea who we had as witnesses. I don't have any little thing from that day, no photo, not even a piece of paper. That's how it was. That's how I married your grandfather.

There were no celebrations. The shame of Eddy leaving the priesthood ran underneath everything. We couldn't talk about it together. We just had to move forward. You have to understand, in our hearts Eddy and I knew from the beginning we had committed a terrible sin. The teachings of the church were in every one of our bones. Still, we knew that it wasn't that way for everyone and thought we could move forward and forget. Others were living their lives without so much heaviness from the church. We wanted to be that way somehow, change into different people.

Andrejs, your uncle Andrew, was born on 18 July 1947. How joyful it was to have my little baby! I cradled him and kept him warm. Eddy showed him off to all the other Latvians in the camp. They clapped him on the back but I knew Eddy still wondered what people might be saying about our past.

I was not very good with my hands but still I sewed a coat for Andrejs from pieces of another big coat someone gave me. I did a decent job. He looked very smart in it, so I took him for a walk around the camp. I remember feeling proud of myself and feeling that I might become a good mother.

When Andrejs was about one year old he fell very ill. He could eat no food without throwing it up. Days went by and, eventually, Eddy went into town to find help. He found a German doctor at the hospital who agreed to come to the camp.

When he arrived, the doctor picked Andrejs up from his cot and cradled him carefully. 'Oh, my little child,' he cried. I saw his eyes were wet with tears. He gave him some medicine to settle his stomach and then turned to us. 'You must follow my instructions exactly or he will die.'

I was shocked. I knew he was very ill but had no idea he was close to death. The doctor told us it was probably the germs in the milk we were giving him that were making him sick. He told Eddy he should walk across town each day to collect food for Andrejs from the hospital. They made him mushed boiled carrots.

After a week or so the doctor came back to our dorm and showed me how to make the carrots myself. I was embarrassed! He made me practise in front of him. I thought the doctor must think I was a terrible mother for not knowing how to serve Andrejs clean food. But that was how we nursed him back to health.

Eddy was very good. He did not blame me and thanked the doctor very politely and earnestly. 'You saved his life, God bless. You saved his life,' Eddy kept saying to him.

All the doctor wanted in return was flour and chocolate from our *paciņas*, food parcels. You see, many Germans were starving. They saw the food we had in those DP camps—Nescafé, spam, vitamin tablets and cans of tuna. It was not much but a lot better than the Germans could buy on the streets.

We were trying to get news about our parents, but at first no one could send letters. We were scared the Russians would read the mail and our families would be punished. Later, I found out through a Polish schoolteacher that my parents had made it through the war and were still in Kraslava.

But there was no way I could go back to Latvia. I knew the Russians might deport me to Siberia because I'd worked for the Germans. I also knew it would break my parents' hearts if they found out Eddy had been a priest, or about Lauris and Ruta. We knew we had to leave Europe and make a life where people didn't know our business. That is what everyone in the camps was trying to do. The conversations started about where to go.

'There are already too many clever people in America,' said Eddy. 'We will go to Australia. They need smart people there.'

I agreed because I wanted to make a new life, but I didn't know if I deserved one. What sort of person was I? I had no skills. I was not confident in myself. Sometimes I think about that doctor and how he watched me making those carrots, and feel such shame.

30

Life in the camps

I made plans to visit my uncle George again. It was hard to reconcile the little boy, Juris, holding Grandma Milda's hand, with the leathery beachcomber in front of me. I could see, though, that he perhaps still had some of the same sadness behind his eyes.

We sat on his deck, this time with strong coffee.

'Can you tell me more about what it was like in those camps in Germany?' I asked.

Uncle George shook his head. 'Not much, but maybe I've suppressed things. I was in the camps from when I was about two to six years old so I should remember more. It must have been traumatic. From what I gather, your grandma sat around the dorm all day for months after the war ended when she wasn't searching for Rudis. That can't have been good for me. It was after she started sewing again and attending more Latvian events that she pulled herself together. Actually, my only clear memory of Germany is of the elephants.'

I looked up, eyebrows raised.

'Yeah, big grey elephants. They were using them to knock down the half-bombed-out buildings. They tied thick ropes around their stomachs; then, as the elephants slowly walked forward, the walls tumbled down. I suppose it's the sort of image that sticks in a little boy's mind.'

'Oh, I never imagined people used elephants for that. You don't remember anything more?'

Uncle George leant back and I realised his hands were pressed into his lap. He was not as relaxed as I had first thought.

'The way I've pieced it together is that Mum started making clothes for other people in the camp. That put a bit of life back into her. There were lots of Latvians with skills in music, literature and art in those camps. She must have felt some pressure to get involved.'

'Did she start to sew her tapestries?'

'No, that came later. It was just simple clothes, but well made. She gained quite a reputation. After a while she got a job as a bookkeeper in the central camp kitchen. That was important, as we had no breadwinner. She needed to show she could support my brother and me so another country might accept us. It was no good being three dependants. We were in a bit of a pickle without Rudis. Don't forget we also had the Old Battleaxe and Granddad, who were too old to be chosen for resettlement by most countries. I remember America wouldn't take them, which was a real punch in the guts. My grandfather had tried hard to show he was employable. He'd worked as a camp policeman and then as a kitchenhand, but we had no choice. Your grandma wasn't happy. She'd seen pictures of Australia and thought it looked like the back of nowhere, a place full of hicks!'

'Did Grandma think she might go back to Latvia?'

'Everyone did at first but after a while it dawned on them there was no going back. Rumours swirled that those who had returned had been arrested and sent to Siberia. We were stuck in those DP camps for a long time, four years. People tried to entertain themselves the best they could. Everyone was always putting on bloody Latvian plays and concerts. *Bearslayer*! You know that one?'

'The one with the Latvian gods and all that?'

'Yep, I saw that one many times. The Bearslayer, *Lāčplēsis*, is a hero. The Latvian gods use him to defeat crusaders. Everyone in the camps lapped that one up because it was about Latvia winning out against evil hordes. It was the male Latvian gods in the play that were the most interesting to me. *Pērkons*, God of Thunder.

123

Patrimps, God of Plenty. *Pakols*, God of Death—he had a skeleton horse and was supposed to be scary, but I'd seen so much death that I didn't bat an eye over a skeleton horse.'

'Really?'

'Kids were desensitised. One time I was playing with some other boys just outside the main fence of our camp. We had found some berry bushes and were stuffing ourselves. We had red juice running down our chins and we were all lurching around, pretending the juice was blood. Mum came looking for me, took one look and started yelling.'

'Did she think you were hurt?' I asked.

'I reckon she thought we'd hurt something else . . . maybe an animal. Kids were used to death and blood.'

I reached out for my coffee. It had gone cold. I shivered and tried to change tack.

'Did Grandma ever think of trying to find another husband?'

'I don't think she wanted more romance, but I'm sure she would have tried to find someone if we weren't accepted into Australia by ourselves. She became a more practical person while we were in Germany. She had no choice. It was her old boss from Riga, Eriks Jansons, who sponsored us, as he had already settled in Melbourne. That's how it worked in the end. Lots of people wrote to other Latvians who had already settled in Australia to find sponsors.

'Things got better once your grandma heard word of her brother, Rudolfs. He'd fled to Copenhagen with his wife and they now had three children. All those visits to the camp noticeboards gave her some good news in the end. Rudolfs was also planning to emigrate from Denmark to Australia. A plan was made for him to sponsor my grandparents, so everyone was sorted. It's amazing how it came together.

'Mum was good at arranging things when she set her mind to it. On the tenth of July 1949, we were told we had approval to travel to Australia. We had to get to Naples to board the boat. The Old Battleaxe and Granddad had to wait in Germany as it was necessary for Rudolfs to settle in Australia first before they could follow him. We all had to go for medical tests. That was a tense time, because I'd been sick a lot. It was a fairly rigorous process and they didn't let Latvian doctors check other Latvians; you had to get someone else, like a Ukrainian doctor, to check you out so there was no cheating. Mum was worried that my X-ray would show signs of damage from tuberculosis, but I was given the all-clear. Then we had to traipse off to the Lutheran pastor to bless our voyage. People tried to get excited but it was all a bit forced. True happiness was a rare thing at that time.'

'You remember a lot, actually,' I ventured.

'It's hard to know what I remember and what I've been told. All I know for sure is that I loved Australia from the very begin-ning. I started to thrive once I could run around on the beach all day. I always dragged my feet home because I knew I'd get a tongue lashing. Your grandma saw things differently.'

'She didn't like it here?'

'For one thing, she hardly ever came down to the beach. Too rough for her. She always went on about Jurmala, where she used to go with Rudis. It was a European beach, where people prom-enaded down a main street of cafes and hardly ever went in the water. No waves at all. Getting dressed up to go to the beach was more her thing.

'She wanted me to be an upstanding Latvian boy. Surfer was not what she had in mind, but I had to get healthy some way and leave all that Bearslayer crap behind. All those bloody Latvian plays and poems weren't any use to me trying to get on with the kids around here, but that was something your grandma Milda never understood.'

'So, you all made it here in the end.'

'We almost didn't. We went through the Augsburg processing centre in late 1949 and then left for Naples. But, I tell you, it was a disaster when we turned up at the ship.'

125

31

 Grandma Milda

The American officer

The boys could not believe the sight of the big grey American warship, the USS *General Harry Taylor*, up against the docks. Nor could I! My eyes followed it up into the sky and then I looked down to see little Janis's eyes were like saucers. Juris couldn't stop coughing, but he too was moving his head back and forth to try to see everything.

I took hold of both boys' hands and joined our group. An American man told everyone to place their suitcases on the trolley to be taken up onto the ship. 'All your suitcases,' he shouted. 'You will get them back when we board.' Of course, no one wanted to do it. We had been keeping an eye on our belongings for years. Now he expected us to just trust him? But, in the end, we had no choice. I followed his instructions, telling myself all would be well. Then I took the boys by their hands again and we lined up to board the boat.

When we finally arrived at the head of the queue, I handed over our tickets. A young sailor with a kind face consulted his passenger list. Then he shook his head, confused.

'Our turn,' I insisted. The sailor looked even more confused. I repeated: 'Our turn.'

A second man now came over to see what the problem was. I just stood there as they talked back and forth. The second man finally took me by my arm and led the three of us off to the side.

126

'I'm sorry,' he said. 'You cannot board now. I will tell the office. Someone will come.'

My heart by this time was racing. I knew something was very wrong. I stood there holding my little boys' hands with no idea what to do. Our suitcases were already on the ship!

A Latvian lady saw what was happening. She told me that someone had probably stolen our places. 'It happened to my brother,' she said. 'He wasn't allowed to board.' I just looked at her and thought: *This is not right!*

I sat down on the dock and the boys huddled up next to me. My hands were shaking as I tried to peel an orange that I'd bought from an Italian man earlier that day. I willed myself to stay calm. The boys shared the orange but Juris was coughing and crying so hard he could barely swallow the pieces. He knew what was going on. For more than an hour, I watched as everyone else walked up the plank to the ship. I felt sick.

Finally, I saw an American officer walking towards me and I knew this was our last chance. His uniform was neat and he looked important. My legs were wobbling as I stood up and tried to explain the problem one more time. Pointing to our tickets, I smiled. I begged. I knew I just needed to keep going.

Eventually, the officer nodded. He told me to wait and walked back up the plank into the ship. It seemed like he was gone for ages. Eventually, the boys and I were the only people left on the docks. My entire body felt without hope, but then I saw the officer walking back down the gangplank. I jumped up.

'Come aboard!' he shouted. My mouth fell open and I quickly got the boys up on their feet. The officer went to them, putting Janis on his shoulders and taking Juris by the hand.

We all walked up the ramp as the waves rocked against the big grey ship. Sailors were tossing off the giant ropes and getting ready to leave. The officer took us up some stairs to one of the upper decks, and we headed down a corridor into a cabin. There was a bed and the grey blankets looked soft. There was a bowl of fruit on a small polished wooden table.

'We stay here?' I asked as I tried to understand what was happening.

'Yes,' he replied. I simply didn't know what to say. It was then I realised this must be his room.

Without warning, the ship's horn blew. The officer took us all up onto the deck, but I didn't know what to think. I wasn't sure if I could trust him. I watched him carefully and decided he was good with the boys. He held them up to look over the side at the water, and they seemed to trust him. People were throwing streamers and my boys cheered with the crowd as the ship steamed away from the dock.

I nodded my head in thanks. The officer tickled Janis, who laughed out loud.

But later that night Juris started sweating and shivering. 'He is not sick,' I told the officer straight away, worrying we would get into trouble.

'He has a fever,' the officer told me. He insisted we take Juris to the ship's infirmary. The doctor told me he had pneumonia. They put him in a bed with cool white sheets and gave him penicillin. I knew then that we had made it, whatever was going to come next. Juris had the medicine he needed and was going to stay in the infirmary. And Janis was just a little boy, happy to be on a big ship.

32

What is real?

Uncle George was not able to tell me much more about the situation with that officer on the ship.

'I don't know why he helped us,' he said. 'Maybe that bloke did not help us for nothing. Anyway, we got on that boat!'

I felt queasy, my mind full of competing ideas about what I could choose to imagine, and whether or not it was okay to imagine anything at all. I simply didn't have enough information to go on. Questions kept running through my head: *Why did she stay in his room? Was there some sort of bargain? Did the officer want something from her in return for his help? Was she scared of him? Was it an acquaintance based on kindness? Was there some attraction?*

The reality was I didn't know what Grandma Milda had thought about him at all. She'd certainly never told me directly anything about him. The only thing I knew for certain was that she'd boarded that boat and the American officer had been involved. Somewhere in those years in Germany, she had grown stronger, and in the end, she had done what was necessary to press on.

Grappling with the uncertainty surrounding my grandmothers' stories in the DP camps and their voyages to Australia, I started to cast out for further sources of information. I searched the online records of the Arolsen Archives based in Germany. The Archives are better known for their records on victims of Nazi persecution but I'd discovered they are also home to thousands of documents from the DP camps. I found the names of Milda and her two boys on the passenger list for the USS *General Harry Taylor* that left Naples in January 1950.

I applied to the National Archives of Australia for my grand-mothers' immigration records, organising for them to be sent to my home address in Darwin as I'd arranged to go back for a few months. It was pouring with tropical rain the day the records arrived. I pulled into the driveway to see a big white envelope sticking out of my letterbox getting soaked. I knew straight away what it was. I jumped out of the car and ran, the rain beating pellets on my head. I pulled the envelope out and shoved it under my T-shirt to lie pressed against my skin.

As soon as I reached the kitchen, I carefully cut it open with a butter knife. The envelope was wet, but the green and white folders inside were miraculously undamaged. The words 'National Archives of Australia' were emblazoned in tall, bold olive letters across the front. I could barely contain my excitement as my mind kept spinning: *These papers could have stayed hidden forever. How is it that no one else in my family has ever asked for them?* It hit me that it was the strangest thing in the world to be opening those documents in Darwin, about to discover the details of events on the other side of the world more than 60 years ago. I opened the first folder, took out the bundle of pages and started carefully turning them over.

It was the photos that struck me first—photocopies of passport photos of my uncles, Juris and Janis, as small boys. They looked solemn and neat in their woollen jumpers. I ruffled through and found Milda, her dark-brown eyes looking steady and serious but in a much softer heart-shaped face than the one I'd come to know.

In the second folder was a photo of Nanna Aline looking directly at the camera. She was classically beautiful with her hair pinned back with curls resting on her shoulders. She looked young and uncertain.

I started to read. There were over 50 pages of informa-tion detailing names, birth dates, eye colours, medical records, education, work history, DP camps, stamps and signatures. I kept turning the pages and then turning back to make sure I wasn't missing things, telling myself to slow down. There were neat type-written pages mixed with scrawled handwritten text. I pored over the documents trying to take in all the information.

Grandma Milda's records had a list of places and DP camps she'd been through in the American zone of Germany, including Bamberg, Hanau, Büdingen, Dieburg, Darmstadt, Babenhausen and Memmingen. I quickly flicked to Nanna Aline's records, to see if there was a match with any of those on Grandma's list, and found different ones, largely in the British zone—including Alt Garge and Kassel–Bettenhausen—and Butzbach.

I took out an atlas to try to find them all, going back and forth, taking into account changes in place names over the last 70 years. A few hours later I decided that Grandma and Nanna had been less than 50 kilometres from each other at one point, but their paths had never crossed.

I stretched my back and kept going. There was no mention of any mix-up with Grandma Milda's tickets for the USS *General Harry Taylor*.

But a final wrench came on the last page of Grandma Milda's documents, with a declaration she'd had to make in 1949 in order to come to Australia.

I, Milda Masens, depose and say:

That I am married with Rudolfs [Rudis] Masens, born 15.7.1910, Latvian subject, engineer.

That my husband is missing since September 1944, when I was deported to Germany together with my children, but without my husband, who at the time was sent to forced labour to another part of Latvia (Liepaja).

That I have no news about my husband since a.m [aforementioned] date and that all my tracings for my husband have been without any results.

Affirmation Record, International Resettlement Organisation 1949

Courtesy of the National Archives of Australia,
NAA: A12004 1032–1034

The documents made it real. It was there in the papers before me.

Part Four: Harsh Light

1949–93

All my best songs
Left me on the road:
But I'll gather other songs
As I walk this foreign land.

Latvian folk song

33

Blue-eyed Balts

Between 1947 and 1952, about 20,000 Latvians immigrated to Australia from displaced persons camps in Germany, part of a much larger program that saw Australia accept approximately 170,000 people from displaced persons camps over those five years.

The Minister for Immigration at the time, Arthur Calwell, saw the potential of these migrants in helping to rebuild Australia's farming and industrial sectors after the war, but also understood the pre-existing Australian population was wary of his plan. He used young and healthy-looking people coming from Latvia, Estonia and Lithuania—his 'blue-eyed Balts'—to promote his scheme to the broader population on the grounds they looked similar to the British and thus might appear more familiar—a plan that had links to the broader, nefarious White Australia policy of the time.

Both Grandma Milda and Nanna Aline felt as if they were nothing like the Australians they met who had completely different styles of dress, behaviour, backgrounds and customs. Most Australians had no idea where Latvia was or what had happened to the country. On this point my grandmothers were united and often spoke about feeling as if they'd landed on another planet.

On arrival in Australia, the Latvians and other DPs stayed in migrant camps before they were assigned to undertake compulsory two-year work contracts as labourers on projects such as the Snowy Mountains Scheme, railway expansions and large-scale farming endeavours. Many DPs felt the Australian government had no interest in their former occupations, but simply saw them as a source of unskilled labour. Nonetheless, they were surprised and grateful the government provided housing, language lessons, education and other services during this time. Standard wages were also paid by the government, in the hope the migrants would save the money to start building new lives.

Nanna Aline and Grandma Milda separately entered this scheme, landing on opposite sides of the country. Nanna Aline disembarked in Western Australia in July 1949, and Grandma Milda in New South Wales in February 1950. There was a vast expanse between them, and it would be several more years before they met.

————

There is a famous artist, Imants Tillers, whose Latvian parents came to Australia from the DP camps of Germany after the Second World War. His artworks are huge landscapes made from arranging multiple small canvas boards into huge grids. On these, he paints giant webs of connection across landscape, time, place and memory. His works bring together Latvian and Australian words and images along with those from many other places and cultures. The effect is his paintings act to mark chapters in some great human story telling of the unlikelihood yet inevitability of many different worlds joining and blending with history and migration. They also serve as a reminder that the past, and all its deep sentiments and cultural references, often stays living just under the surface of the present.

My grandmothers had entered the strange unfolding world of the Latvian diaspora in Australia on their arrival in this country but it took the work of Imants Tillers for me to start to under-stand what it truly meant. On my trips down to Canberra from Newcastle, I found myself visiting the National Library of Australia in the mornings and the National Gallery of Australia in the afternoons.

Looking up at his various pieces my eyes jumped from an image of four pale elongated heads set white against the maroon-coloured background of Latvia's flag, symbolising shared trauma and memory, to Christian iconography and towering Roman numerals, and later Australia's deserts, waterholes, Aboriginal art and placenames. My mind reeled at the sense of shared context and mystery: *All of this in the Latvian diaspora? All of this in my grandmothers? All of this in me?*

I tried to decode the artworks' secret messages: deciphering the intimate cultural fragments, patterns, words of destiny and awful ruptures, catching glimpses of meaning and then wondering what else was there that I didn't understand: *Maybe this is not of me?* In some parts, his paint was thick like flesh; in others, it seemed thin and stretched as if reaching out just beyond the fingertips to connect the sites and symbols.

But back in 1950, all of these connections were tentative, still in their infancy. It was as if Nanna Aline was on one side of one of his giant artworks and Grandma Milda on the other, the panels etched with faint pencil lines, yet to be painted in. My grandmothers were both yet to discover the ways in which Latvia and Australia would end up entwined, how our family lines would join and grow roots in this new place.

34

Graylands

We left Naples in late June 1949 on our ship, the *Amarapoora*. What did we have with us? God, it was ridiculous! Eddy had a new suit he'd bought on the black market. All the men in the camps wanted to have a good suit. We also had a wooden chest packed with a little tin bath for Andrejs, a quilt we'd bought in Germany, maybe some pots and pans. To think we were carrying those things around as if they were precious. I don't know what we did with that bath. We traded the quilt for fresh fruit for Andrejs at one of the ports on the way.

When we first boarded the ship, I could not believe my eyes. There were blue carpets and lamps on the walls in the dining room. The tables were clean. And so much food! White bread and strawberry jam for breakfast. Dinner with meat and potatoes. None of us had seen such food in years.

I am sorry to say but that poor ship didn't look so good by the time we got to Australia. The carpet was ruined and the lamps were broken. I felt ashamed! What must the Australians have thought of us? But we'd all been stuck on that ship for weeks, all squashed in together for every meal.

Most of the Latvians who came to Australia went to the east coast, but we ended up going to Western Australia. It's crazy, but we had no idea that's where the ship was taking us. Everyone thought we were going to Sydney. Once we realised, Eddy and I thought maybe it was not such a bad thing because there would be very few Latvians who knew anything about us in Western Australia.

But another lady started screaming when she found out where we were going. You see, her son was in Sydney and she'd been waiting every day for a year to reunite with him. Now there would be thousands of miles between them, even more distance than when they'd been in different DP camps. The sailors had to give her brandy to calm her down.

When we sailed into Fremantle harbour, Eddy and I took Andrejs up to the deck so we could get our first look at Australia. In the beginning, all we could see were other boats and buildings but, as we came closer, we realised there were hundreds of people waving at us. Some ladies even had flowers in their hands. 'Are they for us? How they welcome us!' I cried.

Our arrival turned out to be a big event. The government had organised a brass band. You see, they were trying to convince Australians we were good people. Lots of Australian families had come to have a look at us.

I remember one small thing. As our ship docked, Eddy spotted a man near the edge of the crowd. Eddy started jumping up and down and pointing at him. 'Look Aline, how that man is peeling an apple with a knife. See how he is cutting into the skin. Just like I used to do at home!'

Our migrant camp, Graylands, was not far from Fremantle, maybe only 6 miles. Still, it took us most of the day to get off the boat and board the buses. All our enthusiasm had worn off by the time we arrived. All day I'd tried to make sure my spirits remained high to keep Eddy happy. I'd talked to distract him when I saw his eyes narrow at new things he did not like the look of. You see, Eddy didn't like feeling out of control.

139

It was when we were standing at the entrance to the Graylands camp that I realised how worked up he was. The sun was hot and there were hardly any trees, but it was the ground that really brought Eddy low. It looked like ash. He wondered how anything would grow and said he'd never seen anything like it. He kept muttering over and over, '*Pelēkā Zeme, Pelēkā Zeme*—Graylands, Graylands.'

Andrejs was sleeping against my shoulder, and there was lots of dust and sand blowing off the road. I was worried it would get up his nose and in his ears. The camp huts looked like they'd been picked up by a giant and dumped in an empty field, nothing like the buildings in Germany. I was wearing my best cream dress and Eddy was wearing his suit. He'd made me put that dress on because he wanted us to make a good impression with the camp officials, but now it was getting dirty.

Eddy's eyes kept jumping everywhere. There was too much going on in his head. 'We should move closer,' he said.

I tried to calm him down, but I just made him angrier. I said, 'Eddy, there is room for everyone.'

He sneered at me, 'I should trust you?' I went cold when he said that. I knew he was saying I was not a trustworthy woman. I knew what he meant.

A group of camp officials came out of their offices. Eddy picked up our bags and stood straighter. When we finally reached the front of the queue, one of the men took our papers. He only said a few words to us. 'Dinner is at five o'clock. Here are the rules.' He handed us a small square of paper. That was it.

Eddy began trying to speak in English, but the man waved him off. You see, Eddy wanted to prove he was smart but didn't get the chance. He was furious! Andrejs woke up but luckily he didn't cry.

Eddy and I were put in a dormitory for families on the east side of the camp. Each dorm had five partitions made from hessian sacks arranged to make little rooms. One of these was ours. The other people in the dorm were all Latvians, Lithuanians or Estonians. They seemed good people but I was shy. They told us we had to go and sign papers to get our supplies. There was a formal procedure for everything. It was a big deal to go back to the office to get even one extra cup. No one wanted to seem careless or stupid in front of everyone else.

I was surprised how cold it got that first night. It had been hot all day, but the dorm walls were thin and there was a gap where they didn't quite reach the floor. I woke up to check on Andrejs in the middle of the night and his little arms were freezing.

I shoved Eddy. 'Wake up! Andrejs is cold.'

He just ignored me.

'Please, we need another blanket. He will get sick.' I had to keep pleading with Eddy for an hour.

Finally, he stomped off and brought back a blanket. I knew he was worried he was not making a good impression on the camp officials by asking for it. He thought I was wrecking things for him.

In the afternoons, I started to walk with Andrejs to the other side of Graylands that shared a fence with a mental asylum next door. When Eddy realised who our neighbours were, he joked with some of the other Latvians, 'The Australians store the Balts and loonies next to each other!' But I didn't think it was funny.

I started going around to that fence at about three o'clock each day. That was when an old lady from the asylum would walk out with her nurse and sit on a bench in the shade under the gum trees. She was thin and frail and always wore the same loose white dress. Each time after the nurse left her, the lady would reach into the pocket of her dress and pull out a rosary of white beads. She slid her fingers along them very carefully. It was such a small movement, while the rest of her was completely still.

If Andrejs was quiet, I'd stay close to the fence to be near her. Sometimes I imagined Mary was watching both of us. I'd say the Lord's Prayer to the rhythm of the lady's beads, just quietly to myself, because I didn't want to disturb her.

One time when I returned to our dorm, Eddy confronted me. 'I know where you are going. You'd better stop it. Do you want to end up like that crazy lady?'

A rush came into my chest. 'Well, if you are not careful, one day I will end up like her!' He walked off.

I kept going over to the asylum fence.

It was hard for Eddy sitting around Graylands with not much to do. After a few weeks, he wanted to get out and see Perth. I was nervous but he convinced a group of Latvians it was a good idea and so six of us went. We hadn't received our money from the government yet but Eddy had a carton of cigarettes he'd bought in Italy. He had the idea we could trade them for wine or spirits. There was no liquor sold at the camp canteen and people wanted to have something to drink.

I left Andrejs with an older Latvian lady. We got passes out but had no idea where to go. We just started to walk towards Fremantle. Eddy thought if we kept to the train line, we wouldn't get lost. We had no hats or sun cream, nothing like that, so we were all going red. We must have looked ridiculous.

We walked for an hour or so and then we came to a street of shops. There was a grocer and a baker. I was happy to recognise these places. We were in Claremont.

All the men started to argue about who would go to try and trade the cigarettes. Everyone found it embarrassing to try and talk to Australians. Nobody could understand us.

'They're your cigarettes. You do it!' one man said to Eddy. His ears went red but he went in.

We all watched through the window as he marched up to the shopkeeper and pointed at a large bottle of something and tried to explain. They gestured and talked and then Eddy came out smiling from ear to ear. He had a flagon of some sort of wine. Maybe it was a bad trade and that's why the shopkeeper agreed so quickly.

We stood around, talking about where we could go. There was a park across the road with huge pine trees, so that's where we went and we sat under one of them. It was much cooler in the shade. We each took turns to sip the wine. It was very sweet, maybe port or sherry. In no time, everyone was much happier.

Even Eddy relaxed. Perhaps we were even laughing, because everything seemed funny all of a sudden. What were we doing sitting in this park on the other side of the world? It seemed the strangest thing. How could this have happened to us?

I don't think we were too loud but it must have been a sight, all of us there in that park. No one else seemed to be doing things like that in Australia. The grass and pine needles were scratching my legs, but I was having fun. From then on, we all knew that if we sat in the sun and drank, it would make us silly for a while. It would make all the problems go away.

35

Chocolate City

Grandma Milda disembarked from the USS *General Harry Taylor* in Sydney with relief. In its last weeks at sea, fights had broken out between pro-Communist and anti-Communist DPs, and the ship had become a tense place. Uncle George told me he remembered the American officer cheerily waving goodbye as they walked down the gangplank and then him quickly walking away as if to get the ship ready to sail off to another port.

Grandma Milda and the boys were part of a group taken to Greta camp, about 30 miles north-west of Newcastle. The camp consisted of two parts: Silver City, made up of corrugated iron huts, and Chocolate City, made up of oiled brown weather-board huts. Grandma Milda and the boys lived in Chocolate City in a dorm for women and children, which housed Latvians as well as Lithuanians and Estonians.

Within a few weeks, Grandma Milda found a job in the store-room keeping track of the sheets and blankets lent out to everyone. While her surroundings were foreign, the tasks were familiar from her time working in the German DP camps. She started English classes. The boys went to camp school each morning and then explored the bush surrounding Greta in the afternoons.

'Mum had worked to build her confidence and she was pretty capable by then,' Uncle George told me. 'She was certainly bold enough to voice opinions on everyone and everything—our living quarters, the noisy birds, green tree frogs in the showers, and especially the food. There was lots of white bread, mutton and boiled vegetables. She kept saying she couldn't understand how the Australians made everything tasteless, but my brother and I loved the food.'

'How did she think she would financially support you all?' I asked.

'It helped that she had a two-year contract to work in the camp at Greta. Those were mostly given out to the men but she got one to look after us. That provided us with a base. Soon she was one of a group in charge of the way things ran in the camp, and that gave her a sense of security.

'Lots of romances were also being formed in the camp and I suppose that, too, provided a path forward for Mum. Lots of men without families came periodically to Greta. Some were working on the Snowy Mountains Scheme up near Kosciuszko. Occasionally they used Greta as a place for weeks off to rest. I think Mum believed we needed a father and so that was on the cards.'

'Right, that makes sense.'

This lined up with what Grandma's friend, Aleksis, had told me when I'd visited him. He first met Grandma Milda when he was in his early teens at Greta; he and his parents were also housed there when they arrived in Australia. Edgars Berzins, an older man who drove the blue camp bus, took him under his wing. It was clear to Aleksis that Edgars was smitten with Milda from the moment he met her, and that Grandma might have welcomed his attention as a practical way forward for her and the boys.

'We saw your grandma every day,' Aleksis recalled. 'We had to help transport the clean sheets from the laundry to the storeroom, and Edgars would help Milda put them away. After a while, he'd stay on to ask about how Juris and Janis were managing. Then he began taking the boys to fish down at the river near Greta, but I put a spanner in the works.'

'Why? Because you liked Grandma?'

'No! Well, I thought she was beautiful, but I was way too young. No, I wanted to go to work in the Snowy Mountains on the hydro-electric scheme. Edgars joined me working there for a while, to keep me out of trouble, but all he did was talk about Milda. I didn't like the work much, so after a few months we decided to get assigned back to Greta. I remember him being worried that she would have found someone else in the meantime.

'Edgars was a labouring man. He'd finished his education in Latvia at primary school and then worked as a truck driver and an auto-mechanic. He was a good man, Edgars. I spent a lot of time in the bush around Greta with him, sawing trees and chopping wood for the camp. We'd talk as we worked alongside each other and it was clear to me he was a thoughtful person. He knew how to take care of people and was patient. Perhaps it was the incident with a little girl who ran into the fence at Greta that convinced Milda he was the one she should choose.'

36

 Grandma Milda

Beginning a new life

I could see all the children playing on the hill at the back of the camp through my office window. I spotted Juris and Janis running around in the long yellow grass, both having grown taller in the short time we'd been there. It was a Sunday afternoon but I was happy working. I smiled as I went back to carefully cross-checking the numbers in the logbook to ensure nothing was missing.

The boys were at the camp school during the day and taken care of very well by the teachers. My work was not hard. I enjoyed it. Sometimes, all you need is to know what you are doing each day. It gave me the certainty I needed.

The sun was beginning to set when I looked up and saw all the children heading to the very top of the hill. I wondered what they were doing up there but then watched as they started taking turns to run down, one by one, their little legs windmilling too fast. I knew straight away someone was going to hurt themselves, so I went outside to tell them to stop.

As I came out of the office, I saw that one of the littlest girls— only five years old—was running straight into the barbed wire fence at the bottom of the hill. She put her arms out in front of her to try to stop herself. I started running towards her but it was too late. She began screaming like a siren as soon as she hit the barbed wire. When I reached her, she was sobbing and her hands were already covered with blood.

I looked around and felt panic rising inside my chest. Then I saw Edgars jumping out of his blue camp bus with his good white Sunday shirt on. He ran over with his first-aid kit and took command. He pulled out a bottle and poured some liquid over the girl's hands. She cried harder. He started to sing softly to her in Latvian and she began to calm down. *Aijā žūžū lāča bērni*—Hush-a-bye, hush, my bear cubs. Tears came into my eyes. I knew it must have been how he had sung it to his own daughter who was lost to him back in Latvia.

Edgars bandaged the girl's hands and gently picked her up. I could see brown spots of blood staining his white shirt.

'Aleksis and I will drive her to Maitland Hospital,' he said. 'You take the other children to have something to eat and drink.'

I nodded and asked whether the girl would be okay.

'I will sing to her the whole way,' he replied.

I watched until the bus drove off in a cloud of dust.

It was only a couple of weeks later that Edgars and Aleksis went off to work in the Snowy Mountains. I was sad to see them both go and, for a while, I could feel myself slipping backwards. It became harder to go to the office each morning. The boys missed them both too. It didn't help that it was getting colder and I knew it would soon be winter. Still, I was surprised when we woke up to frost on the ground. I hadn't imagined there would be frost in Australia.

Then a couple of months later, I saw Edgars behind the wheel of his camp bus again. He drove over to the office and stopped outside. Straight away things felt different between us. He had bought two little toy cars for the boys and yellow roses for me.

'*Labdien*, Milda, do you have time for a proper talk?' he said.

We sat down on the bench in front of the office. I felt nervous but excited too. He told me he wanted us to marry but that he needed to tell me his story first. He started trying to get the words out about how he'd been in the Latvian Legion fighting in Germany and had become separated from his wife and two children, who could be alive back in Latvia. He was mumbling and apologising. Of course, I already knew his story, that he'd been in a prisoner of war camp and that he still had no news of his family. Edgars was shivering and getting very distressed.

I put my hand on his shoulder to stop him from trying to go on.

'My Rudis is also gone. I will marry you and we'll start again together,' I said.

He fell against me and I held him until we were ready to go back to work.

37

Pig heads and railways

After a couple of months at Graylands, Eddy was told he had to work on the railway at Collie to complete our two-year contract. The officials did not care that he was an educated person, only that he was a man with arms and legs. Off we went with four other Latvian families in the back of a truck.

A Polish woman who had already been to Collie told me the forest near the town was filled with snakes and the summers were way too hot. 'All I could do was sit in a tub of water, sweating like a ham in brine!' she said.

I was concerned but Eddy laughed when I told him. He said she was speaking rubbish, but even he started to worry once we left Perth. The fields were empty, with dead trees lying on the ground. I wondered why people did not come and take the wood? In Latvia, a fallen tree would not last one day before someone would chop it up for firewood.

Some men were pointing at smoke on the horizon. When we got closer, we saw the land was burning and the trees were all black. It looked to us like bombs had been dropped in Australia as well. The driver told us the fire had come from a big lightning storm. We were amazed such a thing could happen. After a while we entered a huge forest. Trees reached up to the sky, but they were nothing like the ones back in Latvia. All the leaves drooped down. I remember one woman saying, 'All these trees must be diseased!'

When we finally arrived in Collie, a small group was waiting for us outside the main station. I could see on their faces that they were all thinking: *What sort of specimens will get out of the truck?* As we'd driven through the town, I'd seen some fine houses and a big Catholic church. I knew these people were proud of their place, and I felt like an intruder.

We were taken to some canvas tents on the far side of the railway line. We got two—one with camp beds for sleeping, and the other containing a small wooden table, basin and meat cooler. The floors were made from railway sleepers, but the tents were better than the dorms we'd been living in at Graylands.

The biggest problem was the snakes. In Latvia, there's only a single kind of poisonous snake, but in Collie we saw many different snakes. Once Eddy had to chase one out of our tent. He ran around after it with a shovel while Andrejs and I stood on the table. 'Get out, get out!' he shouted. Thank God we didn't get bitten.

Eddy soon became a leader of the men. His English was better, so he could translate a bit between the railway bosses and the Latvians. Sometimes he would mess around to make people laugh. The Latvians would curse at the bosses and, when the Australians asked him what they were saying, Eddy would make something up about how they were angry because they were trying to get the track laid just right. I was worried he would get into trouble for being too smart but nothing bad happened. He could be very charming when things were going his way.

Things were harder for me. Eddy often got mad because I couldn't do things properly. I'd never really learnt how to take care of a family. I became friends with the other women and they tried to teach me how to cook, but I was always making mistakes. We had to throw away one of our best pots because I left it on the stove and burnt the macaroni.

Another time I tried to make bread and put too much water in the bucket. I had to keep adding flour to make the right consistency for dough. It started rising and rising. I ended up with way too much dough, but I couldn't throw it out. I was very upset.

'Who could make such a mistake? Only you!' said Eddy, but I was lucky he thought it was funny that time. He told some of the other men and they decided to have a few beers and bake the bread to share across the other families. They took hours to do it. Eddy was drunk by the time all the bread was made.

I didn't have much confidence but I wanted to be useful. Everyone was trying to earn money to buy a piece of land. One of the ladies in the town offered me some ironing work. It was something I knew how to do from boarding school.

When I got to the lady's house, she talked to me as if I was a little girl. She asked me to show her my hands. I held them up and she carefully examined my fingernails to see if they were dirty. She sniffed and told me they could be cleaner, so I had to wash my hands in front of her. From that day on, I scrubbed my hands if I was going to her house. I didn't want her to turn her nose up at me.

One day I got up the courage to go to the Collie butcher with some of my wages. I wanted to make Eddy some brawn. I practised saying, 'Good day' and wanted to get it right. I walked there in the midday sun. I was hot and my heart was pounding when I arrived, but I pushed the door and went inside.

I said, 'Good day', but then the butcher said something I couldn't understand and it all went wrong. I couldn't see a pig's head in the counter window. I tried to explain what I wanted but the butcher just stared at me. I had no idea what to do. He went off somewhere out the back.

A few minutes later he returned with a pile of different meats on a tray. There was a pig's head but also livers, kidneys, brains and big strips of fat. I pointed to the pig's head and took my purse out but he shook his head. I worked out he wanted to give it to me for free. I think it was because he usually just threw the head away. I remembered to say thank you and headed out into the hot sun.

The walk back to the tents took a long time. The flies could smell the pig's head and lots of them started buzzing around me. In Latvia, there are hardly any insects, but here, of course, they went crazy with the smell of the pig. Then what a swarm came into our tent once I started boiling that head! There were hundreds of black dots all over the walls. A couple of times I almost burst into tears.

Somehow, I cooked that head and got the meat and stock into the icebox to set. I shooed the flies out. Eddy couldn't believe it when I showed him. We hadn't had brawn since we'd left Latvia. It was delicious.

When I look back now, those years in Collie were some of the best we had in Australia. Eddy was happy most of the time because he was saving money and thinking about the future. That's the key. You can try new things and survive quite well if you are making plans. After a year we bought a couple of acres of land on the edge of Collie from another Latvian family. There was no sewerage or electricity out there, but we wanted to build something on our own land.

Every weekend we went out there to work. Lots of other families helped us. We used railway sleepers to fix up a garage to be our home and bricks to build a stove. We worked quickly because I was pregnant again and we didn't think there would be room for a new baby in the tents. We made a place we could live in. We had a kerosene tin to boil washing because Eddy was always dirty black when he came home from the railway. We had our beds and our icebox. I even made a pillow using material from an old dress.

Soon your dad, Peteris, was born. I was pleased to have another boy because I thought it would be best for Eddy. We had a christening party for him in our new place. It was quite a big thing. All the Latvian families came and even some of the Italians and Australians. We had beer and wine.

An Italian lady from town bought Peteris a small teddy bear. It was such a thoughtful thing for her to do. I thanked her over and over. Eddy said it was embarrassing how I went on. He told me to stop but I felt so pleased about that little bear.

After another year in Collie, Eddy finished his work contract. We had to decide whether to stay or move. Eddy didn't want to work on the railways for the rest of his life. He wanted a proper profession. Also, there was no high school in Collie and we wondered what sort of life the boys could have once they were older.

Maybe it was because we felt more confident or because no one had mentioned Eddy's past to us for a long time, but we started to think about moving to the east coast. I knew my old best friend, Marta from Kraslava, had settled in Newcastle near her sister, Herta. I thought they might help me learn how to run my house properly, and I begged Eddy for us to move there.

I was surprised that he agreed, but he wanted to study at a university and we needed a proper school for the boys. We sold the block of land and Marta told me we could stay with her in Newcastle while Eddy found a job. We knew there was work in the coalmines that would do until Eddy got some Australian qualifications.

To get to Newcastle we had to take the train across the Nullarbor Plain. The land was empty, just orange and red ground for days. The sky seemed to be everywhere. Eddy couldn't believe it. He kept saying that we were crossing one of the greatest deserts on Earth.

Once, when we stopped for fuel, the train conductor told us to stay on board away from the Aboriginal people. He said there was a group who always surrounded the train when it stopped. Maybe they were angry we were on their land, I don't know. I remember seeing one woman sitting off to the side with her two small children. She seemed to be staring at me. I thought maybe she was hungry so I tried to throw my orange to her out the window, but it just rolled into the dirt and sat there a few metres from her.

All these years later I still wonder what that woman thought. Maybe she thought I was throwing food at her to be cruel. Maybe that's why she didn't get up. I feel ashamed at that memory now.

38

 Nanna Aline

Settling in Newcastle

Things might have been better if we'd stayed in the bush at Collie. We wanted more for our lives but perhaps we were too greedy. We should have known how it was going to be.

When we arrived at the main station in Newcastle, the first thing Eddy said to me was a sign of things to come. He shook his finger and said he hoped Marta and Herta didn't know our business.

Well, of course, they did! Marta was my best friend. I'd written to her from Collie. She knew Eddy had been a priest. I didn't want to lie, so I had to confess to Eddy. After I told him, he stared at me with eyes like ice.

A few minutes later we were on the platform, with Marta and Herta kissing and hugging us. I could see from the way Eddy's mouth was set that he was angry. Oh, he shook their hands and was polite, but I could see he was not sincere in his heart. I turned away to try to hold myself together. Everyone thought that I was just overcome from seeing Marta, so they laughed.

Herta's husband drove their car to the front of the station so we could put our suitcases in the back. Eddy jumped to it, picking them all up so no one had a chance to help. He thought they were looking down on him. That was always the thing—when he felt stupid or not good enough, he got angry.

I was impressed when we arrived at their place. It was a proper house with a rose garden, nothing like our place in Collie.

Marta was very kind and had organised mattresses for us to sleep on the floor. But after the first night, it was clear Eddy didn't want to be there. He complained about everything—their food, their conversation and even their little dog.

Eddy got moving. He started working down the coalmines around Newcastle. Within a few weeks, he'd organised a place for us to rent at Redhead by the beach and bought a block of land out at Argenton. He didn't consult with me before he bought that land. I was worried it was too far out of town but Eddy said it was all we could afford. We got a loan from the Colliery Building Society. It was a good deal, a special rate they had for their workers. I went along with it. What else could I do?

After that, we spent every weekend at Argenton building our house. Marta, Herta and their husbands often came. Eddy was kind to their faces, but behind their backs he complained to me. 'They want us to fail, Aline,' he'd say. 'They think they are better than us.'

Perhaps he was right. There's a Latvian nursery rhyme about a farmer who is very poor. He is visited by a fairy who grants him a wish. Instead of wishing for something for himself, perhaps a pig or good crop, he wishes for his neighbour's cow to die. The rhyme ends with the line, *Vārna vārnai acis neknābs, bet latvietis latvietim gan!* A crow wouldn't peck another crow's eye out but a Latvian would! There's a lot of truth to that. That's how it often was, even with our friends.

Eddy was rushing to build us a new life, but he never stopped to get my opinion. He wanted to prove himself. That's how he got caught up in problems with furniture for our flat at Redhead. We didn't know what we were doing, see? We didn't know how things worked in this country. Some Australians took advantage of people like us. Eddy lost more than seven weeks' wages, all our savings. The worst thing was when the company came to take back Peteris's red pedal car. He loved that little car.

39

Hire purchase

It took me a while to work out how Granddad Eddy had been ripped off. Finally, I managed to piece it together after digging around in newspaper archives. In 1952, a man named Leslie Leonard Gray agreed to rent his flat to Eddy on the basis that he, as the landlord, would supply all the furniture, including an ice chest, electric iron and toys, including a child's push pedal car, and it was Eddy's to keep.

The problem was the furniture didn't belong to Mr Gray. He'd obtained it on a hire-purchase agreement. When no one paid the instalment, two men came and repossessed it all. I discovered the details from an article I found:

Six months for fraud

Leslie Leonard Gray, alias John Roberts, 34, labourer, was sentenced to six months gaol yesterday when he pleaded 'Guilty' at Newcastle Court to having obtained £71/10 from Edward Putnis by falsely pretending that he owned certain furniture and floor coverings . . .

The Magistrate: Have you received any of the money back?
Edward: No, I put it down to 'experience'.

Newcastle Morning Herald and Miners' Advocate, 19 February 1952

There was no way Granddad Eddy would have put it down to 'experience' when he first realised his error. He must have pounded his fists into the wall in fury.

Reading that article, I wished Eddy could have had more time to stand tall in his flat surrounded by new things before they were all taken away. I wished he could have had time at Redhead to look out at the ocean in satisfaction at all he had managed to achieve for his family. Maybe then he wouldn't have gone on to cause such damage.

The reality was that life was often challenging for post-war migrants, even many years after their arrival in Australia. Often social and business transactions were extremely difficult for them to negotiate. Latvians commonly had to rely on others for advice as they all tried to nut it out together, but Granddad Eddy was, in many ways, a lone wolf and would try to figure things out for himself.

When I was little I mostly stayed out of his way, although I thought he was interesting. His worn hands always stood out to me—he knew how to do things with them. He used them to open big burping gaseous jars of his homemade pickled dill cucumbers, carve the Christmas ham and sift copious amounts of salt over his red-ripe cut tomatoes. But it was those same hands that carefully held his thick European history books, straightened his Latvian newspapers and held his smoking pipe off to the side so he could make another declaration about how he believed the world worked.

40

Striving to be upstanding Latvians

A Lutheran pastor married Milda and Edgars at Greta camp in 1952. It was one of several ceremonies he presided over that weekend. She made her own wedding dress, a simple maroon A-line outfit that bore little resemblance to the exquisite chiffon dress she'd worn to marry Rudis in Riga all those years ago. Aleksis was proud to be Edgars' best man. They had a small celebration with coffee and sweet red Lambrusco near the dorm afterwards.

Soon they had their own baby girl, Inta (twenty-five years later, she would become my mother). Straight away, Inta was the apple of Edgars' eye and he would sit her on his knee for hours, singing to her. She was his lovely little one.

Grandma Milda and Edgars pooled what they had managed to save from their two-year work contracts. He convinced her they should get a loan and buy a block of land in Newcastle on the hill overlooking Redhead Beach. They hired builders to start on their house, but stayed living in Greta.

Aleksis' family also planned to move from Greta into Newcastle around the same time and he continued his close friendship with Edgars and Milda. He told me a little of the story.

'It was a big construction job. Their house needed strong foundations to get down past the sandy soil. Your grandma was worried about the cost, but when she saw it finished, she knew they had done the right thing. The house stood tall and was made of good red brick. Some Latvians thought one of them must have had money stashed away from Germany to build such a place, but your grandma always denied it. She told people off, saying they managed to build it because they never wasted their money on drink and cigarettes!'

I have a blurry black-and-white photo of Grandma Milda's first day living in Redhead. After they'd moved in with their few suitcases and some furniture they'd collected from other Latvians, Edgars took her and the children down to the beach. The photo shows Grandma Milda standing on the rocks near the ocean. Her hair is curled around her face and the wild sea is crashing in the background behind her. Perhaps Edgars imagined that they would have many times together at the beach in their future, but after that day Grandma Milda hardly ever went. The wind was too fierce for her.

Uncle George told me that he, his brother and Edgars all loved the beach from the beginning. They spent a lot of their time catching mullet and eels in Dudley Creek behind the sand dunes. They were always talking about the best methods for catching eels—flicking them out from under the sand with a stick, casting out fishing lines and even throwing gelignite in the water to stun them. They'd then hang their catch up on wire in their homemade smoker in the corner of the yard and stand around for hours, watching proudly as the smoke was funnelled through the hole they'd dug in the soil and successfully drawn up through its metal chimney.

Edgars also worked in the Newcastle coalmines and gave Grandma Milda his pay envelope each week. Aleksis told me the only time they ever seemed to argue was when Edgars slipped other people money without asking her first. He was always doing favours for other Latvians, mostly lending them cash and fixing their cars. He just bowed his head when she tried to lecture him about it. She sometimes found his generosity infuriating.

Life became harder when Grandma Milda's mother Marija, the Old Battleaxe, and father Andrejs came to live with them.

Even though Grandma Milda's brother had sponsored the old couple to come to Australia, Rudolfs and Milda decided they would share the responsibility of having their parents live with them.

Edgars built a bedroom under the house for Grandma Milda's parents. It had a small sitting area, but it was clear from the beginning that her mother wanted full run of the place. The first thing her mother did was try to sort out the garden. Grandma Milda told her nothing would grow properly in the sandy soil, but her mother didn't listen. She did manage to get a few things to grow in summer and also constructed a large chicken coop.

From the stories Aleksis told, I could see that both women tried to keep their Latvian traditions alive in their own way. Grandma Milda's mother practised old peasant remedies and brewed awful herbal drinks, while Grandma Milda focused on the Newcastle Latvian community and organising social and cultural events. Edgars was president of one of the Latvian societies for a time, but Grandma Milda always felt she had to do everything in the background because he didn't have a head for organising things.

When they had a telephone installed at the house, Grandma Milda was forever on it, helping to solicit donations and find volunteers. She came to know all the Newcastle Latvians very well. She renewed her close friendship with Alise, the young woman who had helped her flee to safety all those years ago and now lived in Sydney, as well as others she'd met in the DP camps in Germany. Alise was still a warm and generous woman who continued to play a significant role looking after the boys, particularly Janis as he grew up.

Grandma Milda also started hosting Latvian parties, always making sure there was plenty of food. When she bumped into Latvians at the Charlestown Shopping Centre, they were grateful to receive an invitation and often asked whether they might bring new Latvians who had arrived to settle in Newcastle.

'That is how Milda eventually came to meet your nanna Aline. It was at a Latvian concert in the old Rotary Hall at Broadmeadow in 1953. I don't think she thought too much of her and Eddy at first, to be honest,' Aleksis admitted.

41

 Grandma Milda

The Old Battleaxe

I can remember Edgars came with me to the Newcastle train station to pick up my mother and father. It was raining but I was excited to show them the progress I had made in building a new home and to introduce them to Edgars. They were the last ones to get off the train. My mother looked just the same, her face stony and as determined as ever, but I was surprised to see how old and thin my father looked and felt concerned.

Of course, my mother started up straight away with me after meeting Edgars. 'What is this weather? You're soaked, Milda. Why didn't you wait for us inside?' I felt immediately like I was a young woman being pushed around again. Edgars and my father just nodded and smiled at all she said.

Within a month, my mother was really getting on my nerves. One day I was reading a magazine when my nose caught a whiff of a disgusting smell. At first, I thought the boys had brought home something dead from the beach, but then I found my mother with a red handkerchief over her nose shovelling chicken shit in the garden, trying to fix the soil. I had already told her we'd tried but she would not listen. We had a big argument.

'You think you don't need a vegetable garden?' my mother yelled. 'Look at Edgars, he's always working. He's a *zelta cilvēks*, a man of gold. Stop with your magazines and help!'

I was upset. My mother did not see all the work I was doing making clothes and organising Latvian events. It was typical of her to just focus on the importance of working in the garden. I admit she did get cucumbers and tomatoes to grow, but the garden was never much good and died back late every summer in the salty wind and heat.

Another time she caught a cold and tied an old smoked cod around her neck to try to cure it. I found her wandering around the front yard with it on, stinking of smoky fish. 'What am I supposed to say to the neighbours if they ask?' I said. 'The Australians already think all DPs are not right in the head!'

Then one day, I went out into the backyard to tell my mother I was going into town to buy some shoes. My mother was with the boys and they were all hunched over a stray dog. I wondered what they were doing, then I heard her say: 'This dog curled up next to me in the night and I used him to take all the pain away from my bones. My old magic put my aches into the dog's body.' She was going on like a witch about the old Latvian ways. The boys were listening to her, and I could tell they were fascinated and wanted to believe her. She pointed over to that sorry dog who was now trying to run away. It did not look well at all. 'He's the one who is limping now!' she cried out, pleased with herself.

My mother looked up and saw me watching them. Just at that moment, my little dog, Mimi, started running around in strange circles. My mother gave me a curious smile. 'Oh Mimi! Mimi!' she said. 'Come here, my head hurts. Will you cure my headache?' I had to rush over to Mimi and take her inside. I did not believe my mother could really put her headache onto Mimi but I could not stand any more of her nonsense!

Edgars simply did not see that my mother was trying to take over our place. He was pleased she helped with the cooking and cleaning, and laughed when she chased the boys around with her broom after they had brought sand from the beach into the house. Sometimes I felt outnumbered and would go to my room to get some peace and plan the next Latvian event. Of course, I did!

But it was good for the children to get to know their grand-parents. The boys called her the Old Battleaxe! I did laugh at that. They got it right; that's exactly what she was.

42

 Grandma Milda

Meeting Aline

Before our Latvian concerts, I always had to rearrange the food table and make sure everyone's plates were properly presented. All the other ladies relied on me to get everything just right.

The day I met Aline and Eddy, I was busy doing this when I noticed two new people arrive. Though we hadn't met before, I knew straight away it was them. I didn't feel I had time to stop and go over to say hello, so I kept working.

After a while, I looked up and saw that Aline was still standing in the doorway in her plain yellow dress, with her little boys behind her, although Eddy had already joined the other men. I couldn't ignore her any longer, so I put on a smile and walked over. '*Labdien*, you must be Aline, come in.'

I looked down to see a very small plate of *pīrāgi* in her hands. I brought her over to the food table and watched as she tried to slip those *pīrāgi* towards the back. I said, 'No, they must be at the front. People will want to taste them to see how you can cook!'

When Aline turned pale, I had to tell her I was joking, but of course I wasn't! I waved Janis over to take Aline's boys to play with the other children.

We had to talk about something so I asked about her people. She told me about her father being an organist and about her days in the choir, so I suggested she might sing a solo at one of our concerts, but Aline started to go to pieces. I thought she was going to faint! I led her to the metal chairs I'd arranged in rows at the front of the stage so she could sit down, and then gave her one of the booklets that outlined the event's proceedings.

She didn't say a word even though I had worked on those booklets for a long time. To fill the gap in our conversation, I explained, 'It's a light program, a few musical pieces, and afterwards we will hold a raffle to raise money for the Latvian Cultural Sunday School for the children.'

Aline blushed and said that next time she would make something for the raffle.

'That would be good,' I agreed, patting her hand, then decided to leave her alone for a while.

When the proceedings got underway, I was busy organising all the prizes on a table on the stage, including Latvian cushions and books and a very good-looking electric kettle. I had managed to collect a lot of those prizes and felt quite proud. Edgars was in charge of the raffle draw, and I watched him spin the wheel and carefully announce the winning numbers.

Suddenly, I heard a shout. I turned around and saw Eddy at the back, waving his wine glass around and shouting his ticket number: 'Sixty-two! That's us,' he said. 'Go up, Aline!'

Fui! What an oaf! It was clear for all to see that Aline didn't want to, but she felt she had no choice. She wound her way through the chairs up to the front. Edgars beamed as he passed her the electric kettle, which she held very tightly to her chest.

I must admit that I shot him a dark look as I had wanted that kettle for the final draw and hoped I might win it.

The rest of the night passed quickly. Everyone ate all the food I'd organised. My mocha cream cake was the first to go. Eddy was drinking steadily, raving on about German books and music. I could tell he was clever, but didn't like his rude jokes. Then he went on about Australia not recognising Latvian people's education or their good standing. I smiled a bit at that: did he think we didn't know he was a fallen priest?

Towards the end of the evening, Eddy spilt red Lambrusco over my good tablecloth. Aline's face rumpled like cottage cheese. I insisted on removing all the glasses and taking it to soak right away, as there was a purple watery stain across half of it.

Eddy couldn't help himself. He kept telling me to put salt on it instead of soaking it, but I ignored him and told Aline that her boys should join the folk dancing group.

'You must also join the choir,' I said to her.

'Are you sure?' Aline asked, glancing over at Eddy.

'No matter what, we Latvians must stick together,' I replied and reached out to squeeze her hand.

43

Not good enough

All the Latvians judged each other one moment and forgave the next. Not just your Grandma Milda, although she was one of the worst.

We were content in Argenton for a while. Eddy found a Catholic school in nearby Boolaroo. Our decision to enrol Andrejs at that school was important. We couldn't participate in his First Communion, because we were sinners in the eyes of God, but we had an idea of what most schools in Australia were like. No discipline, no control—we had heard stories about students jumping from windows and running away from their classes. We wanted our boys to go to a proper school. On that Eddy and I agreed.

They also went to Latvian Cultural Sunday School and Peteris learnt piano. All of us who came to Australia after the war did that. We all worked to make sure our children were educated and had ways to keep our Latvian culture alive.

But the one thing I have learnt in my life, well and truly, is that things come back around. You reap what you sow. Do you remember I told you about my cousin, Jekabs, who stayed with us in Kraslava while he was training to be a priest? After we arrived in Newcastle, I found out that he'd become a Jesuit priest and was living in Sydney! A Jesuit is not like a parish priest who knows how to talk to people; Jekabs was more like a theologian. That was what Eddy had wanted to be, so of course he was jealous and hated him.

Jekabs eventually came to visit us in Argenton. It was a shock when I saw him on our front doorstep in his black suit. I hadn't seen him for over ten years and he'd become very fleshy in the face. He looked at me with such pity. I remember exactly what he said: 'Aline, it is God's will we meet again. We need to pray for your soul.'

You see, by those words he was trying to tell me he knew everything about Eddy. What could I do? He was family, so I welcomed him into my home.

We went into the front room and I introduced Jekabs to Eddy. It must have been very hard for Eddy, but he shook Jekabs' hand and stayed with us for about half an hour. We all tried to talk, mostly news about other Latvians, but there was such a strained feeling.

Eddy kept his face straight and spoke like he was on the same level as Jekabs, like they were just two men talking, but I knew he was boiling inside. After a while Eddy said he had to go and find the boys, who were off fishing down at the lake.

I'd spent the morning cooking, so I invited Jekabs to have something to eat. He kept waving the dishes away and told me he had a fussy stomach and couldn't eat our tomatoes. But he liked my *pīrāgi* and said they were just the same as my mother's.

Then it started. 'Aline, it's good that Eduards has left us alone. He has turned his back on God to be with you. What sort of house is this to bring up children? You need to leave him.' He leant across to pat my hand and I saw his fingernails were too long.

He went on and on like that. 'They are not his children. They are God's children. God makes all children from the sparks of his great stone hammer.' I could see he really believed that. I kept trying to say Eddy was their father, but Jekabs was serious. He thought Eddy had no right to the children and that they belonged to God!

I listened to him go on. I was not very strong, you see. I felt ashamed that he was right in front of me; he was a member of my family who knew what I had done. Looking back now, I think I should have laughed.

Children are the sparks from God's hammer? That is typical of silly priests—no thought for anything practical. How could I leave Eddy? Where would we go? I had no money. Eddy was the children's father. Women didn't leave their husbands in those days.

Eventually Jekabs told me he had to leave. As he was gathering his things, I grabbed his arm. I pleaded with him to write to Rome to help us seek forgiveness. You know what he said? 'Your sin is too great.' I knew straight away what his problem was. He was worried that writing such a letter would damage his own reputation.

He left and I didn't hear from him for more than a year, but I did hear from someone else—my mother! By then people had started writing to family again, always careful because we knew the Russians might read everything. About six months after Jekabs visited, I received her letter in the post. I will read it to you.

Dearest Aline,

I received your letter and photos of you, Eduards and the boys.
Thank you. That is my only happiness in my miserable life.
I believe that owning half the world would not be the same
worth as having my one child back with me.

But what if that precious child injures her mother's heart?
Then it is a hard life for her mother.

I am talking about the state of your marriage. You know
very well our Christian rule. I don't need to remind you that it
is forbidden to only have a union registered in an office. What
did you think when your son went to his first Holy Communion
and you were not allowed to go with him? It is unthinkable!
Maybe you will find it in your heart to let Eduards go back to

his post? Or perhaps you can write to seek a special dispensation from Rome?

I am terrified to think about your life after death. If you happened to die before me, I would no longer be happy to die. I now need to live so I can pray for you every day and night. I keep your situation a secret. I will not even tell Aunty Adela. Not in this world would I tell her. She would be shocked to know you live in sin. I am happy your father died without knowing.

Your mother,
Apolonija Balulis

When I read that letter, my legs went weak and I almost fell down. You can't imagine the pain. That is how I found out my father was dead. I didn't show that letter to Eddy, because I didn't want him raging and yelling. I just hid it and tried to keep on living, but sometimes I felt like I couldn't move forward. That letter hit me every day.

I couldn't believe that Jekabs had written to my mother. But at least one good thing came of it all. My mother wrote to Jekabs and convinced him to write to Rome. He loved my mother, so he did it.

When I finally told Eddy what had happened, I thought he was going to explode. I had to plead with him not to ruin our chance for peace. You see, Eddy thought Jekabs had only agreed because he wanted to prove how powerful he was. He hated that we needed help from him.

In the end, Jekabs' letter worked. We got a letter back from Rome that formally excommunicated Eddy from the Catholic Church but also allowed him to return to the faith as a layman. It meant we could be properly married.

I remember our wedding day. Eddy had been staying at the monastery in Mayfield for the previous ten days. You see, we had to have an artificial separation first, away from the marriage bed, to wash the sin away. In the morning, I sent the boys off to Marta's for the day. They had no idea what was happening. I got dressed in my best skirt and jacket and, when I was ready, I walked alone to the bus stop. The ceremony was to be at the convent church in Mayfield and I had to catch two buses and then walk up the hill for quite a bit because the church was not on the main road.

I felt very hot when I got there and nervous because I was all alone. I entered the church, but couldn't see Eddy, only Bishop Toohey and his secretary, Monsignor Sims. The church felt empty—no flowers, nothing to make it seem like a celebration. They told me to kneel with them and pray.

I was like that for twenty minutes, listening while they recited prayers and read from the Bible. My knees were aching and I felt too warm in my suit. Finally, they stopped and Eddy came through a side door. We were married properly with the full rites even though we were the only ones there. When we were finished, we caught the two buses back home together. That was that.

Would you believe, when Eddy died almost 50 years later, it was the same Monsignor Sims who conducted his funeral service? One of the old nuns organised it. I was talking to her about who might do it because we didn't have a proper parish priest then. She told me she'd found a priest who was retired but had agreed to perform the rites. When I saw him at the church, I knew straight away who he was. 'Do you remember?' I asked him. He looked straight into my eyes and nodded. I was embarrassed, but he gave Eddy a very good service. He came to the reception afterwards, had a few glasses of wine and even asked me for a kiss as he was getting up to leave. What a thing! I didn't know what to do, so I leant over and kissed his cheek. What did he mean when he asked for that kiss? That I owed him gratitude, or that all was forgiven?

44

Scarves and prawns

My mother finally started writing to me again after Eddy and I were married, but it was hard reading her letters because she described how poor she'd become now my father was gone. She couldn't tell me directly. It was dangerous to write letters complaining, because the Soviets read the mail. But she was clever, my mother. Instead she wrote: 'Oh Aline, I am happy. You remember Mrs Bergmanis? Now I have all the things she used to have.'

I knew straight away what she meant. When I was a girl, Mrs Bergmanis had been the poorest woman in Kraslava. I remember her standing at the markets every week, waiting to see what people might give her. Can you imagine what it was like to find out my mother was a beggar like Mrs Bergmanis? I went to Eddy and told him. He agreed we needed to try to help her, and I was grateful for that. You see, he understood how dangerous life was for my mother. His own father had been deported to Siberia in 1953 and his mother had gone with him. They made it back but many people did not.

We thought the best thing would be if she could come live with us in Australia. In Latvia, children look after their parents when they are old. That's the proper thing to do. Of course, we knew it would not be easy for my mother to come here.

We wrote to Sydney and received the papers to fill out, but there were too many things my mother had to do. She needed to get documents from the Russians—identity and police records,

175

things like that. She had no one to help her. She wrote to people but couldn't get all the papers. In the end, the Canberra immigration people said she couldn't come.

A few years later we thought it might be easier, so we tried again. But the rules had changed. We found out my mother had to go all the way to Moscow to be questioned before she would be given the papers she needed to leave. My uncle, Boleslavs, had been arrested for being an enemy of the state. She wrote to tell us she just couldn't face going to Moscow and sitting through the questions, that her fear was too great.

The only thing left for us to do was send her things. At first we tried to send money but people stole it, and big packages never made it through. Then one time I sent her a cream silk scarf folded in a letter. It was so very thin that you couldn't tell it was there. She got it! I thought she might wear the scarf to feel a bit better, but she wrote and told me she'd sold it at the Riga market. That's how the plan started. I decided I would buy scarves to send her and then she could earn money by selling them.

I wanted to get the best ones I could, so every month I caught the bus into Newcastle to buy them at David Jones. It was a big trip, especially if Eddy came with me. He would always try to rush me. I would stand there thinking: *Which one is the right colour? Which pattern will get her more money?* There were racks of them. Sometimes I would stand there for so long that I'd get a stomach-ache. A couple of times Eddy ended up choosing them. He thought the patterned ones were better than the plain colours.

When I arrived back home, I would write a letter to my mother. I remember exactly how I did it each time. I'd sit at this kitchen table and write two pages. That was the hardest part. What could I tell her that was true about my life? In the end, I always found something to write, mostly about the boys, something positive.

When I finished, I'd stand near the laundry sink and unfold the ironing board. Next, I always washed my hands. I didn't want any dirt or oil getting on the scarves, none at all. I'd take the scarf out of the packet but leave the tags on. Sometimes I thought I should cut them off to save a bit of thickness but the tags made the scarves special. It showed they were new from overseas.

I'd take my time, lay the scarf out and iron over and over until it was completely flat like a piece of thin paper. The edges were tough. If the iron was too hot, they curled up and I would have to go over them. I would stare at the patterns as I ironed—brown and grey rings, red squares or little flowers. Sometimes I developed a swollen feeling in my chest as I imagined my mother looking at them and thinking her daughter had chosen such pretty and clever patterns. Not all of them reached her, but it was the only thing I could do.

I was upset about my mother, but life did improve for a while after Eddy and I were properly married. Little Karl came along, and he was a good baby. Andrejs and Peteris often spent their days away from the house, somewhere off in the bush. Parents did a lot less with their children back then. I often worried I was not a good mother, but every week I washed and mended their uniforms for school. I stood and watched them go every morning, but sometimes I wonder what they got from me. A mother should do more than patch up your pants.

The boys often went prawning up near Teralba, and I always cooked everything they caught. I'd tip the prawns into a big pot of boiling water, throw in handfuls of salt and then, after a few minutes, drain them into the sink. The prawns were salty and sweet.

One night the boys and I were all sitting at the kitchen table with our feast when Eddy swayed in with a big smile. I could see his eyes were lit up from drink, but they were not angry. He wandered over to get a plate. 'Good I came home when I did,' he said, and took a pile of prawns.

The boys kept their eyes down, but Eddy was in the mood to talk. He wanted to hatch plans with them to make money. 'You boys are smart,' he said. 'You caught these prawns. Now let's get something else.'

He told them his plan to head down to the mine after payday. He'd noticed that some men got too clumsy grabbing their money and often dropped a few coins between the wooden planks of the office floor. He thought the boys would be small enough to wriggle under and find them.

I'm not sure the boys really wanted to do it at first but he kept talking and they got caught up in the idea. So, off they went the next Friday. One thing I have to admit: they did come back with a fair bit of money!

Other times Eddy would come home from work in a bad way. He hated that coalmine. There were often arguments about whose fault it was when accidents happened. He thought the whole thing was beneath him. Still, he did his duty. That was a big thing.

Once he came home with a brown paper bag and I knew it was drink. I could see he was wound up, talking to himself about all the bastards he worked alongside, and I asked him what was wrong.

'Somebody let a slip go. They think it was me,' he said. He explained that a carriage had gone down the rails and someone had been hit in the back. The boys just sat quietly.

I saw Eddy's fingernails were still black and realised he must have got out of there quickly. I tried to tell him everything would be fine, but he yelled at me, 'What do you know? Shut up, woman!'

You see, a lot of the men at the mine didn't like him. Eddy never joined the workers' union, because he thought they were only a few steps away from being Communists. Lots of Australians didn't like all us refugees from Europe and called us reffos.

Eddy got mad when people stared at him or called him names. He thought he was better than them. The other workers in the mine knew he thought that and it made them suspicious of him. He was not easy in the company of others, could never just be one of the men.

I think that is why he tried so hard to show how smart he was with other Latvians. 'At least they should understand,' he'd say. But he never could make proper friendships with people. He was good company and made people laugh, but he always went too far with his drinks and jokes.

45

Stockton ferry

After hearing Nanna's stories about Granddad Eddy, I started to wonder whether we should slow down. I knew she was taking little white pills for her back. I'd seen her reach for her glass of water to wash them down, her hand tentative as if the glass might slip out of her hand at any moment.

'Is your back getting worse, Nanna?' I'd ask.

'No, it's the same, love.'

'Can I do something to help? Do you want to rest?'

'I can't rest all day, it's just old age. We can keep talking,' she'd say.

After these exchanges, I'd pause, my mind a jumble as I tried to guess what was best for both of us. Mostly Nanna would take the lead and we'd end up continuing on, but one morning, the idea of staying in the house to talk seemed too much for us both. We took our time with breakfast and then I slowly washed the dishes, in no hurry to figure out the day ahead.

'Do you want to go for a drive to the Newcastle wharf to see the ocean?' I asked. Nanna's eyes widened. She paused as if checking in with herself to ensure she was up to the idea.

'Yes, fresh air,' she announced. 'I have to go while you're here to drive me. Years ago, I might have caught the bus but I'm too old now.'

An hour later we got into the car and headed down the main arterial road into town. Nanna stared out the window as we went past the Subaru outlet, Officeworks and Dan Murphy's. I kept my eyes on the road and drove slowly. I could sense her frail body in the seat next to me and it made me more tentative.

'I can't believe how busy everything is,' she said looking out the window. 'It was all bush when we came and awful paspalum grass, you know it? It has sticky seeds. They always caught on the boys' clothes. I had to pick them out before I could do the wash.'

I mumbled in acknowledgement, watching as a red Nissan Patrol turned out of a side street in front of us. I quickly put on the brake and then eased it off as the cars adjusted into a steady flow.

'When we first moved here, it was not easy to get around because we didn't have a car. I worked in the laundry at the Wallsend Hospital and had to catch two buses to get there. It was hard work. The sheets were heavy when they came out of the big washing machines. I almost couldn't lift them.

'Sometimes the boys would walk down to meet me at the crossroads when I was coming back from work. I would come around the corner and see them standing there. So little, by themselves. I was grateful they did that.'

I nodded, trying to listen and at the same time work out where we should stop.

'Do you want to get out at the wharf, Nanna? There's a cafe now.'

'Yes, love.'

When we arrived, I parked the car next to a path running along the sea wall towards the wharf cafes. I stretched and breathed the salt air. Nanna slowly put her arm through the straps of her handbag and got ready to walk. It was windy and wisps of Nanna's hair fluttered around her face. The water slapped against the rocks and grew dark as the clouds came across. I looked up towards the lighthouse on Nobbys Head. It seemed precarious up there on the small hill. We stopped to watch a yellow-and-green ferry dock at the wharf. Only a handful of people were going each way.

'Where does that ferry go?' I asked.

Nanna twisted her head towards me, her eyes sharp. 'You know. It's the Stockton ferry.'

My heart skipped a beat.

'We sometimes used to catch it when we went on Sundays to visit Irene.'

I glanced at Nanna. Her eyes were focused on the Stockton buildings across the harbour. A couple of times over the years I'd heard whispers of Irene, my dad's little sister and Nanna's youngest child, but didn't know the full story.

'It's windy. Should we keep walking?' I asked to give us both a way to keep moving but Nanna stayed put, staring at the people getting off and on the ferry. 'It's all right, Nanna, we don't need to talk about Irene now,' I said gently.

Nanna turned to me, her hair fluffed up around her. Her eyes looked poached and watery.

'No.' Her voice was firm. 'It's okay to talk.'

I looked out over the water as Nanna took a breath and pushed on.

46

Nanna Aline

Irene

I knew when Irene was born that something was not right. The doctor pushed on her chest and eventually she started crying. After a few days, we took her home and I tried not to worry.

When she was about six months old, she started to have fits in her bassinet. Then we realised she couldn't follow things with her eyes. We took her to a doctor and he told us she had brain damage and epilepsy.

What could we do? We took her home and tried to look after her. We cared for her quite well for a time but her seizures grew worse. She would have weeks where her medicines helped but then things would go backwards. We just couldn't cope. Eddy started to block her out. He couldn't bear the sight of her shaking with her seizures. When he drank, he went on about how Irene was God's revenge for our sins. After a while he couldn't even look at her.

We couldn't take care of Irene. That is the truth. In those days, it was different. Children like her were sent to hospital. They didn't stay with families. But I wonder, maybe if things were calmer in our house . . . maybe we could have kept her with us? It was as if we were caught in a huge storm and our whole house was breaking apart.

But why did it happen in the first place? That's something I will ask God in the end. I was in labour a long time and maybe Irene didn't get enough oxygen, but I wonder whether it was because I didn't deserve a healthy girl after everything that had happened in Germany.

When Irene was about six, we took her to Stockton Mental Hospital. We thought it would be safer for her there. At first, we visited every Sunday. Sometimes she came home with us for a night or we would all go up to Nelson Bay for a picnic. I would cook good food and we would sit under the trees. Sometimes it would be okay for a little while. I would look at my family and think we could manage. The boys tried hard with her, Peteris especially, but slowly she got worse. It was hard at home with Eddy drinking and there wasn't enough money. We visited less and less.

After Eddy died, I went to Irene again. She didn't recognise me, but I think she liked it when I sat with her. They were good to her at Stockton. Many of the nurses were very kind. Now her ashes are next to Eddy's. I will be on the other side of her when I die. The three of us together.

When Eddy was alive it was hard to speak about her. He wanted to forget. Now I keep her photo on my bedside table. She is beside me when I wake up every morning.

47

The houses they grew up in

I remember the trip home from the Newcastle wharf after Nanna had spoken of Irene. She wanted to go the long way via the Merewether Ocean Baths. There we pulled over for a while so we could watch the surf, rough and spraying over the rocks into the pool. There were only a few lone swimmers. Nanna found her voice again as we arrived back in Argenton, away from the wind.

'I sometimes wonder if things would have been better if we'd stayed in Redhead. It would have been good for Eddy to be able to walk on the beach.'

I turned off the engine, reached for Nanna's soft papery hand and kissed it.

Tears welled in her blue eyes. 'But I am grateful for all my children and grandchildren. Your dad, my Peteris, he always tried very hard to help me when he was a boy.'

In that moment, I knew with certainty that I'd already waited too long to speak with Dad. If I wanted to delve any further into my grandmothers' stories, I needed to recognise I'd entered the territory my parents grew up in. It wasn't right for me to be there any longer without reaching out to them.

———

Most refugee stories become largely about the next generation born in the new land. Thousands of words have been written about how the DPs who arrived in Australia turned their minds to the education and welfare of their children as soon as they were able. Thousands more words have been written about how hard it was for the children of DPs to straddle the worlds of their parents' pasts as well as try to fulfil their dreams for a better future.

Trauma often passes down the generations. The children of DPs grew up with a terrible knowing and not knowing of the terrors that had come before them. In order to survive, they often used a combination of techniques: embracing the narrative of the distant homeland as their own; seeking to run as far away from it as possible; and, above all, wanting to do well enough in their own lives to somehow remove their parents' pain. My mum and dad, to some extent, tried them all.

I knew my parents would speak with me if I asked. They'd never denied me anything important, even once in my life.

I turned up at their house in Canberra in 2008, scared yet determined. By unspoken agreement, we avoided deeper discussions of why I wanted to find out my grandmothers' stories and what they meant to me, leaving all that for a reckoning down the track. For the time being we also avoided the topic of what they truly thought about my endeavours. My plan was just to sit down and talk with them and see what happened.

The night before we began, my parents and I spent the evening eating, watching TV and talking of other things. I was to interview Dad first and we both knew tomorrow would come soon enough. Perhaps we were trying to stock up on connection and goodwill before we began. I certainly was. I jumped at the chance to help make chicken stir-fry for dinner and tried to entertain my parents with observations about the politicians on the news.

The next morning, we set up at the big pine table in our dining room, used mostly for special occasions. Dad chose a chair at one end and, since I felt it would be too galling to plonk myself down beside him, I sat at the other end, almost 3 metres away, trying to make myself as unobtrusive as possible. Dad clasped his hands in front of him. I picked up my pen and a small notebook, keeping my eyes down.

I wasn't even able to ask the first question. Dad took a deep breath and started speaking. It was clear from the outset my job was to shut up and listen.

48

Best they could

At first, no one talked about the war years; the time from 1940 to 1950 was out of bounds. Later people started to make more of an effort to build up the Latvian community in Australia, but with that came whispers about 'who had done what' during the war.

Once, after too much booze, it came out at a party that one guy we knew had been named as a Nazi in Russian documents. Then someone said he'd seen that man come back from the forest all shook up and that he might have participated in the shooting of Jews. Everyone thought they knew something dark about each other. All these Latvians were intertwined—Marta, Jekabs, Lina and my mum. They all ended up in Newcastle and Sydney. It was just too much.

One of my first memories is of my parents cooking dinner on a primus stove at Argenton. We were still living in Redhead at the time, but every weekend we all made the long trip out to the edge of town to work on the house. At the end of the day, we sat on benches in the middle of the construction site to eat our meal. You had to pump the stove up with methylated spirits and light it. It was a dangerous thing, that stove. I was always worried it might blow.

We ate simple food. My mum always thought it was a problem she couldn't cook or sew very well. She put it down to being an only child. But my dad wasn't well prepared for life either. Spending your early years in a Catholic seminary doesn't set you up for life as a labourer. They did pretty well, all things considered. We always had a proper meal for dinner, not like some of the kids in the street who had to eat food directly from a can. We ate lots of pancakes, potato ones and sweet ones. I'd race my brothers to see who could eat them the fastest. There wasn't much money but we never went hungry. We always had milk and bread.

Andrejs was the eldest. Everyone except my parents and the old Latvians called him Andrew. He kept to himself and tried to steer clear of my parents when he could. He was smart and had lots of plans to make things and earn money. I was the middle boy, the one my parents called on to help them a lot of the time. My little brother, Karl, was the baby until Irene was born.

The house was a pressure-cooker. Mum would get very upset if something went wrong. If we were washing dishes and someone dropped a bowl, she would carry on like she'd lost the most valuable thing. Basic domestic tasks seemed like a struggle for my parents and they would get frustrated very quickly when things did not turn out.

Some days were ridiculously tense. Once Dad was trying to fix our washing machine, but he couldn't figure it out. Andrew was standing on the patio steps watching him, and I was a bit further down in the garden. When Andrew started laughing, Dad lost it and threw a hammer at him. It seemed to me like he threw it full blast. He might have been aiming it so it wouldn't hit Andrew, but I couldn't tell. The whole incident scared me. It seemed like we'd only narrowly avoided complete disaster.

After we moved to Argenton, Dad got a job underground at the local coalmine just past Cockle Creek. He hated it. He went from being a theologian to putting 'coalminer' down as his job description. At one point, Dad left the mine because he still harboured hopes of improving himself. He tried all sorts of things. He enrolled at the University of New England as an external student to do a degree in philosophy, but he wasn't set up to succeed. He couldn't afford to go to the compulsory residential school.

I used to help him with his essays. He'd write them out on big sheets of yellow paper and I had to correct them at the kitchen table. It was hard because I knew Dad expected me to find all the mistakes. I had to will myself to point out the errors. He'd try to hold his tongue and accept my advice but I would be shaking, waiting for him to blow up. I knew I had to do it or Dad would be disappointed in me when he got his results back. I was only about eleven years old.

Then Dad tried to do a hotel management course by correspondence. He applied for a position at Werris Creek as a NSW Clubs manager. Mum said there was no way we were moving to Werris Creek. It would have been a disaster with all his drinking. Later he sold cameras and then worked for a Catholic company selling insurance door to door. It was very stressful as he only got a retainer wage at the beginning and it was reduced once they thought he should be able to earn enough on commission.

He also did a stint selling the plastic film they made in those days to put over black-and-white TVs to get colour into the pictures. We got one for our TV and we all had to stand around and act amazed, even though the colours weren't right and people's faces looked green. It wasn't like a proper colour TV but we kept our mouths shut.

Dad did all these things to avoid being a factory worker. He really tried, but in the end, he gave up and went to Sulphide Corporation down the road. That was the source of a lot of the trouble. If he could have stuck it out somehow at the University of New England, maybe things would have been different.

What you have to understand is that it all goes back to the strange beginnings of his relationship with Mum. Why did they get together in Germany? Mum was pregnant with Ruta. There was no question of Mum keeping her, as Dad would never have been able to handle it. Why did Dad leave the priesthood? It's certainly not straightforward. Maybe he married Mum out of love, but perhaps there was also some self-interest there, some sort of deal. In the end, it didn't turn out the way he wanted, and he blamed Mum for wrecking his life.

My brothers and I went to Catholic schools—first the Star of the Sea at Boolaroo and then Marist Brothers. We were taught by the nuns, priests and brothers. In the early years, we didn't go to church on Sundays as Dad had been excommunicated. Things got a bit better after he went off on some church retreat. It was all kept a secret but, whatever happened, it meant my parents could get married by the church. After that, Mum took us to church some Sundays but sometimes my parents stayed in bed, sick from all the boozing. Mum too. She could be as bad as he was. When that happened, I found the confusion about what to do overwhelming.

I knew it was a mortal sin not to go to church but I was too young to go by myself. You can't understand unless you are brought up in the Catholic faith. Once I was mucking around under an oak tree at school and ate a bit of an acorn. You were supposed to fast for three hours before communion and I felt I had done something really evil by eating just a bit of that nut. That is how crazy the church made people.

Going to those schools set us apart from the other Argenton families. No question. My parents knew how important education was and it was a big thing to find the money for the fees and uniforms. I think they fell behind once with the payments, but they managed. My life would have turned out very differently if I hadn't gone to those schools. Argenton was a rough place. It was sort of primitive and everyone was on the edge. No one wore shoes. Lots of kids just slept on their back porch after playing all day. School opened up another world.

We were always trying to get money. Andrew came up with the idea of going down to the golf course near the creek and collecting balls in the scrub. Sometimes we'd be overeager and collect ones still in play. We'd hear yells of outrage from the golfers when they realised we'd nicked their balls. We'd take them home to repaint them white so they looked new. Andrew invented a tripod where we'd pincer the balls between two pins. He'd carefully paint around the Spalding and Dunlop letters. They looked so good, the golfers bought them back from us.

We were also good foragers. There were mushrooms near Speers Point, but the best was prawning and fishing at the Teralba ponds in the evening. Once I almost drowned because I got caught in our net but Andrew grabbed me. That's how it was—we kids looked after ourselves. It was always crowded and stressful at home so we often left to do our own things.

We had lodgers living with us sometimes for extra money. There was one old lady—we referred to her as Babushka—who was someone's relative. We were cruel, calling her a witch. There was also a man, Ivansons, who was kind and played with us. There's a photo somewhere of him pushing me on my tricycle.

We went to Latvian school and folk dancing classes. Rehearsals were every second Sunday. If you didn't go, the teacher would ring up your parents. There was a fair bit of pressure to keep doing these things, to keep up the Latvian culture. I didn't mind the folk dancing. I was good at it, but that wasn't what I was known for. My folks got me into piano around age seven, and I was a very good player. I stood out playing piano and in academic work.

Overall, we managed, but there were periods of real darkness. At one point, Dad went mad. The drinking had always been bad but it spun out of control. He went totally crazy, bringing home drunks from the pub. Dad was one of those drinkers who made people feel anxious and uneasy. He'd get mean. You didn't know what he was going to do.

I remember Mum having a black eye sometimes. The cops were called more than once to our place. That's no small thing when you remember how rough Argenton was. People had a tolerance for a lot of fighting, but still the cops were called to our place. That tells you everything you need to know.

Mum would argue back and scream at him. He'd be desperate for money to gamble. Once he went at my Commonwealth Bank moneybox with a can opener. I hated it when Mum tried to get me on her side. I can remember her asking me to take the spark plugs out of the car to stop him driving and killing himself. She pleaded with me. I was scared he'd catch me, but I crept out in the dark and managed to get them out for her. I would only have been twelve or so.

What you've got to understand is that my brothers and I often felt contempt for Dad. We couldn't stand him when he was drunk. My brothers and I looked after ourselves. We never dreamt of asking Dad for advice about anything.

When they were announcing the results of the Vietnam conscription lottery, I was sitting alone in the garage, hunched over the radio listening for my birth date. I don't remember my Dad being involved or thinking he could help me in any way. Of course, he was a supporter of the Vietnam War because he hated Communists.

After Andrew and I left home, Karl was on his own with my parents. He had to raise himself. It must have been God-awful at times.

The hardest thing was Irene. I once took her to the swimming pool with my friends when I was around eleven. I took her into the water and her body softened. She just lay against my arms in the blue water with the sun shining on us. I was happy to be doing something good for her. It seemed like a moment of peace.

Then it happened. I saw her face tightening and her eyes started to roll back. I pushed through the water as fast as I could to get to the edge. She started to shake. I was worried she would slip out of my hands, but I managed to lift her out. We both lay there on the warm concrete. I held her head in my lap as her body seized in an epileptic fit. My friends all stared. I felt helpless.

Now that I look back, I'm still glad we went to the pool that day. For that one moment in the water, Irene was really relaxed in my arms.

I know it all goes back to the beginning. How did they end up together? All these years, there's been an undercurrent of something bad. Sometimes I wonder how it must have looked at the beginning to the other Latvians—an older priest spending hours alone with a young pregnant girl? What went on there?

War trauma and poverty put families on a tightrope and one wrong step has great significance. My parents did the best they could. It always took so much effort for them to claw things back from the brink each time, but they always managed. Time and time again. They both kept trying.

49

All of this

My conversation with Dad had a huge impact on me. I realised I had been afraid throughout my childhood of not only what had happened in Latvia, but also its reverberating effects on the houses my parents had grown up in. I love my Dad with a ferocity that sometimes judders my bones and the pain sitting behind his words was a lot for us both to bear. I can remember trembling as I watched him wrestle with internal waves of emotion, the sucking froth of memories pulling in and out.

'I'm done talking,' he declared. 'My skull is splitting. I'm going to lie down.'

'Thanks, Dad,' I choked.

I watched him walk up the stairs and then stood up from the table, my stomach aching. I clutched my side and made my way outside towards our green swimming pool, desperate to be out in the sun. The pool looked calm with only one long gum leaf floating in it. I got the net to scoop it up, pain stretching and throbbing down my side. The sliding glass door opened and I turned my head to see Mum coming down the steps towards me.

'The wind is going to pick up. No point. The pool will soon be covered with leaves,' she gently said.

'Is Dad okay?' I blurted.

'He'll be all right. Come back inside and have a rest.'

'All of this is still around us. Latvia, the war . . . all the problems it caused!'

Mum sighed.

'It is and it isn't. Your nanna Aline is living a good life now. You've seen that for yourself. We live a good life now.'

I watched another leaf drift down into the pool.

'It's awful but you have to see how ludicrous the whole situation was for everyone at the same time,' she continued. 'That's the key.'

I looked up to see Mum's steady eyes.

'You'll see when we talk tomorrow. Both awful and ludicrous.'

I followed Mum back inside.

Dad spent the afternoon in his bedroom reading the newspaper. I sat quietly beside Mum in the lounge room, trying to concentrate on reading a book while she did her crossword. Slowly, the pain in my side eased. When it was time to make dinner, Dad emerged.

'Should we have sausages?' he asked.

I jumped up, relief at his back-to-normal tone filling me like cool water from the green pool outside.

'I'll make the salad,' I said.

50

— Inta —

Redhead

When my dad, your *vectēvs* Edgars, turned 50, Mum got all the Latvians together for a big party at the Broadmeadow Hall. I was about seven years old and your grandma Milda sewed me a coat from real rabbit fur. She made me sing three songs. I didn't want to do it because I knew I'd be awful, and I was, but my dad loved it.

I never called my brothers Juris and Janis. No way! Only my parents and the other Latvians called them that. They were always George and John to me. I remember Mum pleading with them to perform something too, but they weren't having a bar of it.

That's how it always was in our family. My brothers, especially George, would wriggle out of Mum's schemes as often as they could, but I was the littlest so I would go along with her. That's how I ended up walking around in fur coats and with huge bows in my hair. John also wore her outfits when he was younger—I remember a blue jumper that had a white collar and big decorative buttons. He was worried he might run into some of the local boys when he was wearing it. I remember once seeing a photo of all the Redhead kids at the local school with T-shirts and bare feet and John standing on the edge wearing a shirt and tie. After he got older, George stubbornly refused that sort of thing. He often looked like he'd just come off the beach.

My mother always wanted things to look perfect. She made such beautiful clothes, it's no wonder she wanted to show them off.

When I came along, she had someone to dress. And then when you and Liana and Mara came along, she turned to trying to dress you.

She was always making lists to figure out how she wanted something to go. I would find dozens of them around the house. And she kept little stashes of papers and postcards all around the place—she never threw anything away. There are still two shoe boxes full to the brim of this sort of stuff somewhere upstairs—letters from friends, my school reports, bits of old magazines and programs from Latvian events. Oh, and money. She was always squirrelling away money in old bags and between the pages of books. I'm still finding it ten years later. Roubles, Latvian lats, Australian dollars . . . I will bring it all down later.

———————

On Sundays, she'd be ready for church at least half an hour early. It drove her mad that George would turn up five minutes before we needed to go and refuse to comb his hair. She'd get angry, saying to him, 'Have you no pride? Have you no shame?' She would nag at him but he was very stubborn. Often he would get away with it and I would end up with another large bow in my hair.

My mother's brother, Rudolfs, lived in Melbourne after he immigrated to Australia. We went to visit him once a year or so, and to see my grandparents as well, once they'd moved to live with him. The whole family would pile into Dad's green Volkswagen and we'd head off at the crack of dawn. Mum would make a picnic lunch, packing everything so we could eat like royalty on the side of the road. The Australians thought we were mad.

Once she cooked a chicken and put it in a big pot in the boot of the car for us to eat on the way. When we stopped for lunch she went around the back to get it, then we heard her scream, 'Edgars! Come! Maggots!'

We all raced to get a look. The squirming white worms were wriggling all over the brown chicken skin. Mum glared at Dad. 'Flies must have got into the car when you packed it!'

George and John started to laugh. They got sticks and started poking at the chicken. They accidentally flicked some of the maggots into the boot of the car.

'*Fui!*' Mum cried. 'Stupid fools!'

Dad threw the chicken into the bushes. He wiped out the boot with some oil, then we all piled back in and kept going. Mum sat stony-faced while John, George and I cackled in the back.

Mum was proud of both her sons. She doted on them despite telling them off all the time. Sure, she wanted them to go along with her ideas about how to be good traditional Latvian men but I also think she secretly admired how at home they were in Australia. She liked how confidently they went about Newcastle. John and George were always in the bush, out fishing or involved with the surf club. They sometimes brought home fruit they'd nicked from someone's orchard. They knew how to take care of themselves, and Mum would turn a blind eye. It was really my brothers who looked after me a lot of the time, especially George. He would often be there to meet me when I got out of school or ballet classes. He had a soft and gentle side to him. He was a good painter at school, I remember that.

A few years later, Sue and George's wedding caused a huge fight. George started seeing Sue when he was spending all his time at the Redhead surf club. He got into surfing and went out every day. He moved out of home into a flat above the local shop right next to the beach so Mum would stop hassling him about it.

Mum was devastated when George told her Sue was pregnant and they were getting married. Their relationship had been a secret up to that point. George had never brought Sue home to meet my parents. I remember Dad listening and quietly accepting the news, but Mum shrieked and went on. 'I didn't drag you through Germany so you could turn around and waste your life!'

Mum couldn't stand the thought of George being with an Australian girl. Back then, she thought all Australians were hicks really. She was quite rude to people she thought were lower down the pecking order than herself. She'd say things like, 'I can see who you really are. I can see what is really going on here!' She'd waggle her finger at people like she was some great moral arbiter but then be all smiles when people fell into line.

Mum sat and sewed for days following the news that George had asked Sue to marry him, her mouth all puckered up. She was in a real state because she couldn't decide what to do about the wedding. She wanted nothing to do with Sue, but she couldn't stand the idea of George getting married without a proper ceremony and party.

In the end, her need to save face won out. I felt sorry for Sue. She was only seventeen. Mum gave her hell when she sat down to talk to her before the wedding and told her how things were going to be. Mum made her dress and organised all the food. The first time Dad laid eyes on Sue was at the wedding. Sue loved George with all her heart and stuck by him, and George worshipped Sue. They were meant for each other. I think Mum understood that in the end.

Things did not go much better when John met Flora. I think Mum had always held hopes that John would marry a Latvian girl. He participated in a lot more Latvian events than George ever did. Sunday Cultural School lessons, folk dancing, old fraternity get-togethers, playing chess with our Latvian neighbour Mrs Svetkis. For a few years he went around with the Latvian crowd in Sydney after he went off to university to study engineering. He took me out with him some nights. We'd go to dinner somewhere and eat piles of crabs and prawns and then go on to pubs in The Rocks on the harbour. They were some of the best nights of my life.

John met your aunty Flora at a party in the early seventies. She was a no-nonsense nurse from England and was planning to go back there but John convinced her to stay.

Apparently early in their relationship John invited Flora to come over to dinner where he was living temporarily in Aleksis' flat in Sydney. Mum turned up unannounced on the front doorstep after having caught the train down from Newcastle. She spoke entirely in Latvian, didn't say a word to Flora and insisted John take her out late-night shopping. Poor Flora ended up sitting in John's bedroom all night reading a book as he dutifully took Mum around the shops.

Flora tried to fit in with the whole scenario but it was tough. Mum would just click her fingers and John would drive up to Redhead from Sydney almost every weekend to fix things around her house. Flora started to go with him so Mum put her to work making food for Latvian parties and doing the washing-up. One minute they would be getting along okay—thanks largely to Flora's efforts—and the next Flora would be left stranded in the kitchen as all the ladies filed out to enjoy the food, talking exclusively in Latvian.

Mum disapproved of them living together and when they announced they wanted to get married, she tried to put them off. A part of it was that Mum was worried Flora would take John away to England. But in the end, they got married and their wedding was beautiful. It was held outside in the rose garden at the Cardiff nursery as it was owned by a Latvian couple at the time. Mum insisted all her Latvian friends be invited but that meant there was not enough room for Flora's friends. In the end, Flora just agreed to keep the peace.

But your aunty Flora was a strong person even when she was younger. She eventually got fed up with all of Mum's interfering, especially after your cousins were born. Flora drew a line and Mum backed off a bit, she had no choice if she wanted to stay a part of their lives.

Mum was proud of John when he bought land and a house at Dora Creek on Lake Macquarie. From then on he was often out on his boat, catching crabs and fish. Mum thought it was a bit glamorous, John owning that boat. I think it reminded her of some of the adventures she'd had with Rudis when she was younger. Not that she went out with John many times, if at all. Those days were over for her.

It was different when your dad and I told her we were getting married. Of course, she wanted to be in control of all the arrangements. But Mum had known your dad since he was a little boy and watched him play piano and folk dance at countless Latvian events. She had always looked down on your nanna and granddad for being Catholics, but she overlooked that because she knew your dad was going to be a university professor one day. He was Latvian and well educated—he still ticked the boxes.

We got married at the house in Redhead. We had to have both a Catholic blessing and Lutheran pastor, which took some negotiating. I was still in the bath when the guests arrived. When Mum came in, I was sitting in the water. She hissed at me to hurry up and get ready, but she was all smiles for the ceremony. It was a proper Latvian wedding and I could see a triumphant gleam in her eye the whole time. She made my dress and it fitted perfectly.

What I remember most was how proud my dad was of me. He came from the earth, my dad, a practical man. But he was also quite a soulful person. He could play piano and violin by ear and had a terrific tenor voice. He never put himself forward; he was always in the background, smoothing things over and making sure we all had everything we needed. My mother loved us but Dad was special. I was his girl.

Some people couldn't handle my mother but I never had a big

problem with her. So what if she pushed for things to be nice and proper? So do I most of the time! No one could doubt that she was very skilled. She was one of the best in Australia at stitching Latvian tapestries. That big olive green and red one she had hanging in her lounge room at Redhead is a masterpiece. She had a very strong image of herself as an upstanding, skilled and cultured Latvian woman and all that it entailed.

My mum liked festive events to have a sense of ceremony about them. When we were little, we all had to stand next to the Christmas tree and recite a poem before we could open our presents; that's a Latvian tradition. She also fancied herself as something of a classical music expert, though I don't think she really knew that much. But so what? Lots of people aspire to be more than they are. Any grace we all have, we get from her. No doubt about it!

Do you remember when we'd go shopping at Pacific Fair for groceries, she always wanted to have a nice lunch too? I often didn't have time but we'd all end up in some cafe anyway and then she'd want to order cake and coffee. You and your sisters loved it.

She was stubborn, but she had to be to make a life in Australia. She never talked much about the war and wanted to move on from those times. Good on her! I think she had the right idea. All those nights the old Latvians spent drinking too much and singing patriotic songs didn't change anything. Your grandma Milda was careful, she didn't want to get sucked back down into all that stuff. She was very selective about how she remembered Latvia and upheld its culture.

But God, I tell you, it was a shock when Rudis turned up! Mum liked telling her version of what happened after she got over it all, but I think it really upset her at the time. The idea we all had of Rudis being some sort of prince with exquisite taste and manners burst like a bubble! Turns out he was a pragmatist above all.

51

 Grandma Milda

Back from the dead

I hung onto the arm of my chair as our lounge room seemed to rock. I looked down a second time at his name on the back of the small white envelope—RUDIS MASENS.

Slowly picking up my letter knife, I started to cut, but the blade caught and ripped the far corner. The sight of the torn paper made me wince and I went even more carefully, until I could ease out two very thin pages.

I tried to read his letter, but my eyes kept jumping forward before I could finish each sentence.

> . . . I survived the War . . .
> . . . live in Riga . . .
> . . . such a joy to hear you are alive . . .
> . . . one true love . . .
> . . . found out your address from Stefans Feldmanis . . .
> . . . I want to come to Australia to see you and the boys.

Everything came flooding back. The hours I had spent looking at those square cards on the noticeboards at Hanau DP camp for a message. The days I'd spent on my bed in the dormitory, wishing he would appear. It felt as if the last 30 years fell away, as if I was a young woman again. I had such a rush of warm feelings towards him. I thought: *How is it possible that he now shows up like this?*

It must be our fate to meet again! I knew immediately that I would write to tell him to come.

I headed downstairs to the garage and found Edgars standing beside his old Ford in his blue work overalls. The news almost burst out of me. Pride filled my chest like a rush of air at the thought of Rudis seeing his sons, now young men.

When I blurted out what I had just learnt, a look of pain crossed Edgars' face. It was unreasonable but I found myself annoyed, and put my hands on my hips until he at last started to slowly nod.

'Of course,' he said, as if coming to his senses. 'Of course, we will help Rudis to come. The boys should see their father.'

I clattered back upstairs and rang my old friend Alise to tell her the news. My voice was breathless and I could hardly get the words out. 'I got a letter! Rudis is alive and coming from Latvia to see me!'

'Oh Milda,' Alise sighed. 'Imagine how it will be after all these years.'

I clasped my hand to my forehead. 'Which room will I put him in?'

At this Alise laughed. 'He can't stay with you!' she exclaimed. 'It would be too strange. He can stay with me in Strathfield and you can visit him here.'

Again, I felt irritated. 'Are you sure?' I asked. 'Edgars will understand . . . it is not like Rudis and I are still married, that all got sorted out years ago when I told the officials he was no longer alive!'

Alise laughed again. 'Even so, it's not a good idea!'

When the day finally arrived, we all got ready. I fought with Juris to try to get him to put on some decent clothes. I wanted to wring his neck, and couldn't bear the thought of him wearing beach shorts to meet his father. Edgars eventually stepped in and told Juris to put on a proper shirt and pants.

When we all arrived at Alise's house, I saw him on the front porch, wearing a three-piece suit in the blazing sun. I knew straight away it was Rudis by the look of his shoulders. I wanted him to go inside to allow us to get out of the car properly and order ourselves, but he just stood there waiting. We had no choice but to get out in front of him.

Edgars went ahead, to try to break the tension. '*Labrīt*, Rudis,' Edgars said and put out his hand. Rudis shook it and they clapped each other on the shoulders and talked about how happy they were to meet each other.

I walked up slowly behind them. Rudis leant in formally and kissed both my cheeks. '*Labrīt*, Milda.'

My mouth was wobbling far too much for me to form any words. I couldn't even smile.

Rudis turned to face his sons. 'Ah, here they are,' he said. He shook their hands very formally and Juris and Janis gave him nods and half-smiles. As we went inside, I wanted to shout at them to stand straighter, but I said nothing.

Alise had prepared some drinks and snacks, and we all sat in the front room. It seemed uncomfortably hot and I could feel my back getting sticky. My mind was blank. I had no idea what to say and was relieved when Edgars and Rudis started talking about political events.

I watched his face as he spoke and I recognised some of the expressions that I was used to seeing on Janis. I hated the strangeness of it and looked away.

After a few minutes, Rudis turned to me and said, 'How uncultured this country is. You must miss good Latvian music and food.'

I felt heat rising in my chest. 'We are fine. We put on concerts and make our own food,' I retorted.

Rudis nodded, but then he replied, 'But is it always uncomfortable like this? No proper winter. No snow?'

I glared at him. 'There's snow on some of the mountains in winter.'

He looked at me, confused. 'There is? You still ski?' he asked.

What a ridiculous question! I found myself saying something about how Janis liked skiing and then I turned to Juris and asked him to tell his father about his work at the Redhead Surf Lifesaving Club.

My words were ringing in my ears and sounded too sharp. To be honest, I was wondering what on Earth was happening.

After an hour, I realised I couldn't stand it any longer. My mind was jumping all over the place. I kept asking myself whether he had always been this pompous. I got up and went out into Alise's back garden to get some air.

After a few minutes Rudis joined me. 'Milda, the boys are strong men. You haven't done badly,' he said.

'The Communists almost ruined our lives but we've been safe here,' I replied.

Rudis slowly shook his head. 'Actually, you could have had a good life in Latvia. I have worked, and every weekend I've gone to the beautiful forests to walk and, in winter, ski.'

I stared at him. I couldn't believe what I'd heard him say.

'You speak like the Russians have been a good thing,' I said. 'After everything that happened?'

Rudis shrugged his shoulders. 'It was bad for a time, but things moved on. Here, there is no culture. You, of all people, to end up in a place without culture.'

I felt tears pricking my eyes and let loose a flood of words. 'What choice did I have? You promised you were coming back. You have no idea what it was like on my own, pregnant and with Juris so little.'

Rudis looked away. 'You could have waited. It might have been better. Do you know what it's been like to live without my sons? They are both my sons, aren't they?'

My mouth hung open. I couldn't believe him!

Suddenly I felt a hand on my shoulder. I turned, surprised to see Edgars standing beside me.

Edgars cleared his throat and then spoke firmly. 'No, they are my sons. I have raised them. Milda, it's time to go.'

Relief swept through my body. Rudis threw his hands up in the air and walked off to the back fence. I leant on Edgars as we walked back into the house. We then said our goodbyes to a stunned Alise, got in our car and drove home.

I was relieved when Rudis cut his visit short. Before he left, he travelled to Newcastle to see the boys and they took him down to Redhead Beach together. Janis even invited him on a day trip to the Blue Mountains and then out to Dora Creek. The boys tried their best. It was not easy because Rudis was not a good English speaker and George, in particular, only had a basic level of Latvian by then. They couldn't have any deep discussions.

The last time I saw him was at a Latvian event in Sydney before he flew back to Latvia. I watched appalled as he raved on about some of the benefits of the Communist system. Can you imagine? We stayed in touch with letters for a few years because that was the polite thing to do.

Then we stopped writing to each other. I remember feeling sad but also relieved.

52

Hard times

The boys were always trying to do the right things to keep the peace, but sometimes it was no good. There were a couple of years when things got bad in our house. After a few drinks Eddy would blast me. 'My life went downhill as soon as I laid eyes on you! You ruined me!' Perhaps he was right. Often I just sat at this kitchen table and cried.

Eddy started drinking most nights down at the Argie pub. Herta's husband would come around some mornings to see how I was after Eddy left for work. He was a kind man and knew how this house was for me. Well, it happened, we were together a few times. I was ashamed.

One night I sat down and told Eddy. I thought maybe we could forgive each other for all the mistakes we were making. Eddy said he understood and forgave me. We knelt and prayed together side by side at the foot of our bed. We did the rosary. We both were very honest with one another. I remember being hopeful things would get better.

A couple of nights later we were at a party. Eddy got drunk and told everyone what I had done. I remember Herta yelling at me, 'How could you be so stupid?'

She was angry it had happened but even angrier that I'd told Eddy. 'It is the craziest thing you've ever done, telling him. Now everyone knows!' she said. It was horrible. I went home by myself and started drinking. I wanted to drink so much I'd never wake up.

I didn't know it was possible but things got worse. Eddy started playing the pokies and drinking at the Workers' Club all the time. He went crazy, spending all our money. He brought all sorts of people into the house. Refugees like us from Europe but also Australians. Most of the time I just listened to him go on at me, but sometimes I argued back.

One time he received his bonus from work and he gave me a five-pound note. I hid it in a canister at the back of the cupboard. Later that night he came home from the pub so drunk he could hardly talk. He was spitting and slurring. 'Aline, give me my money!' he yelled.

I just stared at him.

'You stupid woman!' he cried.

Well, then he started. He brought up everything from the past—how I was a loose woman, how tired he was of looking at me, how I was not a good mother, how I had trapped him. I tried to get away from him but he punched me in the eye. It felt like he'd thrown a rock at my head. I just went mad. I was sick of him.

He lunged at me and I grabbed the small knife he used to slice his tomatoes. 'Get away from me!' I yelled.

I pushed that knife towards him and cut his neck. At first, I was afraid of what I'd done but then I saw it was hardly bleeding. Eddy just laughed at me so I reached into the cupboard and pulled out the five-pound note and ripped it up in front of his face. 'There. Now you can't gamble it away!'

Now, when I think about my sons, I wonder how they managed to survive all that and become such good men. Kind to their wives. Good men. They must have found the way on their own.

One thing I was grateful for was finding out news of Ruta. It was at one of Milda's afternoon parties. I was there alone because

Eddy had refused to go. When I knocked on the front door, no one heard me. I could hear everyone laughing and talking. I felt out of place and was wondering whether I should turn around and leave when Milda came out and saw me. 'Don't stand there, come in,' she said.

I followed her and when I got to the doorway, I saw her coffee table was completely covered. *Pīrāgi*, scrolls, nuts, ginger chocolates, sandwiches and eggs with herrings. It was as if Milda had expected 50 people, not ten! '*Labdien, labdien,*' everyone got up to kiss my cheek.

'No Eddy?' one of the Latvian ladies, Mrs Vilks, asked. I told them he was not feeling well. Mrs Vilks patted the couch next to her and I was grateful.

Milda poured me a glass of white Lambrusco. As I drank it, I started to relax. In many ways, it was better being there without Eddy. I didn't have to worry about him doing something wrong. I watched Milda eating ginger chocolates. She kept reaching into the bowl for more when she thought no one was looking. Everyone talked about recent events in Europe. I had another glass of wine and then started to feel unwell and got up to go to the bathroom.

It was cooler out in the hallway. I felt better being away from all the food. For some reason, I went towards Milda's bedroom and looked in. I could see her dressmaking dummy in the corner with beautiful brown silk material pinned on it. Then I heard laughter from the sitting room and jumped away from her door, knocking the telephone she had on the little table just outside her room. It tinkled a few notes. I held my breath, waiting to see if anyone would come.

That is when I glanced down and saw the photo in the *Latvija Amerikā* newspaper resting near the telephone. Goodness me! I knew it was her. Straight away. She looked just like me. My daughter! I checked the caption to make sure and saw her name—Ruta. She was still called Ruta! Her folk group had been dancing for the recent *Jāņu Diena* celebrations. She had flowers in her hair and was smiling.

I wedged the newspaper under the big pile of magazines sitting on the floor next to the table so it would be safe. I rushed to the bathroom to wash my face and then paused as I looked in the mirror and started to wonder: *why was that paper there like that? Did Milda leave it out for me?*

I wiped my hands, told myself it must be a coincidence and slowly walked back to the sitting room. 'Are you all right, Aline?' Mrs Vilks asked as I sat back down. I told her I was tired. 'We can drive you home,' she said. I wanted to be by myself and catch the bus but she insisted. 'No, you might be getting ill if Eddy is already poorly. You look very pale.'

As everyone was saying their goodbyes I slipped back out to the hallway, pulled out the newspaper and stuffed it into my handbag. 'Thank you for coming,' Milda kissed me on the cheek. She leant in and whispered in my ear, 'You leave that Eddy in bed out of the way as long as you can.'

Sometimes I think she must have left that newspaper out for me on purpose. I never asked her. I suppose I was ashamed to find out she'd known about Ruta all along.

After seeing that newspaper article, something changed inside me. But for many years I did nothing. I wanted to wait until she was a grown woman.

When my mother died in 1976, I felt lost for a time. It all seemed too difficult to look back and try to make things right. It was some years later that a Latvian woman who knew the story told me that Ruta had emigrated from Germany with her parents to England after the war. It was a surprise for them when years later they applied and won a place in the lottery to live in America.

I then heard that, as an adult, Ruta moved to Frankfurt in Germany. But there were rumours around the Latvian community in Frankfurt that she'd had a hard childhood. How those rumours hurt when I heard them! You can't imagine the pain.

Eventually, I could not stand it anymore. It was around 1984 that I asked a trusted friend who lived in Frankfurt whether he might pass Ruta a letter from me. My hands were shaking so much when I wrote it, I could hardly hold the pen. When she wrote back a few months later with such kindness and told me she'd had a happy childhood, it was like a giant heavy stone rolled off my chest and away down the hill. I thought perhaps it was enough to know at least that.

53

 Grandma Milda

A man of gold

Your nanna Aline had some very hard moments. Of course, I knew of Ruta. Latvia is a small country. We all knew a lot about each other's business. We all knew people in America and back in Germany. I felt excited when I saw that photo of Ruta in the newspaper. By then, I knew how difficult Aline's life was. I left it out for her to see.

But my world was about to change too. One morning I went downstairs to Edgars' garage because I had been calling him and he hadn't answered me. I found him sitting on the concrete floor with his head in his hands, unable to speak. I wasn't sure what had happened but I knew it was serious. I ran across to Mr Svetkis's place and he came in his dressing gown and slippers. 'Call an ambulance!' he urged me. But it took over half an hour to arrive.

The ambulance men took Edgars off to hospital. Mr Svetkis had to go across the road and change his clothes so it took a while for us to get organised and follow. When we arrived, we had to wait several hours for the doctors to finish examining Edgars. When a young man came to speak with me, I couldn't work out what he was trying to say. He kept mumbling that he was sorry. It was Mr Svetkis who told me Edgars had suffered a stroke.

Back in those days people who survived a stroke were often sent home only a few weeks later without any rehabilitation. I turned my sewing room into a bedroom for him. I helped him when he needed to go to the bathroom, out to his favourite chair and then back to his room. Day after day. At first, I wasn't able to fully understand what he was saying and we both became very frustrated that he had to ask me over and over for things. Eventually, I learnt to work out what he wanted and we settled into a new way of life. In some ways, we were closer than we had been when we were younger. He'd stayed by my side all through that business with Rudis. I knew what a good man he was.

I looked after my Edgars at home for twenty years like that. That was my duty. At times he was worse and at other times he was better, but steadily he went downhill. His car stayed in our garage because I couldn't drive and eventually Juris sold it. All his hundreds of tools sat there until Janis took them.

There were two things that kept me going all those years— my sewing machine and my visitors. If Edgars was well enough, I would help him get up and have him sit with me while I served coffee, biscuits and chocolates. If he was no good, he stayed in his room. It was full of Latvian newspapers; he never wanted me to throw them out. He would try to sit up in bed and read what he still could. I learnt to manage on my own.

In the late 1980s, I decided I couldn't take care of him alone anymore. I was getting too old myself and my back would start aching for hours whenever I had to lift him from his bed. That was when it was arranged for us to move in with Inta and Peteris. To leave Newcastle and live on the Gold Coast.

Edgars didn't want to give up the Redhead house, but what could I do? We couldn't go on the way we were.

It was an immense effort getting the house ready to sell. Janis, Flora and Sue helped but there was way too much to do. It was a truly awful time. Then Edgars wouldn't go easily when we left to stay the night at Janis's place at Dora Creek, the day before Peteris was due to pick us up to drive to the Gold Coast. I had to plead and talk to him for a long time to get him out of that house. Flora and Sue were really upset having to witness it all.

The next morning, Edgars woke up and insisted he wanted to go back to the Redhead house. I asked Peteris if we could drive back there to see the house one last time before heading north. I thought it might help.

We got out of the car at Redhead and I watched in horror as Edgars shuffled over and put his arms around the grey telegraph pole in front of our house, hugging it tight. His mouth was open in silent protest, tears streaming down his face. All our suitcases were in the car. There was nothing in the house. All that was left to do was to say a final goodbye.

'Come on, this is ridiculous,' I scolded him. 'We must do this. Foolish man!' I looked up and down the street, but luckily there was no one around other than the two of us and Peteris.

'People will come out and see you making a scene!' I said to Edgars, but he slowly shook his head and held on.

Peteris looked down at the ground. 'How about I walk around the block, to give you some time?' he suggested.

It was all I could do to nod. His heart must have been breaking because mine certainly was. I watched Peteris walk off up the hill, and then I turned and moved closer to Edgars. 'Please, I know, but we have no choice,' I reassured him. 'It's time. I can't take care of you alone.'

I tried to pull at his arm, but he wouldn't let go of the pole. 'You will hurt your hands. Come on,' I pleaded. 'Please, we have had a good life here. You will now see Inta and the girls every day.' But he kept his arms wrapped tightly around the old wood.

'Fine! You stand there, on your own!' I said finally and, waving my arms as if to be rid of him, I walked back into the shade near the letterbox to wait for Peteris. Five minutes later, I saw Peteris come back over the hill and take in the scene. I knew he understood what needed to be done and I nodded to him, giving him my approval. Peteris squared his shoulders and walked slowly over to Edgars. 'Come now, Edgars, we have a long drive,' he said gently. I watched as he unclenched Edgars' fingers from the pole, trying not to hurt him.

Peteris then half-lifted and half-dragged Edgars, his feet trailing uselessly along the yellow lawn, over to the car. 'Thank you,' I choked as Peteris clipped Edgars' seatbelt. I could see his hands were shaking with the effort.

Edgars moaned and tried to turn his head back towards the house as we drove up the hill and away. I was grateful when Peteris stopped, turned the car around and drove back down the hill so we could have one last look.

Our home. It looked strong, almost as it had when I first saw it finished all those years ago, but it also had many parts Edgars had added over the years to try to make our lives better. The front balcony, the room under the house for my parents, and his garage. I placed my hand over Edgars' hand and looked out at the blue ocean in front of me. To have come through the war and built that house meant everything to him. He'd laid many of those bricks with his own hands.

54

Grandma's part

I was sitting with Nanna Aline on the back patio when I finally asked the question that had been knocking around in my head for a few days. 'Did Grandma Milda like living with us on the Gold Coast?'

'Of course, she loved being near you girls . . .' she paused, 'but that first eighteen months before he died, Edgars was very sick.'

'Yes, I remember we were scared of him. Too young to understand. We didn't really start spending time in her granny flat—"Grandma's part", as we used to call it—until he passed away,' I mused. 'Then we were always in there for the first few years after that. We used to joke we liked hanging out with Grandma more than our parents.'

Nanna nodded.

'Poor Milda. She was very sad when Edgars finally went. He had been wonderful to her. She knew that. But he was free from his pain at last. That was a comfort.'

I squirmed at the realisation that I had almost no memory of how it had been for *vectēvs* Edgars at the very end, despite being eleven years old. The mix of grief and relief Grandma Milda must have felt had not been apparent to me at the time.

Nanna Aline looked up to the ceiling, lost in her thoughts. 'I used to imagine how lovely it was for her to have you girls around. Your little faces and bodies. She told me that she tried to teach you some Latvian customs—like how to make our special Easter eggs—but that you became too busy with your own activities as you got older.'

I smiled guiltily as I remembered Grandma Milda asking me and my sisters to help her make them every Easter. At first we'd complain when she called us into the kitchen. 'Not now Grandma, *Neighbours* is about to start on TV.'

Then she'd huff and cajole until she got her way, and soon we would be caught up wrapping the eggs with onion skins and stuffing them into old pieces of her stockings. 'Now, one of you girls tie the ends with string.'

'They might stink of feet, Grandma,' we'd giggle and she would glare at us.

Soon the table would be scattered with dry brown onion skins, segments of grey floppy stocking and oddly shaped trussed eggs. She would bring them to the boil slowly so none cracked. When they were done, we would crowd around to watch her open up the soggy bundles. She would snip at the stretchy wet stocking and brush aside the wet skins.

'Aha! There.' The eggs would be stained with deep golden and brown marbled patterns created by the onion veins. We would take them all out, marvelling at how each one was different, then rub them with bacon fat until they gleamed.

I blinked as Nanna raised her index finger and continued, 'But one thing Milda complained about: she was no longer in charge of her own house!' Nanna's words rang true. I knew my parents had done their best but they'd set boundaries early on to give everyone the space they needed to function, and Grandma Milda had been hurt by some of these, perhaps with no memory of the same tussles she'd had with her own mother.

For example, a few months after Grandma Milda and *vectēvs* Edgars moved in, my parents started to close the door to the granny flat when they came home from work. At the beginning, it had stayed open all the time, but Dad didn't want them seeing him relaxing with a beer in front of the TV in his undies. Eventually, after a silent war between Grandma and my parents of opening and closing the door, it settled into being open on weekdays and closed around 5.30 each night and sometimes on weekends.

Our house was in the hinterland behind the Gold Coast and wasn't on a main bus route. In Newcastle, Grandma had caught the bus by herself to Charlestown to do the shopping, but on the Gold Coast she could only go places if my parents or her friends took her. It must have been painful for her to watch my mum's eyes tighten when she reminded her of an appointment or of something she needed to buy.

It was hardest for Grandma on special occasions. She always played a major part, but once the festivities were done, she was expected to go back to her granny flat and leave us to it.

One Christmas after *vectēvs* Edgars died, Mum made a bountiful lunch, but to Grandma Milda it must have been nothing like the old days when her parties had gone on all day and late into the evening. My sisters and I went off to our rooms after lunch was done to play with our new toys, and Mum and Dad went to lie down.

Grandma must have had some extra energy running through her, perhaps from the champagne. In the evening she decided to make an early supper and invited everyone to come and join her. After Mum's lunch, we were not ready to eat much more but we all went in to do our best.

55

❀ Grandma Milda ❀

My last party

Yes, I can remember how you all came into my granny flat as if you were facing a firing squad! Still I smiled and welcomed you in. I had organised many treats—eggs with anchovies, cherries, mixed nuts, liverwurst on toast and chocolate éclair sweets. My big square coffee table was covered with tasty food. It had taken me hours to prepare.

'What a treat! It looks magnificent,' Peteris declared. He took a small plate with half an egg and a liverwurst toast. I could hear the tiredness in his voice but at least he was trying.

I nodded at him and then turned towards you girls. 'Come on, now.'

'We are full from lunch, *Vecāmāte*,' you complained. Only those who had never known hunger would say such a thing! I wanted you to enjoy yourselves but there you sat as if you wanted to be anywhere else in the world.

Inta was trying to prop herself up on the settee with her glass of white wine. She couldn't even stay upright! Her body kept leaning as if she was about to topple over and fall asleep. *Fui!* I knew she'd had too much to drink and felt angry. I wanted to shout at her to pull herself together! But I could see you three girls were worried about your mother. Maybe you were even embarrassed for her? I certainly was and did not want to make it worse.

I got up to put some Christmas carols on my cassette player, and chose the tape of the St Andrew's choir. Their beautiful high floating voices filled the air but it didn't help at all. We all stopped talking to listen to those choir boys. Those wretched piping voices actually made things worse.

'You must eat something,' I tried to urge you girls again. I had to watch you nibble at my chocolates with small smiles plastered on your faces. It was simply no use.

All my life I felt the best when I was hosting my parties. Those lunches in the early days at Redhead used to go for hours. There would be smoked eel and salmon sprinkled with dill on my glass platters, three types of herring on black rye bread. Of course, people smoked and drank, but we were polite and tried hard to enjoy ourselves. We knew how to have a good time and understood the importance of a beautiful occasion. Sometimes, there was such wonderful conversation and people shared memories of the old days in Riga.

That Christmas I wanted to show you I could still arrange a lovely celebration. I wanted you to understand there are important rituals no one pays attention to anymore. It is a wonderful thing to greet people properly, accept flowers and food from your guests, perhaps organise for someone to give a little speech, and set a table for all to enjoy.

Ha! I am glad I did not go to the trouble to make one of my cakes! No one made cakes like me in Newcastle. I remember telling you girls, it's the most beautiful thing to make a proper cake for a party. I'm not talking about one you put together out of a packet. I'm talking about a proper torte—one made to sit proud and tall in the middle of a table. Three layers, the sponge soaked in Cointreau or Kahlua, and then covered in pineapple or mocha butter cream to match.

In the end, your dad helped me put plastic wrap over the food. Your mother went to bed and you girls ran off to watch one of your television shows. I sat listening to that choir until I'd had enough and switched them off!

I should have been happy enough. I had my friends. Old friends, like Aleksis. I had you three girls. I would never have believed back in Germany after the war that such a life would have been possible for me.

But I wanted that supper to be special. As I sat with you all around the table, it was clear that part of my life was over.

56

 Nanna Aline

Friends in the end

When you girls got older, your grandma Milda often rang me to talk. Sometimes she was lonely. Of course, she was grateful to be living with you and loved that little dog your mother gave her. What was his name? Boobsie?

The few times she came back to visit Newcastle she stayed with me. Of course, she turned her nose up at everything. She didn't like the toast with liverwurst I made her each morning for breakfast. She kept putting her hand to her stomach. Once I remember asking her if she would prefer something else but it took her a week to tell me she wanted *All-Bran*. Such a simple thing! Why didn't she go down to Glendale to buy it for herself?

But I got used to having her stay with me. We spent a lot of time talking and looking at old photos together. We chatted about you girls and how it was for her living with you. I suggested maybe she could teach you some Latvian or how to sew tapestries. '*Pah*, you know what young people are like,' she said. 'They are doing their own things and aren't interested.'

She liked being back in Newcastle among all her old Latvian friends. Lots of people came to visit while she was here, and she liked all the attention, everyone asking how she was and catching up on all the news.

It was good to have Milda there for my card games with Lina. Yes, the same Lina who was with me when I gave birth to Ruta!

She ended up in Newcastle. That's how impossible it all was! How did I ever think I could leave the past behind?

When I met her in Newcastle, Lina and I shared a few angry words and tears, but we became friends again. That's just how life had to be. Lina had tried her best for me when we were in Germany; it would have been silly for me to hold a grudge. She never changed who she was, though—always talking and interfering in other people's lives, even in Newcastle.

During one of Milda's visits, Lina came over to have lunch and play cards. After a few rounds of Joker it became clear that she was cheating, keeping extra cards rather than putting them back in the pile. I didn't say anything but I noticed Milda winking at me. She could also see what was happening! Milda and I were smiling at each other. We played for a while, but it became ridiculous. Lina was winning every hand, so I thought we should end it. However, Lina didn't want to. 'But I am doing so well, we must keep going,' she said.

It was obvious Milda could hardly keep from saying something. Then Lina laid an ace, two and three of hearts on the table. 'Here! I won again,' she cried.

Milda and I started laughing and couldn't stop.

'What is so funny?' Lina asked. She had no idea we knew.

An hour later, Lina's husband came to pick her up and, as soon as she left, Milda burst out, 'How she cheats! Does she think we can't see her?'

I said to Milda that we should let her win because it made her happy. She looked at me and said, 'Lina is lucky you're still her friend after what she did back in Germany.' I knew that meant Milda wanted me to talk about Ruta, but I just nodded.

She left it alone. We ended up talking about other things and laughing the whole afternoon. It was the nicest time I'd ever had with Milda. In the end, we shared so many things—our lives in

Latvia, our coming to Australia, you girls. We understood each other.

You know, I can remember your dad carrying your mum on his back around the Broadmeadow Hall at one of our events when she was only three years old. He was looking after her even then. They grew up together—life partners in the truest sense. It was the most sensible thing for me and your grandma Milda to become good friends in the end.

So, that is how it was. We became two old women who could confide in one another. There was no time left for pride or that type of silliness anymore. We got along much better once we stopped judging one another and started to talk and laugh about everyone else!

Part Five: Twilight

1989–97

In song I was born, in song I grew,
With song I lived all my life,
Singing I glimpsed my death
In the garden of paradise.

Latvian folk song

57

Swallowed up

When I was younger, I thought Russia had swallowed Latvia and it would stay that way forever. That's how one of my school textbooks described it. Swallowed up.

At the end of the Second World War, the Iron Curtain slammed down. I didn't believe it would ever open. Only a few brave Latvian Australians sought to visit Latvia when it was part of the USSR. A deep fear of the Russian state flowed in the blood of most Latvians back then; it still does for many.

I can remember Grandma reaching out to other Latvians as speculation began that the USSR might crumble.

'Mum, Grandma's on the phone again,' I complained once when I wanted to talk to a school friend.

'Let her be. There are changes happening in Latvia. She's speaking about it with her friends.'

When she was off the phone, I asked, 'What's happening, Grandma?'

'The USSR is getting weaker,' she said with glee. 'There are big demonstrations. Millions of Latvians, Estonians and Lithuanians have joined hands to protest for freedom. They are standing in a big chain, hundreds of kilometres long. It is beautiful! They are calling it the Baltic Way. Can you imagine it?'

I nodded but couldn't really see it in my mind. For too long, I had imagined Latvia as a place of occupation. Freedom seemed like an elusive dream.

'What are they wearing, Grandma?'

'Some are in folk costumes but mostly normal clothes.'

I tried again to imagine the mix of young and old people standing in an unbroken line, holding hands, their bodies symbols of both historical and modern-day Latvia.

A few months later I remember watching the Berlin Wall fall on TV. As people scaled the concrete wall and tore pieces of it down, I looked over to see Grandma's eyes were wet.

'That I have lived to see such a sight! Latvia might soon be independent!' she cried in awe.

I reached out to grip her hand. 'It's fantastic, Grandma! Does that mean you would go back? To visit?' I asked, trying to process the news in my head.

'How would I go all that way?' she retorted. 'Who would take me?'

'We would, Grandma,' I enthused. 'Mum and Dad.'

'*Pah!* I don't think so. You are all too busy with your own lives. I'll never get to go back. It would not be a good idea, anyway.'

58

No return

In May 1989, my old Riga friend Tedis wrote to tell me that he and Edite were finally travelling back to visit Latvia. They had emigrated from Germany to America after the war but we'd found each other back in the 1950s and managed to stay in touch. Tedis felt that the USSR's grip on Latvia was loosening and that it was now time for them to return. I wrote back and instructed him to tell me the truth about what he saw. No rose-tinted glasses!

When I received his letter, though, I wondered whether I had the strength to read it. I sat in Edgars' old black rocking chair with it in my hands for at least half an hour before I opened it. It was a fat bundle of pages. I knew Tedis would have prepared it very carefully, and there would be no un-reading it.

Eventually, I decided I must do it before the girls came home from school and so I began to read.

Milda, we travelled on the Tallinn–Riga road, the momentum building every minute until finally at 7 p.m. on 5 July 1989 we crossed the Latvian border. We all sang *Še kur līgo priežu meži*. Everyone was crying and babbling and laughing. The countryside was so familiar. Our special green fields were dotted with little white flowers! Then I saw Juglas Lake where my father used to take me boating when I was a boy . . .

When we got to Riga, we travelled straight down *Brīvības Bulvāris* to the centre of the city. I recognised it immediately but was confused at how run-down it now seemed. It hurt my soul to see such familiar sights now twisted and different. We arrived at the Riga Hotel at 9.30 p.m. but none of us could dream of sleep. Our memories allowed for no peace. Edite and I walked to *Vērmanes dārzs*. Do you remember we used to sit there together with the red roses? There were no flowers but the stone lions were still there! At midnight, we found a shop on the corner of *Brīvības Bulvāris* and *Merķeļa Iela*. We bought a bunch of daisies and walked to the Freedom Monument. It took our breath away when we saw it—the same column soaring into the dark sky. We laid our flowers at the base . . .

Everything is mixed. Today we went to Edite's church, which has been beautifully kept. I took a photo of her standing in the same place she stood on her confirmation day. Do you remember? She was next to the marble column. Could there be a bigger or more wonderful experience for her than to return after fifty years and stand in that same spot? But that afternoon we went to my *Jāņa* church. The walls were water damaged and the place was sad and dark. The service was just us and a few old ladies. I thought about how you were with me the day of my confirmation in that church—10 April 1938—well before it all began. You were full of love and congratulations. Now this is a place of loneliness and lament. Everywhere I turn there are ghosts and memories . . . We wandered back to our hotel and suddenly it was all too much. I had been blocking it for days but I couldn't any longer. Russian faces, Russian signs, Russian shops, Russian language everywhere! If it weren't for that, perhaps I could ignore the dirt and feel like I was home . . .

I couldn't bear Riga any longer so we left for Jurmala. My first sight of the coast was like a cool wash for my heart—the sight of water and pines. But then Slavic faces and Russian shapes. All the old summer houses have been taken over by Russian organisations. All the children building sandcastles were speaking Russian.

232

Trying to talk to somebody just wasn't possible. No one had a Latvian tongue. At the end of the main street there was a beautiful memorial park for heroes fallen between 1940 and 1945. Can you imagine our shock when we found only Russian language and Russian names? It was sickening. This rewriting of history weighed heavily on me. It was one thing to hear about all those years of occupation from a distance, but it was another to see it with every step I took around my beloved homeland.

I am sorry. I wish I could bring you better news. Perhaps things will be different soon. The young Latvians I met felt certain that independence was just around the corner . . . A part of me wishes I'd stayed away. To have my memories touched with present reality brought me pain that even now I am back in America I can't shake. But to see Edite in her church was really something special. For her I was very glad . . .

That is the thing. For each person who visits there will be pain on one side and joy on the other. For each person, it will be different. Milda, I know how much you loved everything when we were young. Perhaps leave your memories in peace.

I folded the papers quickly and put them under a magazine on my table. The letter confirmed what I already knew—the Latvia of my youth no longer existed. It was not possible to go back in time.

I looked around my granny flat and decided it was good enough for me. I knew you girls would soon be home with your faces full of sunlight. My Inta would then come home from work and later Peteris, who would be interested in learning of the letter and talking seriously with me about it.

I knew it would not do you girls any good to see your grandma crying. I decided to lie down for a while until you came to my door.

59

Latvia is free!

'What was it like for you when Latvia was declared independent in August 1991, Nanna?' I asked.

'Eddy and I were still half-asleep when some friends rang from Sydney with the news. They'd been up half the night celebrating.

'I had to work hard to get this idea into my head. Latvia is free! I had to shake myself. Latvia is free! After we hung up the phone, Eddy and I just stood there. It was hard to know what to do. We had a few tears but then had our breakfast of ham on toast, just the same.'

'It must have been a very strange feeling after so long,' I murmured.

'I had no idea what I was supposed to feel! But as the day went on, I got into it. At 10 a.m. we turned on our little radio to listen to the *Latvian News Hour* on SBS. Eddy had to fiddle with the dial to make the signal clear. Then it came through loudly. I heard the huge roar of crowds in Riga, singing and dancing. I could see the streets in my mind, filled with flowers and our maroon-and-white flag. Such a thing! That Latvia gained independence in my lifetime!'

'Did you celebrate, Nanna?'

'At lunchtime, your uncle Karl rushed in with bottles of champagne under his arm and hugged me. "What a day, Mum!" he cried. He ran to the living room to get the good glasses and popped open the champagne. The first glass bubbled all over my tablecloth. It was a really good thing Karl did, coming to celebrate with us. He had such a happy face.

'Slowly I felt more and more a part of it all. Then the radio filled my kitchen with precious songs about land and freedom. I'll sing one to you.'

What is land if you don't have your language?
What is language if you don't have your land?
What is freedom if you don't have land
And land if you don't have freedom?

I looked across at Nanna singing in her clear, reedy voice, with her eyes closed. In that moment, it felt to me as if the world was rushing into her small kitchen. When Nanna opened her eyes, they were glowing.

'As the music played, memories came to me of my people—my mother, father, aunts and uncles. So many faces, all gone. I started to cry, and Karl got worried. "Oh, Mum! Don't be sad. Invite over some Latvian friends. Call up Mrs Freijs. See if she wants to come over," he said.

'I felt silly but Karl kept pushing and, in the end, I rang her. I put out some of my *pīrāgi* and boiled some eggs to go with herrings and we opened the second bottle of champagne. Mrs Freijs and her husband came over. So did your Aunty Helen. After a while, it did feel like a party. Karl kept hugging me. "What a day, Mum. You've waited your whole life for this!" All he wanted was for me to feel truly happy. Well, I suppose I was.'

I reached out for Nanna's hand. We sat in silence for a moment, until the world left the kitchen and it felt like it was just the two of us again. Nanna cleared her throat and I could tell she was ready to move on.

'For the first months after Latvia became independent, everyone was very positive. People were happy they could talk to their relatives openly on the phone. Everyone passed around stories about each other—who had been reunited, who had done well, who was poor, what had been discovered. Some people began taking trips back to visit their families.

'But that positivity didn't last! Many Latvians became upset with the Latvian Australians who went back. They thought we'd return and bring all our money. None of us were rich enough! Of course, we gave what we could. Many of the Latvian Australians of my generation who went back were also disappointed. The country was run-down. There were hundreds of ugly concrete Soviet buildings and many places were nothing like people remembered. Fifty years later, too much had changed!

'The biggest problem was that Latvian Australians still hated Communists. However, the Latvians back home had had to live somehow through that time, when you couldn't get into university or get a good job without being a member of the Communist Party. For the Latvians living in Australia, it was hard to trust people who had done what they needed to do to get on in life.

'I thought I would never go back to Latvia; I wondered how I could possibly travel such a long way. But by then Andrejs had reached out to Ruta and they had become good friends. Andrejs suggested we all meet in Latvia. At first, I couldn't imagine how it would be, but I couldn't get the idea out of my head. I was younger than many Latvians who had already gone over, so I told myself to just go.'

'Were you afraid, Nanna?'

'Goodness, yes! I was worried about what Ruta would think of me. Andrejs told me Ruta didn't think like that at all. He said she was a lovely person and was curious to meet me, so I decided it was the right thing. It seemed such a gift that she wanted to meet me, and Eddy agreed that I should go. That was one very important thing he did for me.

'I wanted very much to see my parents' graves. There is a

golden rule in Latvia: children must take care of their parents' graves, and I grew up believing that rule. I had never visited the graves of my parents. It was something I needed to do before I died.'

60

 Nanna Aline

Back to Latvia

I travelled by myself on the plane to Latvia in June 1995. How I cried when I saw my cousin Emilija standing with flowers in the middle of the Riga airport terminal. She was the one who had taken care of my mother when I wasn't there to do it. She'd taken her to live with her in Riga when my mother could no longer stay in Kraslava alone. Then she'd buried her in 1976 when I was not there to do it. Now she'd brought flowers for me. It should have been the other way around.

I clung onto her and cried. She said the kindest words: 'Aline, I remember your face. You are home now.'

Emilija was only about eight years old when I left Latvia but standing before me now was a woman in her sixties. It was lovely of her to say those words to me. She knew there was no one else left to say them, to tell me I'd come home.

We left the airport and got into a little white car belonging to her son, Martins. It was very tight with all my suitcases and bags. Emilija held my hand as I looked out the window. She could tell I was both upset and surprised. Riga was such a different city from the one I had left—highways and service stations, all those things they had now.

We arrived at Emilija's apartment, which was a dark-grey building with hardly any windows. When I walked through the front door, all I could see was a narrow flight of stairs. And the smell! It was as if those stairs had been used as a toilet.

As I started to climb, I wondered how my mother must have struggled to get up and down with her sore leg. There was hospital-green paint peeling off the walls. I could see huge patches of concrete. I was huffing and puffing to get up those stairs. Emilija asked me if I was all right and helped me take the final steps.

When we got inside the apartment, I was immediately relieved. It was cosy. Good chairs and rugs. Then I saw the dining room table. Oh, my goodness! It was laid out with food—eels, eggs, bread, ham, tomatoes and brawn. My stomach was still full and a bit unsettled from the plane. I wondered how I was going to eat any of it. Emilija was not rich and the food must have cost her a fortune. You see, she was trying to show how welcome I was by putting out such food.

It was only lunchtime but we had some wine and looked at old photos of my parents and relatives. Emilija was very warm, despite all she had been through. But after a while I felt dizzy with everything. I was ashamed but I had to lie down. It was too much!

In the evening, I took out the presents I had brought from Australia—warm jumpers and slippers and a bottle of Bénédictine. I gave a small envelope of money to Emilija. It was not enough—a couple of thousand dollars I'd saved from my pension. I was worried she might be disappointed, but she hugged me and thanked me. It really should have been more.

I was relieved when Andrejs and your cousin Jan arrived a couple of days later in Riga. They were able to help eat all the food and Andrejs was very good keeping up with the conversation. You must understand, it was strange for us all, trying to understand what Emilija and her family wanted to do in each moment and what their expectations were. Our lives had all turned out very differently.

It was agreed we would go on a small trip into the countryside as we still had a day or so before Ruta was to arrive. Our first stop was to visit my mother's grave on the outskirts of Riga.

She was resting at the Salaspils cemetery beside her brother and sister, their places marked with one big granite stone. Small vases of white daisies and carnations dotted their plot. I knew Emilija had placed them there days earlier as part of her constant care of them. Such a mix of gratitude and shame filled my chest. I was relieved that my mother was being looked after but ashamed it was not me doing so.

As soon as we got out of Riga, I felt like my heart was being even further squeezed. One moment the houses and fields looked beautiful, exactly like I remembered, and I would feel high. The next moment I would see something that didn't fit in with my memories, like a big factory with tall chimneys, and I would feel out of place. Some parts of that trip were very sad. Emilija took us to see the memorial stone to the thousands of Jewish people taken from the Riga ghetto to Rumbula Forest and killed during the German occupation. I felt overcome to be standing there, mourning Latvia's terrible history, so far from the home I had made on the other side of the world.

Emilija brought blackberry wine for the drive home so we could have a few nips on the way. Andrejs thought it was a ridiculous idea, but it helped me to cope. I leant into Emilija as we drove along and eventually I began telling her stories of my childhood—happy memories and sad memories. I knew she understood. She grabbed my hand and kept crying out, 'Really? That really happened?'

On the Saturday back in Riga, I woke up with my stomach tight and aching. Finally, the day had come. I was going to meet Ruta. Andrejs went off to the airport to pick her up. The plan was to bring her back to Emilija's apartment. I took a long time to get ready. My hands wouldn't work to do up my buttons and my hair looked thin and awful. Finally, I gave up.

When Ruta came through the door with Andrejs I just froze. I watched them for a few moments, brother and sister. Ruta's hair looked shiny. It was blonde-grey and neat. She had on a white blouse and black pants with boots. She looked very fashionable.

When she turned and saw me, my heart stopped. She came right over and hugged me straight away. It happened fast and I felt like the world was spinning. When I looked down at her hands, I saw she was wearing Latvian rings. It was like I was looking at my own hands. I was shaking like a leaf. Perhaps Ruta thought I was going to have a heart attack. She kept hugging me, not letting go of my arms. I did not know what to say. Andrejs and Ruta both talked over my silence to smooth things out. Suddenly, there was another table-full of food, with Emilija fussing around trying to make everything special. I was overwhelmed.

It took several days for me to get used to being around Ruta. I could tell she was a thoughtful, competent and clever woman straight away. She had organised to hire a car so that we might all travel to my birthplace, Kraslava, together. The next morning we all set off, Ruta and Andrejs in the front and Jan and me in the back.

Ruta was good at travelling. She'd already been to Latvia many times and knew her way around. When we finally arrived in Kraslava, Ruta had called ahead and organised for me to visit my old church. I felt such happiness when I saw the familiar statue of Mary but then started to shiver as I looked up at the big tree in the church grounds to see a dead crow hanging from one of the branches. 'Goodness me!' cried Ruta. We knew it had been placed there to warn off other crows but it felt like a bad omen to me. I wasn't sure whether I should go in after seeing that crow but Andrejs and Ruta convinced me that I must. I had come such a long way.

When I walked through the doors, it was dim inside. The windows were dirty, blocking out the light. I felt as if I was in a dream. There had been some renovations but mostly everything was just as it had been. Ruta had tears in her eyes as I showed her where my grandmother had sat when she came to our church, where my mother and Aunty Adela stood in the choir and where I put my Bible on the ledge. For a moment there was joy in my heart but after a while I started to feel empty. I began noticing things that had been damaged. The paintings looked dark, as if they were still covered with soot. All the pews were chipped and cracked, and the altar was bare. It was such an odd feeling to have returned to a place so familiar yet unfamiliar at the same time.

That afternoon we went to visit my father's grave under the big oak trees. His headstone was also clean and polished. The path was neat around him, pressed dirt with no weeds at all. Emilija's son, Martins, had organised for someone to come each week and take care of it. I was again filled with thanks as I put my lilies on his grave and then stood up, wondering if I should say something. I felt strange with everyone there, so I just closed my eyes and said a few prayers to myself.

Eventually Andrejs said we had to keep driving, but the feeling came over me that I didn't want to go. I wanted to sit down right there and just be alone, next to my father, my hands touching the earth. Andrejs led me over to the car. I wasn't able to tell him I wanted to stay.

That night, Andrejs and Jan went to bed early because they were not feeling well. Ruta and I opened a bottle of wine. I think I had a few cigarettes. The day had been so full that I no longer had the energy to be nervous around Ruta. We smiled at each other and then began to talk easily. Suddenly, I had to get my thoughts off my chest.

'I am sorry,' I said.

Her eyes went wide and she looked startled. Ruta reached out to grab my arm. 'I have had a good life.' She said it fiercely, over and over. 'I have had a good life.'

I could tell she was speaking the truth. You remember that years ago, I had heard from friends that Ruta's life had been hard. At the time, it had been like an arrow to my heart and I'd worried that I had given her away to bad people. Ruta and I talked further about it and she became really angry. All of a sudden, I felt like I was the child and she was the one looking after me. 'Don't worry,' she said. 'My parents were good to me.'

Ruta said we should talk about our lives, so we really knew how things had been and not worry about what anyone else thought. I wondered maybe if I should tell her again how sorry I was but she brushed all of it away. I found out that Ruta had never known about me while her mother was alive, but that her father told her when he was dying. Maybe that was the best way. I tried to tell her everything I could about my family so that she could get an idea of her people. She listened very carefully. That moved me so much, that she would care about my people after everything that had happened.

Those first days, perhaps I even thought I could be a bit of a mother to her, but slowly I understood. We were two adults really, just trying to get to know one another. We couldn't become mother and daughter—that time had passed. It made me sad but also perhaps a bit relieved. Ruta was a grown woman. She was a good person and had her own life. That became clear to me.

Ruta told me that she'd also made contact with her father, Lauris, here in Riga and that he sent me his best wishes. You see, she had the warmth in her to weave all the people from her past back into her life story. To know that she had contacted Lauris fixed something that had been broken inside me.

A few days later, back in Riga, we were on the steps of the *Galerija Centrs*. It was towards the end of our time in Latvia and I was doing some final shopping for gifts to take back to Australia.

That is when Ruta saw him. He was old and walking in the distance with a cane, but she knew it was Lauris. 'Quick, before he walks away. Do you want me to go after him?' she asked.

I wondered for a moment whether I should speak to him, but then I just shook my head. 'Leave it be,' I said. 'I have his good wishes and that is enough.' We stood there together and watched him walk away.

What a thing for Andrejs to have taken me to Latvia to meet Ruta! What did I do to deserve a son like that? That trip helped heal some old wounds.

61

Becoming strong on my own

I was the wrong woman for Eddy, that's for sure. Even now, I don't know why he married me. He knew about Lauris and Ruta, but he still wanted me. He had full knowledge of everything so it was awful, him turning around and carrying on as if I'd tricked him. Like I was an apple that looked good on the outside but was rotten. When I was young, his words really hurt me. He made me feel very small.

One day, Eddy's younger sister Ilze arrived from Latvia to stay with us for a few months. I was astonished when I met her, even though I had known her story for years. Her husband had moved to England after the war and made a new life but he never managed to send for Ilze and she was left in Latvia. I thought she might be bitter, but no! She was a cheerful and busy woman. On and on she went—washing our floors, mowing our lawn, all the time talking. Ilze also had good eyes, and she saw how Eddy was treating me.

One evening we were on the back patio after dinner. Ilze was sitting next to me on the little couch and Eddy was on a white plastic chair. He'd been to the pub that afternoon so he started up, talking about how his life had been wasted. Then he started to go at me, 'You stupid woman! Not good for anything. Dragging me down!'

I felt my cheeks going red. I couldn't believe Eddy was saying these things in front of his own sister. He went on and on, spitting away at me. It was as if he didn't even see Ilze as he went on: 'Why did I let you bring your filth to my name? You are a waste.'

I was ashamed but Ilze put her hand gently on my leg. It felt warm. She leant over and whispered in my ear, 'Let's record him. We can play it back in the morning so he hears how he is.'

I was very surprised! But she smiled at me in such a way that all the bad feelings just went away, out into the night.

Eddy was still going on, but it was just noise. I wondered, could we do such a thing? I looked at Ilze and she smiled again. I leant into her and whispered back, 'The cassette player is in my room, along with blank tapes. If you get up, he won't even notice.'

Ilze left and I sat still to keep Eddy's eyes focused on me.

After we started recording, everything changed. It was like the more worked up he became, the better. A few times I had to squeeze my lips together to stop myself from laughing. Ilze and I sat and sipped our drinks until he slowed down and then left, slamming the screen door behind him. She turned off the tape and gave me a big hug. We went to bed and left Eddy by himself.

The next morning, I woke up early. I couldn't sit still and kept going to the fridge to get more things for breakfast—herrings, brawn, tomatoes and cucumbers. Ilze and I ate, but when Eddy came in, he had very little. I started to lose my courage but Ilze gave me a wink and got up to collect the cassette player. I didn't want to go through with it but I didn't stop her.

I watched her set up the tape recorder on the table and then stand up tall. 'Eddy,' she said. 'I don't know how a brother of mine could speak like this.' She turned the tape on and Eddy's voice spat out: 'You stupid woman! How you just sit there. Not good for anything.'

Eddy's eyes went as wide as marbles. He sat upright and then knocked his chair to the floor as he rushed over to turn it off.

Eddy turned to Ilze, his eyes like a fire. 'How dare you? I paid for you to come and this is what you do in my house?' He looked

as if he was going to hit her but then he came at me. 'And you?
I should record how you weep and carry on.'

I stood up and looked him straight in the eyes. 'At least I have
a heart,' I said.

Eddy turned back to Ilze. 'Give me the tape.'

Ilze looked at me and I agreed. I knew we had made our point.

Eddy ripped it into a pile of brown ribbon on the floor. 'You're
lucky I don't throw you both out of the house,' he said and
stormed off.

Ilze squeezed my hand. 'Don't worry, I'm not going anywhere
until he calms down.'

None of us ever spoke about that tape again, and for a while
Eddy did calm down. He even started to read out loud each night
from a book about Poland. His voice was gentle, reading from
that book. When he spoke Polish, he was nothing like the man
on the tape. It was musical, hearing him read and explain pieces
of Polish history.

Eddy could be very gracious when he wanted to be. I'd like to
tell you he never spoke to me again like that, but of course he did.
The difference was now I could ignore him.

A few years later Eddy went into a nursing home. Some
Latvians thought I should have left him there after all he had done
to me, but every second day I went to that home. 'Oh, Aline, you
are such a good wife to him,' the nurses said.

He hated the food so I always brought him sprats, prawns or
salami to eat, but still he went on at me sometimes: 'You must be
glad I'm out of the house. Tell me which men are visiting. You're
not fooling me . . .'

I'd just shake my head and tell him to keep his voice down.
What did he think? I was an old woman! Of course I was sitting
on my own in the house.

Sometimes he calmed down. He even apologised for making
life hard. He was not a bad man, you know. He did what he could.

I know more than most how hard it can be to survive in this world. But after he died, I could eat what I wanted, visit my church and read my books.

I am a good reader, you know. You have seen all the books I have on my shelves. Your uncle Andrejs has sent many of them to me over the years. I like reading about how other people see the world. You know, I read that book by Sally Morgan, *My Place*, a couple of years ago and I liked it. A few times, when she talked about the land, I could almost see it her way. It took time for my eyes to change after we arrived here from Latvia. The colours of Australia are different. Green is often close to grey.

You see, after Eddy died, I learnt to enjoy my own company. In many ways, the later years of my life turned out to be some of my best. That was something I never expected. I learnt how to become strong on my own.

62

Leaving us

In 1996, my family, including Grandma Milda, left the Gold Coast because Dad had a new position at the University of Canberra. The move coincided with me finishing Year 12 and starting at the Australian National University.

We all moved into a new place, my Grandma Milda no longer residing in a granny flat but rather a large games room we converted to a bedroom next to the downstairs bathroom. She managed to keep many of her Latvian things on display, and those that could no longer fit were stored in cupboards throughout the house. I moved into the bedroom directly above her and could often hear her TV quietly below me.

Our lives went on; my sisters and me taking meals into Grandma Milda's room, and hanging around to keep her company when we could. I was happy she approved of my first boyfriend, who happened to be Hungarian and therefore quite cultured in her eyes.

One New Year's Eve, the three of us shared Latvian goodies and champagne to celebrate, but this time, I was the one who prepared the platters of eggs, bowls of cherries and blinis with smoked salmon. 'Very good!' I remember her licking her lips, satisfied, and feeling pleased she was enjoying our company. But I became anxious she might get lonely when we left her alone a couple of hours later to go to a nightclub in town.

Grandma Milda grew frail but seemed relatively content. I took for granted she would be that way forever.

I was in bed, half-asleep, when it happened. I heard her calling at the edge of an early morning dream.

'Inta! Inta!'

It took a few moments for the sound to register. My mother's name.

'Inta! Inta!'

It came like a slow car crash, the realisation something was wrong. I sprang out of bed, but Mum was faster. I caught her in the hallway downstairs, rushing into Grandma's room. I followed a few steps behind her and saw Grandma was in bed, confused and struggling weakly against the bedsheets to lift her head. Mum shooed me out and raced to the phone.

'Can you come quickly?' she urged down the line. 'I think my mother has had a stroke.'

I stood there, staring at the cork tiles in the kitchen, not knowing what to do.

'She won't want you to see her like this,' Mum said to me and rushed back to Grandma.

It only took five minutes for the ambulance to arrive. I saw her being carried out, small and bound up in a white sheet, black straps crossing her body on the stretcher. I patted her arm and she looked back with watery eyes. She tried to nod, a small head movement, as if to say everything was going to be okay.

Grandma was in the hospital for a few weeks. I was with Mum for most of my visits to her, but once I went on my own.

As I entered the hospital, I was afraid of the condition I would find her in and wondered whether I would be able to sit with her as we had always done. She was in a room with others, so I pulled the pink curtain closed. I looked at her tucked up in a sheet and pale cream blanket, relieved she seemed to be sleeping.

As I used to do when I was little, I pattered on to her quietly about my life. University and poetry, my upcoming birthday and assignments. I told her we were taking good care of her dog,

Boobsie, and that he wasn't lonely without her. When I had no words left, we sat together and I stroked her arm to soothe us both.

'I hope you get better soon, Grandma,' I said as I left.

But when I kissed her cheek, I knew I was saying goodbye.

―――――

Grandma's funeral was at the grand old Rookwood Cemetery in Western Sydney in July 1997. It is a sprawling, majestic place that houses the dead from almost every country in the world, a place of thousands of migrant family stories buried in the earth.

I sat in the small chapel dressed in a navy skirt and white shirt with a lace collar, hoping Grandma Milda could see me looking neat for her. Fountains of white lilies and orchids towered on either side of Grandma's polished wooden coffin. The air felt thick and full of history as the Lutheran priest began speaking in Latvian. I could only pick out a handful of words but what was clear to me was that Grandma Milda was returning to another time and place, back to her homeland.

The last piece of music to play was Albinoni's Adagio in G Minor, one of the saddest tunes in the world. The organ notes started by speaking of the inevitability of human sorrow, then the violins came in softly explaining like a heartbroken mother giving her children news of death.

Though I didn't know as I listened to the lament that day in the chapel, I discovered a decade later that the Saxon State Library in Dresden had held a collection of Albinoni's previously unpublished music in its archives when it was bombed to rubble in 1945. Some claim that the sheet music of the Adagio in G Minor was found in the ashes after the war and then given to the world as a reminder of all that had happened.

My cousin Carl, Uncle George's son, once told me that Grandma Milda had revealed to him part of the story of her long journey across Sudetenland into Germany to escape the

Russian forces. In early 1945 Grandma Milda and her two little boys were sleeping in a barn just off the road one night to escape the freezing conditions when something woke her. She went outside into the cold, still air and saw against the black sky green lights falling in the shape of Christmas trees. Half-asleep and exhausted she gazed at them drifting down from the heavens, marvelling at how beautiful they were. Then she watched as a huge orange glow formed on the horizon. Horror seized her as she realised the lights were falling bombs.

I wonder now whether it was the firebombing of Dresden that Grandma Milda saw back then. Hundreds of thousands of refugees and citizens of the town perished in the flames.

When I listen to that piece of music now, it speaks to me of that bitter night Grandma Milda sheltered in a barn with her sons, watching those sparks descend to deliver annihilation. It also speaks to me of the utter destruction and despair she managed to live through and survive.

Part Six: Reflection

2023

The song was my own in my singing,
But was not of my making;
Grandmother taught me,
Crouched by the fireside.

Latvian folk song

63

Together in Nanna's house

As I sit here writing in my Canberra study, I still find it hard to see my grandmothers as real people, despite how hard I've tried over many years to discover who they really were and understand the arc of their lives. Though I glimpsed more of my grandmothers' lives than many grandchildren do, they nonetheless remain partly fairytale characters in my mind. Perhaps it's the same for grandchildren the world over.

Over many years, every occasion I sat down to listen to Nanna Aline talk about her life felt momentous to me. But each visit to her place also followed a familiar and comfortable pattern, designed to help us weave around, and take care of, each other.

I slept on the fold-out couch wedged between her small dining room wall and her good table. Each morning I'd wake up under a mound of doonas, blankets and pillows. First thing, I'd listen to Nanna shuffle into the bathroom for a shower. 'One fall and it's over. That's how most people go,' she'd sometimes quip. The house would be calm until Nanna turned on the taps, then a moaning and shuddering would start as the old pipes struggled with the water pressure. Nanna worried the sound signified the house would soon fall down around her. I'd hold my breath until the whining eased off as the water reached a steady thrum. Then I'd relax, pull the covers to my chin and think about the best way to approach my questions that day.

After her shower, Nanna would head into the kitchen. I'd get up and pad out to greet her in my pyjamas. She was always ready for me, in a housedress or pants with a floral blouse, her thin grey hair combed and set back with simple silver clips.

'Andra, did you have a good sleep? I hope I didn't wake you in the night.'

I never slept well at Nanna's but always told her I did. 'Yes, I had a deep sleep.'

After breakfast, I'd change into neat clothes for Nanna and we'd set up somewhere to talk, alternating between her kitchen, lounge room and back patio. I'd get us water and set up my notebooks. When there was nothing left to do, we'd look at one another.

'Well, what do you want to know?' she'd ask.

That question always caught me by surprise, despite being well aware it was the reason I was there.

———

The further we went into her story, the more adept Nanna Aline and I became at moving between darkness and light. After hearing about the hardest parts of her life, I'd often watch her, anxiously wondering how I could ease the painful memories I'd just been responsible for bringing to the surface.

On the day Nanna told me of Ruta's adoption, the story had slowly leached the light from her eyes and I'd wanted more than anything for it to return. 'Do you have some Latvian folk songs, Nanna?' I cast about.

'Ah, just put on that *Old Linden Tree*. And get us both a little something to drink.'

I found the Bénédictine and then the CD, and studied its pale-orange cover.

'Nanna, it's Russian!'

'So? All the folk songs are the same. Russian, Latvian, they're all from the Jews and gypsies anyway. They are the ones that have always made the best music. What does it matter?

Your grandma Milda cared about such things. I don't. Good music is good music.'

I put the CD in and the sounds of a soft piano accordion filled the room. I took a sip of Bénédictine, which was sweet and strong.

'We will get tipsy,' said Nanna. 'Have a chocolate.'

I took a strawberry one and opened its silvery red wrapper.

'Sometimes when I'm sick of thinking about my life, I put on music and have a small glass of something to drink. Then I feel better. You know André Rieu?'

'Nanna!'

'What? He's very good. I love to listen to his concerts.'

'Don't you think he looks silly with his golden hair?'

'Maybe . . . but when he plays Strauss, "Blue Danube", you know? I think about how it was when I was a girl at Christmas and my uncles would play music on the wireless. We would waltz.' Nanna closed her eyes and started to sway. 'Such a show André Rieu makes with all the men in tuxedos and women with magnificent ball gowns on stage.'

I scoffed and refilled my glass. Nanna waggled her finger at me. 'Vienna is not so far from Latvia. We knew how to waltz, of course we did.' Nanna's eyes twinkled as she sucked on her chocolate. 'Yes, I could waltz very well. Pour me another glass and I will show you.'

'Nanna!'

'What, you don't want to waltz with your old Nanna? Even the nuns knew how to waltz.'

She pushed herself up from her chair.

I struggled up off the couch and went over to hold her hands. Nanna closed her eyes and we swayed together, listening to the music. A lump formed in my throat. I didn't know whether to cheer or cry.

I would never know what was coming next when we would sit down with my notebooks again. Nanna would often lure me into a false sense that her stories would stay lighter this time around. She'd tell them so matter-of-factly, interspersed with shrugs of her shoulders, hands flung in the air and moments of hilarity, that it often took a while for their full impact to sink in.

As we continued, it became clearer to me that my questions about Nanna's past were feeding her constant questioning of herself and her life. Sometimes she'd peer across, daring me to say something that either excused or judged her behaviour. In these moments, I'd flounder. Half of me was sure it was my job to stay quiet, a witness to the stories she'd honed over many years inside her head. The other half wondered whether I should burst forth with the love I had for her and try to take the pain away.

The moments that were the hardest were when she'd question whether or not she'd been a good mother. Often, her longing for things to have been different squeezed my chest as if it was an accordion box rushing to empty out all the air. One day I couldn't hold my tongue. 'You must have helped your children find their way, Nanna. Just by getting on with life each day if nothing else!' I burst.

Nanna shook her head. 'They mostly did it by themselves,' she said quietly.

I waved my arms around Nanna's lounge room to take in her endless array of wooden and silver-framed photos. They covered the mantlepiece and every other available surface, years of smiling children, grandchildren and great-grandchildren at Easters, Christmases, weddings and graduations. 'Look at how things have turned out. Our families all have good lives. You must have done something right!'

Nanna looked around, slowly taking all the pictures in. 'I suppose that is true,' she marvelled. 'It's remarkable how my children have gone on to live such wonderful lives.'

She leant across to me and lifted her index finger. 'You know, one thing I must say. So many of you have moved to other parts of the country and even out into the world. But your Uncle Karl and Aunty Helen have always been living by my side, looking after me, here in Newcastle, just down the road.'

I nodded and knew she spoke the truth. My frequent presence at her place over the last decade had been a welcome development but Uncle Karl and Aunty Helen and their children, my cousins Liam and Eliza, had been a steady presence, taking care of Nanna in Newcastle all along.

64

Imagining Grandma Milda

After interviewing Grandma Milda's old friends and relatives, memories of us both sitting and talking as she weaved and sewed often rose to the surface of my mind. Sometimes I'd sit in my study looking through my notes, hearing her voice so clearly as I put the parts of her story in chronological order and mused on all she'd lived through. Other times, I imagined her somewhere up in the clouds, still keeping things to herself as there were many mysteries I knew I'd never now manage to solve.

I'd remember the hundreds of occasions my sisters and I had raced into her granny flat straight after school to find her calmly working her needle with a stillness that automatically slowed our steps. We often stood there in our uniforms, whispering to each other about whose turn it was to sit in the chair next to her, bargaining and fidgeting until we all found our spots.

I also often thought about the early mornings before school when I would knock on her door but then barge straight in to find her serenely propped up with her olive bedspread covering her legs, Boobsie by her side, as if waiting for me.

'Grandma, will you plait my hair?' I'd ask.

She'd waggle her finger at me and laugh, '*Pah!* One of you girls has stolen my brush. You bring it back and I will do it.'

I'd give her a small smile and dash off to find it.

Now I think that some of those mornings she must have felt heavy, perhaps having had her sleep interrupted by dreams about the past, but she never gave any sign of it to me back then.

As the years went by, Grandma Milda came to have an aura of magic about her, a calmness that enveloped her as she dedicated herself to her craft. She kept sewing and stitching until she was very old, making dozens of dresses, blouses, coats and ballet costumes for my sisters and me. No one spends years perfecting their art without reaching some higher plane and Grandma's deft needlework made her seem otherworldly at times. Cotton, lace, silk, lycra, tulle and leather—nothing was ever too difficult for her to work with; all fabrics received the same treatment with her needle.

My cousin Carl once told me that when he'd gone to help pack up the Redhead house, prior to Grandma Milda and *vectēvs* Edgars' move to the Gold Coast, he'd been amazed at the mountain of fashion magazines he'd found. 'You know, she had twenty years of *Burda* piled up in the corner of her room,' he said in awe. 'I don't think there was even one issue missing.'

A vision of her towering columns of the fashion magazine with its beautiful models and pages of clothes patterns had filled my mind.

Grandma Milda had always wanted me to understand my Latvian cultural heritage, but I think a part of her also understood my hesitation, born of the fear of the country and its past. I can remember her giving me a traditional Latvian seven-day ring on my thirteenth birthday. I didn't know what was in the little red velvet pouch when she handed it to me and was excited at the thought that it might be a necklace or maybe a bracelet. I felt a pang of dread when I undid the red silken cords and tipped the ring onto my palm. It was silver and had seven small diamond-shaped pendants dangling from it like lucky charms.

'Each one is engraved with a symbol for warding off evil spirits and bringing harvests, strong morals and good fortune,' she declared.

'Thanks, Grandma,' I choked.

'Put it on your finger.'

I slid it on but it felt like a clamp, somehow binding and mediaeval.

'You like it?'

'Yes, Grandma,' I lied.

'Good girl. Now you have your ring.'

As I left her room, I had a squeamish half-proud, half-sick feeling in my stomach. I went straight upstairs, took the ring off, and put it at the back of my sock drawer. Grandma would occasionally ask me where it was. 'Why don't you wear your ring?'

'I don't want to lose it.'

She'd look sceptically at me. But once she went further. 'It represents bravery, not fear,' she said slowly. 'All the girls and women in Latvia wear them. You might want it one day.'

65

Knowing yet not knowing

On the shelf above the desk in my study, I have a photo of my younger sisters and me, aged six, four and three, standing in a row. We are holding hands, walking along a wide bush track, tree trunks looming to form a big wall around us. Sometimes during my childhood, our closeness brought a throbbing to my chest too great to bear. I'd hole up away from my sisters, reading my books, to get rid of the heavy, swirling-water feeling in my stomach. It was a deep sense of foreboding that came from the understanding that I might not know enough to protect them if darkness came for us.

When I was young there were nights I'd wake up to the sound of sad folk songs my parents were playing in the lounge room. The music was always beautiful—the men's voices rumbling in the distance and the women singing over the top—but I'd want them to turn it off. The music made me feel bad inside. I'd squeeze my eyes tight and pray for my sisters in the room next door to stay asleep, curled up sucking their thumbs.

One time when I was about seven, I remember my bare feet hitting the cool cork tiles of my bedroom. I tippy-toed in my Mickey Mouse nightie towards the lounge room, the music becoming louder, rushing in my ears. Dad was sitting in a low-slung leather chair near the fire, a fat brown stubby on the wooden floor beside him. He was bent forward with his eyes closed, straining his head to one side. There was no sign of Mum, which meant she had already collapsed into bed.

I hung in the doorway until Dad looked up and saw me. I rushed over, my bare arms pricking against his hairy ones.

There was wetness in the corner of his eyes, which seemed strangely naked without his glasses.

'Dad, it's the music making you sad.'

He looked down wearily at me. 'I know, but sometimes I want to listen to it.'

One of the old Latvian art books we rarely looked at was on his lap. It was open to a white page covered with thick, inky black lines. There were rows of upside-down hunched U-shapes walking away from a silhouetted roofline of buildings set in the distance, a heavy black cross towering over them all.

'Can you see?' asked Dad.

I gave a small nod.

'Those shapes are people walking. The Russians are coming. They have to leave the city behind.'

The people were just bent lines—no bodies, no faces.

'I don't think we should look at them,' I said.

Dad sighed and nodded. He closed the book and leant down to rest it gently on the floor. I climbed into his lap and we stayed like that, staring at the fire for a while, the coals forming deep, pulsing red caverns. The singing faded away to quiet. We were left with only the crackling of the embers.

———

Somehow, parts of my grandmothers' stories had been living deep in the marrow of my bones long before I knew the details. More accurately, perhaps, not just their stories but parts of the 'Latvian story'. I had known it and yet not known it since I was a little girl.

When I was sixteen, I sneaked into Grandma Milda's granny flat to borrow a book called *Dear God, I Wanted To Live*, one of the only ones in English on Grandma's shelf. I'd never touched it before, because I knew it was about the deportations to Siberia. Curiosity must have overcome fear on that particular afternoon, and I took it upstairs to read.

The book tells the story of a fourteen-year-old Riga girl. On 15 June 1941 she saw a truck pulling up at the front of her house.

> I stood there unable to move. I began to tremble, feeling hot and cold . . . We filled suitcases and sacks with belongings, stuffed wicker baskets with food. The chekists [Cheka] kept rushing us to finish up and get into the truck. When the four of us were finally seated, I spotted our cousin riding by us on his bicycle. He saw us and understood what was happening.

She was taken with her mother and two younger sisters, aged nine and twelve, to a cattle car full of other Latvians, her grandmother also seized by the Cheka.

> We were cramped. Movement was difficult, almost impossible. The air was thick, insufferable. Then someone smashed the glass in the barred windows, and we could breathe.

The rows of cattle cars sat for days in Riga with new prisoners arriving. When the train started at last, the journey was one of never-ending agony.

> All of us suffered most from want of water. The food was too salty, and we were constantly plagued by thirst. Sometimes we got some clean drinking water, but more often it was the dirty yellow ditchwater scooped along the route.

Within the first two years of exile, she lost her mother and grandmother to illnesses associated with hard labour. After enduring five years of unimaginable cold, deprivation and hunger at a *kolkhoz*, a collective farm, named Big Chigas in the middle of the endless Siberian Taiga, she finally received good news—her sisters were being sent back to Latvia. Months later, a big white ship arrived for her: she was free! Once again the difficult journey by ship, train and truck had to be endured. Finally she saw the fields of Latvia.

> In the afternoon we were on Latvian soil. The train drove through Zilupe. How dear to us was this country with its fields and woods, its meadows and towns! We crowded around the windows and the open doors, so as not to miss anything. We viewed our homeland as some long lost and now at last regained treasure.

I remember turning the page, and the afterword slamming into me.

> One day in October 1950, two Russian KGB men entered the apartment . . . As she [Ruta] started to scream the men changed their minds. After warning that a report would be made to headquarters in Riga, they left . . . On January 21 1951 . . . the family then was sent on a slow torturous journey back to Siberia. The prisoners' car built for no more than twelve passengers was crammed with some thirty men and women.

I felt like a wounded animal for hours after reading that book. My head felt hot and all I wanted to do was lie under my bed covers. I'd wanted desperately for it to end differently and thought: *But she picked berries, survived! She was clever and caught fish! It should not have ended that way!*

I never asked Grandma Milda or my parents about what I had read. I just slipped the book back on the shelf and tried to forget it. I felt grubby, like I shouldn't have touched it in the first place.

Of course, I never forgot it. For a long time, I couldn't understand how it was that my grandmothers were among the lucky ones who escaped such a fate. I sometimes entertained fanciful thoughts that they had lived somewhere safe, away from all the atrocities that were being committed at that time, but then logic would prevail and I would think fearfully: *There was nowhere safe back then, my grandmothers must know about these unspeakable things.*

I now think a part of me wanted to confront the fear that my grandmothers could have suffered a similar fate and reckon with the knowledge this type of terror existed on this Earth and still does. It was what propelled me to finally ask for my grandmothers' stories.

66

Seeing Latvia for myself

The Daugava River stretches across Latvia, bending gently around Kraslava, travelling through rolling green farmlands, and past Riga's skyline of steeples and into the Baltic Sea. The beauty of that river and the way it connects the two sides of my family was only something I came to understand when I visited Latvia—first in 2006 and then 2008—to see for myself the places where my grandmothers' early lives unfolded. By design, as well as a little luck, both times I visited Latvia my parents were with me. They had already made the pilgrimage a couple of years prior and now supported me as I wandered around awestruck and bewildered, trying to comprehend all I saw.

At first, it was Grandma Milda I could feel around me. She was there when I entered old Riga, my taxi slowing to bounce along the cobblestone streets. I could feel her quiet joy as I looked up at the Art Nouveau buildings painted mauve, blue and grey, decorated with stone flowers and symbols, glowing in the June summer sun. I could imagine her nodding as she watched my parents waving at me from the balcony of our hotel, *Radi un Draugi*—Relatives and Friends—and at that moment I saw them with new eyes, as if I'd previously failed to focus on all the complex brushstrokes of a familiar painting. They were dressed up as if ready to go out, framed by flowerboxes filled with white and purple petunias, looking suddenly Latvian, like they belonged.

My dad shouted across to me, 'Come on. Bring up your bag. The festival is still on for *Jāņu Diena* in the main square, but not for long!'

As soon as we entered the Riga square, I found the familiar fairytale I'd been after. Hundreds of people were dressed in Latvian folk costumes. The men had oak-leaf wreaths adorning their heads and the women wore billowing skirts woven with threads of red, yellow and green. Bunches of wildflowers, grasses and wheat decorated the stalls. People were selling hunks of fatty pork, baskets of the prettiest strawberries I'd ever seen and huge mounds of yellow caraway cheese.

'I can't believe this has been here the whole time!' I said stunned.

Mum laughed as I stared at all the girls dancing in their costumes, their eyes reminding me of my sisters. The scene matched the stories I'd heard from Grandma Milda growing up. I couldn't believe I was standing there, somehow transported like Alice down the rabbit hole.

'Now you understand why Grandma didn't like you wearing shorts and grubby T-shirts. She was from here!' she exclaimed.

I rushed around with my parents, wanting to join in. I stopped in front of a stall selling delicious-looking cured pink pork hocks.

'Let's get some of that pork. It looks good!' I enthused.

'We already have some things back in our hotel room,' Dad laughed.

I shook my head. 'No, we need that pork.'

When the music started and people joined in the folk dancing, the whirlwind of light and movement and the sounds of the fiddle and *kokle* engulfed me as if I was on a vast merry-go-round, spinning wonderfully but way too fast. When I came back down to Earth, my parents were waiting for me.

'Let's walk past the Freedom Monument,' Dad suggested.

When I saw the slim granite column towering at least 30 metres high, my chest started to pound. At the top stood a strong stone maiden of Latvia, facing west, her hands reaching up to the sky and holding three stars. Dad got his mobile out. 'Let's call Nanna from here.'

I wordlessly nodded and took his phone.

Her thin voice reached through the air from the other side of the world.

'Andra, is that really you?'

'Yes, Nanna, I'm here in Riga, right under the Freedom Monument.'

'Oh, really? You are there!' her voice bubbled.

'Yes, everything is wonderful,' I gushed. 'All the flowers and food.'

'You like it? You like everything in Latvia?'

I imagined her standing in her small hallway in Argenton, phone pressed up against her ear.

'Yes, Nanna. I really do.'

As the days unfolded, I set out on walks by myself, retracing the steps Grandma Milda had taken around her city. I headed over the Akmens Bridge to Pardaugava, pausing to look down at the stormy Daugava and its currents as Grandma Milda must have done so many times before. I found her street but the block of flats she had lived in was no longer there. Other beloved places—the opera house with its tall white columns, *Vērmanes dārzs*, the garden with its stone lions and even the *Otto Schwarz* restaurant with its fragile glass drinks trolley—were all still standing, renewed in recent times yet imbued with the power of her memories.

———————

After a week my eyes started to adjust and look past the wonder to see what else was in Latvia. I began to notice all the giant stone and metal statues installed by the Soviets. They were a blur of heavy jaws, thick necks and iron lips. One of Stalin was particularly horrible, the pupils in his steel eyes cut out and vacant looking. When I walked out past the old city to the Communist bloc flats and saw all the squares of concrete with tiny apartments and streets littered with broken bottles and beer cans, I could feel my skin prickling with warning, uncomfortably alert in the clear northern air. It felt like Grandma Milda was telling me to get out of there to safety.

I did not go back to the hotel but instead found myself outside a towering black box without windows in the middle of old Riga. It was the Museum of the Occupation of Latvia, standing as a reminder of all that had happened.

As I walked towards it, my head felt tight and itchy. I bought a ticket in the dark foyer and walked quickly around the exhibits. My eyes blurred looking at the Second World War photos, Communist propaganda, battered suitcases, children's colour pencil drawings of men in trucks, and aluminium cups and spoons issued to those sent to the forced labour camps in Siberia.

I told myself to slow down, then walked back to the beginning in order to read all the information boards carefully: Nazi–Soviet Pact in 1939; Deportations in 1941; Burning of St Peter's; Occupation by the Germans; and the Riga Ghetto. I read the devastating accounts of the purges and atrocities that had followed after the war, including the mass deportations of Latvians to gulags in 1949, the oppression of the Catholic and Lutheran clergy, and suppression of Latvian intellectual and cultural life. In the middle of one of the rooms was an original cattle car that had the wooden bucket toilet the prisoners would have had to use. I could only look at it briefly.

Another display set out the facts of the Soviet and German occupations from 1940 to 1945: Latvia lost approximately 610,000 people, or more than a third of its population. Many were killed in battle or disappeared without a trace, others were sentenced and deported to Siberia, and the remainder fled to become refugees. *One-third of the population?* To see that estimate set out so clearly was like a punch to the head.

I was about to leave when I walked past a glass case. Inside was a small piece of cloth pinned on a black felt board. It was embroidered with more than a hundred names. One leapt out at me:

Milda.

The small neat letters were traced twice in delicate red and blue thread. *Milda.*

Reading the information plaque, I learnt the handkerchief belonged to Merija Stakle, first deported to Siberia in June 1941 to work in a *kolkhoz*. She was later arrested in 1950 as a political prisoner after telling stories of her previous life visiting the great capital cities of Europe and sharing her love of music. The women with her at the prison camp had each recorded their names there now in different stitches and colours using thread pulled from their clothes. I leant forward and saw little pictures sewn among the names: a bunch of small flowers with stems of light green and buds of yellow, lilac and pink; a treble clef on staves so thin they looked like cuts in the cloth.

Milda.

The name was right there beside them, reverberating through my chest.

I knew that name did not belong to my grandma Milda. But it could have been her among those women if her fate had been different. I stood looking at it for a long time.

———

When my parents and I left Riga for the countryside, it felt like a cool balm soothing me. The sight of the rolling fields and azure lakes calmed me as we drove towards Kraslava where Nanna Aline was born. When we hit a patch of green forest on the outskirts of town I realised it was Count Plater's Forest, where Nanna Aline and Marta had run from the soldier's eyes among the trees more than 50 years ago.

When we entered the town, I could clearly see Nanna's grand white church on the hill, much larger than I had imagined.

Several hours later, I approached its doors and entered to see afternoon sunlight streaming in and dust motes dancing in the air. The wooden pews looked rough and bare but there was a rustic warmth to the place and, at first, I could imagine Nanna peacefully sitting next to me, taking it all in. Yet, after gazing up at the stone statue of Jesus on the altar for too long, the weight of all that had unfolded in her life descended. I shivered and bowed my head.

When I lifted it minutes later, it was to see a little wooden door at the side of the church. Astounded, I let out a breathless laugh, realising it was the door Nanna must have come through when she was a little girl. There, hiding in plain sight, after all this time.

When I eventually walked out of the church into the sun, Dad was in the distance heading down the hill to the banks of the Daugava River. I set out after him and as I drew closer I could see the water calm at the bend, lapping softly at the sides. There were tall reeds at the edge and for a while we watched little brown-yellow finches darting in and out of the stalks in silence.

'Not a bad place for Nanna to have grown up near this river,' he finally said.

67

I know what came before me

Back in Australia, as the years went past, it was my generation's turn to marry and begin our own families. Our Christmases became gaggles of boyfriends, new husbands and wives, and then, later, great-grandchildren, with Nanna Aline the remaining matriarch looking over us all.

When my two children were a bit older, I sometimes went by myself to visit her. We'd sit beside one another in familiar company as she became older: 92, 93, 94, then 95. Each time I left her place I wondered if we were getting close to the end and worried I'd left important things unsaid.

When Nanna greeted me on her back steps in early 2020, she beamed with an uncanny saintliness and seemed particularly fragile as I took her arm. I knew she was approaching the end of her life. We sat out on her back patio in the morning light.

'You've been a good girl to listen to an old woman like me,' she said. 'But sometimes after you'd leave my place after all our talking, there was a word that would come to me.'

My heart skipped a beat. I knew the word. I didn't want to hear the word.

'Shame.'

It smashed into my body.

'I'm sorry, Nanna!'

She shook her head.

'No, Andra. Listen to me. Sometimes I felt ashamed about stories I told you. Some of them stung like bees at me! But then I started to think: why should I feel shame? My granddaughter

274

took the time to really see me. To see our family. When I thought about this, the shame went away. It was replaced with love.

I sucked in air as I fought down rising waves of emotion. 'I've learnt a lot,' I choked.

'What have you learnt?'

I'd practised the answer in my head many times, wanting to be able to tell Nanna when the time was right. I dug my finger-nails into my palm, willing myself to speak clearly and leave no words unsaid. 'Nanna, from you I learnt about how life can be, that events and people circle back around as if there's some great pattern to it all. Your personal stories, the arc of your life—it has held the universe inside it.'

Her lips started to wobble and she looked down.

'I know what came before me,' I whispered. 'I am very grateful.'

'That is something at least,' she replied.

I let out a shuddery breath. 'Anyway, it's not over yet, you're still here.'

Nanna slowly pointed to her chest. 'Yes. I. Am. One of the last old Latvians left.'

My mind turned to the things I'd found here in Nanna's house—rosary beads given to her by her mother when she was sent to Germany, the black-and-white photos of her lost family, and the pile of letters bound with pink gauze ribbon hidden at the back of her cupboard. These things had been here all along, but the journey to uncover them had been longer than I could ever have imagined.

Nanna finally let out a sigh, breaking the silence. 'What will happen to this house when I die? It will have to be sold, that's what. The new owners will knock it down. A corner block like this, they can put flats on it.'

'Oh, Nanna, no, we won't sell it.'

She looked across sceptically at me. 'There's no point pretend-ing. It will all be over.'

I wanted to contradict her, declare that I would take care of the house, but I knew that wasn't how it would go. Nanna was right. My family would keep the photos, the Latvian tapestries, but sell the block.

'All my life the priests have talked about the pearly gates of heaven, but I have been a sinner.'

I shook my head but Nanna nodded to herself gravely.

'Yes, I have. I have prayed my whole life. That instruction to pray was all I had left of my father. But maybe I won't be able to pass through those gates. One thing, I have lived with myself a long time. I love the sinner that I am. I know how to laugh. That must count for something.'

'It does, Nanna. Of course, it does.'

'Ahh! This is silly talk. All I need now is books and music. Sometimes I listen to Mozart or Verdi and I think what a beautiful world it is that people can make such music. Music and memories. The ones when I was a little girl are so clear to me now.

'I often think about how it was when my mother and I went to Sunday service at our Kraslava church when I was five or maybe six years old. My mother would put me in my best outfit, my dress with the strawberry pattern and a little red cape. I had to stand on a wooden chair in the middle of our room so I wouldn't get dirty while she finished getting ready herself.

'I felt like I could see the world from up there. Through the window I could watch all the people from the village coming up the road to the main entrance of the church. I saw how my mother combed her hair and put it up neatly with pins. When she was ready, we followed the priests down our special corridor. As I walked, their black robes were all around me. When the door opened, my ears filled with the sound of my father playing the organ.

'I hope that's what it feels like to go from this Earth. I hope it feels like it did when I was in that corridor as a girl waiting to go through to the other side. It will be such a big thing to finally know. I will say the Lord's Prayer in Polish. That's how I learnt it from my mother.'

As I stared at Nanna, it was suddenly as if I could see every day of her life on her face. I saw her skin cracked with thousands of tiny lines, not the wrinkles of the elderly but the transformation of the very old. Almost back to the elements.

We sat there holding hands until we went back inside.

68

Running over the grass

I still miss Grandma Milda. I wonder what she would say if she knew that I had pieced together my memories of all she'd told me through our years together and then kept searching to find out more about her life. My sense is she'd likely dismiss the importance of her personal story and encourage me to think more about the broader continuing story of Latvia.

Perhaps she would say I should focus on the beautiful music and ancient cultural traditions that tie Latvians around the world to this *pasaule*, this earth under the sun. Perhaps she would tell me to lend my voice to this music?

But perhaps she would also tell me to stay alert, as the world is teetering and the Russian bear remains hungry. Perhaps she would remind me that Russia will always want to extend its territory to the Baltic Sea. I hope she is not aware of Russia's invasion of Ukraine, but maybe she is.

My children know very little about the terrors of Latvia's past. 'Children don't need to know such things,' Grandma Milda once said, and now I agree with her. I haven't completely shielded them from the recent stories of Russia invading Ukraine on the nightly news, but I have never made the connection for them between the events there and what happened in Latvia during the war. Perhaps like my mother telling me about splinters being forced under people's fingernails, a part of me lets them see the news to warn them.

I try to be careful, offering glimpses of what the world can be like, while offering reassurances when their faces grow worried. I hug my daughter to me at the sight of people lining up against a backdrop of apartment buildings with gaping holes exposing their private spaces and belongings. 'That girl in the purple puffer jacket will be safe now,' I tell her. 'See, she's getting on the bus with her mummy to leave the fighting. Let's turn it off and go and brush your teeth.' My voice is calm, but inside I'm rattled at the sight of history repeating itself. When I was in my late teens, Grandma Milda often warned me the Russians would seek to reoccupy former Soviet Union countries, including Latvia. Her deep distrust and fear of the Russian state never wavered through all her years living in Australia.

I must have absorbed her warnings in some measure. Learning of the invasion of Ukraine, I realised I had been expecting Russia to reoccupy its neighbours in my lifetime. A part of me had been waiting for it.

When I watch images from Ukraine some nights after the kids have gone to bed, my eyes always jump to the women and children and what they are wearing. Sitting on the edge of my couch in Canberra, I try to gauge the warmth of their clothes, as if my vigilance will somehow urge them to stay warm and run when they need to.

Maybe Grandma Milda sees those Ukrainian women in their puffer jackets making Molotov cocktails, and marvels at their bravery against the Russian state. Maybe she sees that while some things stay the same, new phenomena emerge. Maybe she sees how hard Ukraine is fighting back. Maybe she believes this time it will be different. It looks right now like it might be.

Where is Grandma Milda now? Perhaps she can be anywhere she wants to be. Maybe she blinks and is at the top of St Peter's, looking out over the wide, stormy Daugava. Then she blinks again and is standing in her garden at Redhead, looking out to the ocean. Then she blinks once more and is on the Gold Coast, watching my sisters and me run under our purple jacaranda tree and over the green grass towards her.

69

Honouring Nanna

It is Sunday morning and I am in my study. The morning rays are shining through my window and I turn to face them, close my eyes and feel bright, red light flood the back of my eyelids. It seems like I am in a warm cocoon.

I open my eyes to see the order of service for Nanna Aline's funeral in front of me. It has the most beautiful photo of her on it, set neatly on the front of an A5 booklet and bordered by white and cornflour blue. It was taken only a couple of years before she died. Underneath is written the incredible span of her life: 30 August 1924–23 October 2021. Nanna is smiling, one of the biggest smiles I've seen in all the photos we have of her. She's wearing a forest-green jumper and has a bright parrot sitting on her arm, its underbelly a vivid red and gold. The image helps me hear her voice, as if she is saying: 'How remarkable, this life. How did I end up here?'

I sometimes imagine Nanna Aline has joined Grandma Milda at a table where they can play the card game Joker and take turns to snort softly at each other's remarks.

It wasn't until I attended Nanna's funeral that I fully understood where we had arrived after all those years of talking. In the months before she died, I woke up at night worried that in the busyness of life, my family might not make the space to fully honour Nanna at her funeral, that somehow we would fall short. 'The Latvians take care of their dead,' she'd often told me.

As my family gathered to prepare the words, prayers and music, I laughed and cried as I realised how well we knew her favourite flowers, music and prayers. We knew her and could celebrate her life. Just like that, all the fears and doubts I'd ever had about asking for Nanna's story shrank, as the immense importance of knowing who she was expanded to fill all available space. All the whispers and elusive fragments of her life I'd grown up with had been made whole.

As Dad, Mum, Liana, Mara and I stepped out of the car at the chapel in Wallsend, I felt like we were finally arriving at the end. The grey gravel glinted in the sun as we took our time to walk across to the foyer. The first person I saw was Uncle John, little Janis now an elderly man himself, with Aunty Flora. I was glad that, through him, Grandma Milda was going to be represented.

As we entered the chapel, I saw Nanna's simple wooden coffin covered with cascading cream roses and knew the letters from her parents were inside beside her. My family gathered around with awkward hugs and sombre waves to the camera that would live-stream the service, for the benefit of those watching from around the world, and sat down.

The priest entered and began the rites. Uncle Andrew's daughter Anna lit the paschal candle, Mara placed the white pall on the coffin and Uncle Karl's son Liam got up to speak. Nanna's grandchildren came to attend to her, one after the other, with Bibles and prayers. Then it was my dad's turn. He looked graceful to me in his light grey suit. His adult shell had come away and he stood there as his mother's son with an aching, loving boyishness. 'She was just fifteen when World War Two broke out,' he said. 'The war totally changed her life. There was a deep sorrow that came from being separated from her parents at an early age.' Dad's voice broke and I looked down, the cream dots on my black dress wavered.

'But she survived. My parents built our house in Argenton to make a new life. Mum treasured that house, her own garden. There wasn't a lot of money but we were definitely the best-dressed children in our area. Each morning she proudly watched us from the front porch. In our well-pressed shirts and uniforms, we walked down Elizabeth Street to the bus stop on our way to school.' Dad's face was soft with understanding at all Nanna had been through, how hard they'd all tried. He paused and found his voice again.

'Once settled, she would not be moved. Even when she was getting very frail, she was determined to remain her own master, in her own home. She succeeded brilliantly, right up to three months ago. In hospital at the end, she told me in Latvian, only half-joking, and now I am translating . . . "I am so old it's embarrassing, almost shameful . . . What am I doing, still meddling about in this sinful world?" Then she had a little laugh. She knew she had to bide her time and the release she sought would come soon enough.'

As Dad spoke further of Nanna's love for her children, grandchildren and great-grandchildren, I pulled my speech out of my bag and steadied myself. When Dad sat down, I rose and stood in front of my family. I felt calm, as if a long and wild storm had blown itself out and given way to air suffused with pink and grey, a clear, reverent dawn.

I spoke of Nanna as a great conversationalist—how she'd often leant towards us or pressed the phone to her ear. How she'd sometimes told us light stories, like her reflections on how busy it was these days down at the Glendale shops. How she'd sometimes told us deeper stories, such as her memories of walking into the Alt Garge DP camp, alone in the world and unable to return to her parents in Latvia. I spoke about how she'd always looked for meaning in the episodes of her life, was hard on herself about many events but still able to laugh and celebrate the beautiful things in the world.

I looked out at my family and knew we were beyond lucky. It was partly the sheer guts of my Nanna Aline that had made us so.

My voice quaked with the enormity of it all when I reached my final words.

'Nanna taught me nothing less than what it means to be human, to earn the grace and wisdom that come from surviving darkness and celebrating light.'

When I sat down, I felt weary exhilaration. Nanna's priest started the concluding liturgy. He explained how he'd seen her at the end, her presentation to her God, nothing hidden, nothing unexamined. It seemed right to me as he explained how it might have felt to her—her ultimate knowing of herself, her heart's desire to be accepted by God, her preparation for a happy death.

Schubert's 'Serenade' was played as Nanna made her final journey in the coffin. I stepped forward with my cousin Eliza to lay white roses to travel with her and then closed my eyes.

All of a sudden it felt as if Nanna and I were both standing outside her church in Kraslava with the cold wind on our faces. Both young girls with the pine trees behind us, a fierce rustling all the way up to the sky. I could sense the statue of Mary with her blue robes high above us. I could feel the immensity of the unknowable future about to unfold.

All those years I'd spent talking to Nanna, I'd always known it was not my place to weigh those heavenly golden scales. As much as I'd wanted to offer relief, it was not a granddaughter's place. My job had been to listen, love Nanna and try to understand and earn the right to be the keeper of her stories.

When I went to Latvia with my parents in 2008, it had been on one of the years the famous song festival was being held in Riga. On our last evening before heading home, we went to the closing concert at the *Mežaparka estrāde*. As we filed into the outdoor stadium, I couldn't believe the sight of thousands of people standing on giant platforms sweeping across the stage. Young and old, they formed a fragile yet immense and unified group of red and white lyric folk.

When the choir began, I finally heard the sound of 14,000 people singing together. It was like nothing I'd ever heard before. The blend of voices brought a timelessness to the music. The singers seemed joined, as though molecules of water forming a great tide across the sky—past, present and future—united as one.

As Nanna Aline's coffin left the chapel that day, on the other side of the world in Newcastle, I wanted to stand and sing. I wanted to sing out as loudly as I could, my voice pealing and chiming across the world so all could hear. I wanted to sing with the force of 14,000 voices.

Ring the bells! Ring the bells! My nanna's soul is heavy and rich with life. Let her pass.

Author's notes

Material in this book

The life stories of Nanna Aline and Grandma Milda weave together material derived from interviews and conversations with Nanna Aline held through the period 2006–2021, memories of speaking with Grandma Milda through childhood and reconstructions of events in her life, family interviews, original letters and historical research.

Family history seeks to track down precise dates, locations and events, but it also involves piecing together oral history, family stories, myths and musings to understand how life might have been, as is the case with this work.

It should be noted that most of these stories are those my grandmothers were willing to tell their granddaughter during my childhood and early adult years. There are some subjects that might have received a deeper and more complex treatment if my relationship with the participants had been different.

Language

In the Latvian language, as a general rule, the stress is on the first syllable of a word. It is a phonetic language as the sounds of all letters in a word are pronounced. This makes it a beautiful song-like language.

The Latvian words italicised in this book include diacritics (accent marks), which modify the sound of the letter they are on or under. However, other proper names of Latvian people and places have been anglicised with diacritics omitted (not italicised), for the ease of the non-Latvian reader.

Readers may wish to note Nanna Aline's name is written as *Alīne* or *Alīna* in Latvian, with the diacritic over the 'i' signifying the need to lengthen the sound. Milda's name in Latvian is the same as appears in the book and is pronounced in a similar way to how it would commonly be pronounced in English.

Photo insert

The photo insert includes a mix of family and archival photographs. These have been selected for their relevance to this work and historical period after careful consideration. An immense thank you to my relatives for allowing me to share family photos. I also thank and acknowledge the following sources for particular photos as:

Page 2, top *Skats uz Kaļķu ielas sākumu no Brīvības bulvāra, Riga. A view of the beginning of Kalku Street from Brivibas Boulevard, Riga, Latvia, 1930s.* Source: National Library of Latvia. Item 92085/24817s.

Page 3, top *A Soviet BT tank with a truck and troops in the centre of Riga, Latvia, 1940.* Source: Wikimedia Commons.

Page 3, middle *Mass deportation of Latvian residents to Siberia, Latvia, 1941.* Source: Wikimedia Commons. Photographer unknown. Original image from the Nazi propaganda publication *Baigais Gads* (Riga, 1942).

Page 3, bottom Damaged buildings of the Riga Old Town, and St Peter's Church 1939–1945. Source: Carl Kadelke, National Library of Latvia. Wikimedia Commons.

Page 4, top *Welcoming German soldiers, Riga, June 1941.* Source: Bundesarchiv, Bild 183-L19397. Photograph by o.Ang.

Page 7, bottom *Aline (front row, left), Milda (back row, second from left) with Latvian community members, Newcastle, 1962.* Photograph by Mr Ozolins, Universal Photography.

Page 9, top right *Krāslavas Romas Katoļu Baznīca, Kraslava Roman Catholic Church, St Ludwig, 1920s–30s.* National Library of Latvia. Item 92085/56122.

Page 9, bottom *Krāslavas, Kombuļas Street (intersection near Aline's family home), Kraslava, Latvia, 1930s.* National Library of Latvia. Item 18766.

Page 10, bottom *National Song Festival, Daugavpils, Latvia, June 1940.* Source: Daugavpils. Choral Festival, 1940, Mara Citko, National Library of Latvia, Item 92085/17758.

Page 11, top left *German Armoured Personnel Carrier at crossing, Latvia, June 1941.* Source: Bundesarchiv, Bild 101I-209-0063-12. Photograph by Hugo Tannenberg.

Page 12, bottom left and right *Aline and husband Eddy, in their International Resettlement Organisation photos, Butzbach, Germany, 1949.* Source: National Archives of Australia, A11657 160–162.

List of names

A family tree, confined to the central family members who appear in this book, is provided at the front. For reference, the details of other key people who appear in this book are as follows (please note that most names have been changed to pseudonyms to protect the privacy of individuals):

Ade—A Latvian girl Nanna Aline met on the road from Kloddram to Alt Garge displaced persons camp in 1945.

Aunty Adela—Nanna Aline's aunty and close adult confidant. She lived with Nanna Aline and her family in Kraslava.

Aleksis—Grandma Milda's long-time friend, whom she met at Greta camp in Australia in 1949. He was a young boy living in Rezekne when the Russians occupied Latvia in 1940. Grandma Milda shared some important stories about her life with him.

Alise—A Latvian girl Grandma Milda met on the train from Gotenhafen after fleeing Latvia in 1944. They reconnected when both immigrated to Australia and Alise settled in Sydney. Alise was a key source of support for Milda and her sons throughout her life.

Boleslavs—Nanna Aline's uncle. He was sent to Siberia likely as part of the 1949 deportations.

Cousin Anna—Uncle Andrew's second daughter—one of his six children and one of Nanna Aline's eleven grandchildren.

Cousin Carl—Grandma Milda's eldest grandchild who grew up close to her in Redhead. He is Uncle George's eldest son—one of his three children. Grandma Milda shared some significant stories of her life with him, including experiences living in Latvia and fleeing the country in 1944.

Edite—Grandma Milda's friend from Riga who ended up in America after the war but stayed in touch and travelled with her husband, Tedis, back to Latvia in 1989.

Egerts—Grandma Milda's lodger in Riga who was taken by Russians in June 1941.

Cousin Eliza—Uncle Karl's daughter—one of Karl's two children and one of Nanna's eleven grandchildren.

Elizabete—A girl from Riga with whom Nanna Aline became friends in a dormitory for girls participating in the *Reichsarbeitsdienst* scheme in Germany.

Emilija—Nanna Aline's young cousin. She remained in Latvia after the Second World War and was able to greet Nanna Aline on her return in 1995.

Eriks Jansons—Grandma Milda's old boss from Riga who sponsored her to come to Australia with Juris and Janis.

Herta—The sister of Nanna Aline's childhood friend Marta, from Kraslava. They renewed their contact after both immigrated to Australia and ended up being close friends in Newcastle, although they fell out after Nanna Aline was briefly involved with Herta's husband.

Ilze—Granddad Eddy's sister who remained in Latvia after the Second World War, and visited Eddy and Aline in Australia in the early 1990s.

Cousin Jan—Uncle Andrejs' eldest son—one of his six children and one of Nanna Aline's eleven grandchildren. He travelled around Latvia with Nanna Aline, Andrejs and Ruta in 1995.

Jekabs—Nanna Aline's older cousin who stayed with her in Kraslava for a period and became a Catholic priest. He reconnected with Nanna Aline in Newcastle after he became aware she'd married Granddad Eddy, a former Catholic priest.

He eventually wrote to Rome to pave the way for Nanna Aline and Granddad Eddy to be married by the church.

Cousin Liam—Uncle Karl's son—one of Karl's two children and one of Nanna's eleven grandchildren.

Lina—A midwife who Nanna Aline met at Alt Garge, Germany, in 1946. She helped Nanna Aline when she was pregnant and arranged for Ruta to be adopted by a Latvian couple.

Marta—Nanna Aline's best friend as a girl in Kraslava. They renewed their contact after both immigrated to Australia and ended up being close friends again in Newcastle.

Martins—Emilija's son who assisted Nanna Aline, Andrejs and Emilija on Nanna Aline's return to Latvia in 1995.

Mikels—Nanna Aline's childhood friend from Kraslava. She ran into him at Alt Garge displaced persons camp after the war.

Rudolfs Seja—Grandma Milda's brother who fled Latvia for Denmark, then emigrated to Australia and sponsored their parents, Marija Seja (the 'Old Battleaxe') and Andrejs Seja, to join them in Australia.

Stani—Nanna Aline's uncle. He was accused of being a Bolshevik and arrested by the Germans in Salaspils.

Tedis—Grandma Milda's friend from Riga who ended up in America after the war but stayed in touch and wrote to Milda about his visit back to Latvia with his wife, Edite, in 1989.

Acknowledgements

My deepest thanks to Nanna Aline and Grandma Milda for sharing parts of your life stories and inspiring me to stop, look back and understand your lives. In working to honour your stories, mine was also changed for the better.

To my dad, mum, sisters and extended family, I want to say thank you for understanding what I was trying to achieve with this book and providing your support. I am grateful beyond words for all your generosity, forbearance and love.

I would also like to thank the following people and organisations for assisting with the research and writing of this book:

For granting permission to use passages from the work, *Dear God, I Wanted to Live*, by Ruta U., published by *Grāmatu Draugs* in 1978, I thank Dace Rudzitis and the Helmars Rudzitis family.

Excerpts from Latvian folk songs are from: *Latviešu Tautas Dziesmas* [Latvian Folk Songs], edited by A. Svabe, K. Straubergs and E. Hauzenberga-Sturma, 12 volumes, Kopenhagen: Imanta, 1952–1956. The excerpts are from volumes 1, 2 and 10 and were translated into English by Peter Putnis.

The texts of Latvian President Dr Karlis Ulmanis's addresses to the nation in 1940 are drawn from historical sources including: *The Occupation and Annexation of Latvia 1939–40*: Documents and Materials, I. Grava-Kreituse, I. Feldmanis, D.A. Loeber, J. Goldmanis, A. Stranga. Riga, 1995; and newspaper articles appearing in *Valdības Vēstnesis*, Nr. 135 (18.06.1940).

For providing my family's post–Second World War immigration records and photos (NAA A12004 1032–1034 and A11675 160–162), I thank the National Archives of Australia and acknowledge the critical role it plays in facilitating family history work in Australia. I would also like to acknowledge the National Library of Australia, National Library of Latvia, Museum of the Occupation of Latvia, Arolsen Archives and Bundesarchiv for historical and archival material.

To Richard Walsh and the whole team at Allen & Unwin, including Elizabeth Weiss and Samantha Kent and freelance editor Meaghan Amor, a huge thank you for seeing the potential in this book and working to help it see the light of day. It has been magical to learn how authors and publishing teams can collaborate to bring books into the world.

For sharing this journey and providing encouragement and mentorship along the way, I will always be grateful to Jan Cornall and the wonderful DraftBusters crew. Thanks also to MARION (formerly known as the ACT Writers Centre), the amazing group of writers from Hardcopy 2019 cohort, and 'BeWriters' Group. The early support of Patti Miller, Virginia Lloyd, Peter Bishop and Varuna: The National Writers' House, and the NT Writers' Centre was also pivotal to getting some early momentum. A huge thank you also goes to Nancy Lane and Ilze Thomas who both provided essential editing and support.

To my many friends who believed I might finally get the book finished one day—and particularly to those who acted as early readers including Biff Ward, Tamara Jacka, Benita de Vincentiis, Caroline Edwards, Caitlin Delaney, Angela Jackson, Michelle Tabone, Julie Armstrong and Katie Puttock—a massive thank you.

Finally, all the love in my heart goes to my partner, Michael, and my children, Talis and Annija. The faith you showed in me is what made achieving this dream possible.